Also by Dr. Wayne W. Dyer

BOOKS

Being in Balance
Everyday Wisdom
Everyday Wisdom for Success
Getting in the Gap (book-with-CD)
Gifts from Eykis
Incredible You! (children's book with Kristina Tracy)
Inspiration
The Invisible Force
It's Not What You've Got! (children's book with Kristina Tracy)
Manifest Your Destiny
A Morning and Afternoon of Your Life
No More Holiday Blues
The Power of Intention
A Promise Is a Promise
Pulling Your Own Strings
Real Magic
The Sky's the Limit
Staying on the Path
10 Secrets for Success and Inner Peace
There's a Spiritual Solution to Every Problem
Unstoppable Me! (children's book with Kristina Tracy)
What Do You Really Want for Your Children?
Wisdom of the Ages
You'll See It When You Believe It
Your Erroneous Zones
Your Sacred Self
Your Ultimate Calling

AUDIO/CD PROGRAMS

Applying the 10 Secrets for Success and Inner Peace
Change Your Thoughts—Change Your Life (unabridged audio book)
Change Your Thoughts Meditation
Everyday Wisdom (audio book)
Freedom Through Higher Awareness
How to Be a No-Limit Person
How to Get What You Really, Really, Really, Really Want
If You Change the Way You Live, the Life You Are Living Will Change (abridged 4-CD set)
Inspiration (abridged 4-CD set)

Inspirational Thoughts
The Keys to Higher Awareness
Making Your Thoughts Work for You (with Byron Katie)
Meditations for Manifesting
A Morning and Afternoon of Your Life (abridged 4-CD set)
101 Ways to Transform Your Life (audio book)
The Power of Intention (abridged 4-CD set)
A Promise Is a Promise (audio book)
The Secrets of the Power of Intention (6-CD set)
10 Secrets for Success and Inner Peace
There Is a Spiritual Solution to Every Problem
The Wayne Dyer Audio Collection/CD Collection
Your Journey to Enlightenment (6-tape program)

VIDEOCASSETTES
Creating Real Magic in Your Life
How to Be a No-Limit Person
The Miracle Mindset
10 Secrets for Success and Inner Peace
What Do You Really Want for Your Children?

MISCELLANEOUS
Everyday Wisdom Perpetual Flip Calendar
Inner Peace Cards
Inspiration Cards
Inspiration Perpetual Flip Calendar
The Power of Intention Cards
The Power of Intention Perpetual Flip Calendar
10 Secrets for Success and Inner Peace Cards
10 Secrets for Success and Inner Peace gift products:
Notecards, Candle, and Journal

All of the above are available at your local bookstore,
or may be ordered by visiting:

Hay House USA: **www.hayhouse.com**
Hay House Australia: **www.hayhouse.com.au**
Hay House UK: **www.hayhouse.co.uk**
Hay House South Africa: **www.hayhouse.co.za**
Hay House India: **www.hayhouse.co.in**

CHANGE *Your* THOUGHTS—
Change YOUR
Life

Living the Wisdom of the Tao

Dr. Wayne W. Dyer

HAY HOUSE, INC.
Carlsbad, California • New York City
London • Sydney • Johannesburg
Vancouver • Hong Kong • New Delhi

Published and distributed in the United States by: Hay House, Inc.: www.hayhouse. com • *Published and distributed in Australia by:* Hay House Australia Pty. Ltd.: www.hayhouse.com.au • *Published and distributed in the United Kingdom by:* Hay House UK, Ltd.: www.hayhouse.co.uk • *Published and distributed in the Republic of South Africa by:* Hay House SA (Pty), Ltd.: orders@psdprom.co.za • www.hayhouse. co.za • *Distributed in Canada by:* Raincoast: www.raincoast.com • *Published in India by:* Hay House Publishers India: www.hayhouse.co.in

Page 142: Poem "Woman with Flower" from *Star by Star,* by Naomi Long Madgett, the Poet Laureate of Detroit (distributed by Lotus Press, Inc. • copyright © 1965, 1970). By permission of the author. Naomi's Website: **www.naomilongmadgett.com**

Page 371: "Wild Geese," by Mary Oliver, published in *Dream Work* (copyright © 1986). Reprinted by permission for all printings of book and CD program.

Wayne Dyer's editor: Joanna Pyle
Editorial supervision: Jill Kramer • *Design:* Amy Rose Grigoriou

Library of Congress Cataloging-in-Publication Data

Dyer, Wayne W.
  Change your thoughts, change your life : living the wisdom of the Tao / Wayne W. Dyer. -- 1st ed.,.
    p. cm.
  ISBN 978-1-4019-1184-3 (hardcover) -- ISBN 978-1-4019-1750-0 (pbk.) 1. Laozi. Dao de jing. I. Title.
  BL1900.L35D94 2007

299.5'1482--dc22   2007000532

ISBN: 978-1-4019-1184-3

10 09 08 07   6 5 4 3
1st edition, August 2007
3rd edition, August 2007

Printed in the United States of America

For my father, Melvin Lyle Dyer.
Even though I've never known you, after
thoroughly digesting the Tao, I finally get it!
It is—and always was—all perfect. I love you.

Contents

Preface xi

Verse Number:

1	Living the Mystery..	2
2	Living the Paradoxical Unity..	8
3	Living Contentment..	14
4	Living Infinitely..	20
5	Living Impartially..	24
6	Living Creatively	28
7	Living Beyond Ego..	34
8	Living in the Flow	40
9	Living Humility..	44
10	Living Oneness..	48
11	Living from the Void..	52
12	Living with Inner Conviction..	56
13	Living with an Independent Mind................................	60
14	Living Beyond Form..	64
15	Living an Unhurried Life	68
16	Living with Constancy..	72
17	Living as an Enlightened Leader	76
18	Living Without Rules	82
19	Living Without Attachment..	88
20	Living Without Striving	94
21	Living the Elusive Paradox	100
22	Living with Flexibility	104
23	Living Naturally..	108
24	Living Without Excess..	112
25	Living from Greatness	116
26	Living Calmly	122
27	Living by Your Inner Light..	126
28	Living Virtuously	132
29	Living by Natural Law	138
30	Living Without Force	144
31	Living Without Weapons	150
32	Living the Perfect Goodness of the Tao	156
33	Living Self-Mastery	160
34	Living the Great Way	166
35	Living Beyond Worldly Pleasures................................	170
36	Living in Obscurity..	176
37	Living in Simplicity	180
38	Living Within Your Own Nature	186
39	Living Wholeness	190

40	Living by Returning and Yielding	194
41	Living Beyond Appearances	198
42	Living by Melting into Harmony	204
43	Living Softly	208
44	Living by Knowing When to Stop	214
45	Living Beyond Superficialities	218
46	Living Peacefully	224
47	Living by Being	228
48	Living by Decreasing	234
49	Living Beyond Judgment	238
50	Living as an Immortal	242
51	Living by Hidden Virtue	246
52	Living by Returning to the Mother	252
53	Living Honorably	256
54	Living as If Your Life Makes a Difference	262
55	Living by Letting Go	266
56	Living by Silent Knowing	270
57	Living Without Authoritarianism	274
58	Living Untroubled by Good or Bad Fortune	278
59	Living by Thrift and Moderation	282
60	Living with Immunity to Evil	286
61	Living by Remaining Low	290
62	Living in the Treasure-house of the Tao	294
63	Living Without Difficulties	298
64	Living by Being Here Now	302
65	Living by Staying Simple-hearted	308
66	Living by Emulating the Sea	312
67	Living by the Three Treasures	316
68	Living by Cooperating	322
69	Living Without Enemies	326
70	Living a God-Realized Life	330
71	Living Without Sickness	334
72	Living with Awe and Acceptance	338
73	Living in Heaven's Net	344
74	Living with No Fear of Death	350
75	Living by Demanding Little	356
76	Living by Bending	360
77	Living by Offering the Surplus	364
78	Living like Water	368
79	Living Without Resentments	374
80	Living Your Own Utopia	378
81	Living Without Accumulating	382

Epilogue	387
Acknowledgments	391
About the Author	395

$\mathcal{P}$reface

*Progress is impossible without change, and those who
cannot change their minds cannot change anything.*

— George Bernard Shaw

Change Your Thoughts—Change Your Life is the end product of my yearlong journey of research, contemplation, and application of the Tao Te Ching, a book of wisdom that's been translated more than any volume in the world, with the exception of the Bible. Many scholars consider this Chinese classic the ultimate discourse on the nature of existence; and it continues to be a valuable resource for achieving a way of life that guarantees integrity, joy, peace, and balance. I recently read about someone who overcame life-threatening addictive behaviors by reading and rereading the 81 verses of this ancient text. Just imagine! In fewer than 100 short passages, it describes a way of living that's balanced, moral, and spiritual; and that works for all facets of life on Earth.

Legend tells us that the Tao Te Ching was authored by Lao-tzu, a prophet who was also the keeper of the imperial archives in the ancient capital of Luoyang. Seeing the continual decay during a period of warring states, Lao-tzu decided to ride westward into the desert. At the Hanku Pass, a gatekeeper named Yin Hsi, knowing of Lao-tzu's reputation for being a man of wisdom, begged him to record the essence of his teaching. Thus, the Tao Te Ching was born out of 5,000 Chinese characters.

In all my reading on the origins of the Tao Te Ching, I never found a definitive historical record of its writing . . . yet today it survives in thousands of versions in virtually every language. In fact, after reading this classic text one morning and then taking in a different interpretation that afternoon, I was hooked. I ordered more translations, five of which were quite old and five of which were more modern (you'll find their titles in the Acknowledgments). Since neither Lao-tzu nor the origins of his verses are historically certain, I was fascinated by the different ways the 5,000 characters were interpreted by scholars in the editions I studied—especially when you consider that many of these ancient Chinese symbols are no longer in use and invite differing translations themselves.

I then felt called upon to write an essay for each verse that showed its valuable wisdom applied to the 21st century. From those ten translations I'd gone over, I pieced together the 81 passages in *Change Your Thoughts—Change Your Life,* based on how they resonated with me. This book is my personal interpretation of the Tao Te Ching, each verse of which gave me an insight into life and nature. As you read on, know that these pages were pasted together from what I *personally* felt were the most useful aspects of those ten different translations I studied, and I apologize for any exclusions (or if the inclusions don't seem to be a perfect fit).

One of the many gifts of the Tao Te Ching is its mind-stretching quality, especially in the way that Lao-tzu uses irony and paradox to get you to look at life. If you think that being forceful is the appropriate response, Lao-tzu urges you to see the value in being humble. If action seems called for, he asks you to consider nonaction. If you feel that grasping will help you acquire what you need or want, he counsels you to let go and be patient.

And just what is this thing called "the Tao"? As we're told in the 1st verse, to name it is to lose it, so here's the best that I can come up with: The Tao is the supreme reality, an all-pervasive Source of everything. The Tao never begins or ends, does nothing, and yet animates everything in the world of form and boundaries, which is called "the world of the 10,000 things."

Commentaries on the Tao Te Ching generally interpret *Tao* as "the Way," *Te* as "the shape and power" (that is, how the Tao manifests), and *Ching* as "book." Every translation I read referred to the Tao as the Way with a capital *W*, and Te as adding light or color to the Way. Well, as I look at the name I've carried with me for over 65 years, *Way*ne Dyer, I realize what may have attracted me to studying and writing these essays! As you can see, the first three letters of my name make up the word *Way,* while a dyer is one who adds light or color. It's no wonder why I've been so totally involved in reading, writing, interpreting, and, most significantly, putting into practice these 81 verses.

In *The Wisdom of China and India,* Dr. Lin Yutang states, "If there is one book in the whole of Oriental literature which should be read above all others, it is, in my opinion [Lao-tzu's] Book of Tao. . . . It is one of the profoundest books in the world's philosophy . . ." As you read *Change Your Thoughts—Change Your Life,* you're going to find your way through Lao-tzu's mystical and practical philosophy, along with the joy of applying it to your life in today's modern world.

Writing this book was a complete surrender to ideas that didn't always seem to fit a linear rational approach, and it has changed me in a way that's like the Tao itself: unexplainable and unnameable. Once I knew that I'd be spending a year on this project, its creation came about in the following way, which I have journaled for you:

> *I awake before 4 A.M., meditate, consume juices and supplements, and enter my sacred writing space. On a table, I have some framed drawings of Lao-tzu: In one he's clad in simple robes, in another he's standing with a staff, and in a third he's astride an ox. I ease into my work and read one verse of the Tao Te Ching, letting the words stay with me and inviting the forces of both the outer and the inner life to inform me.*
>
> *Some of the passages contain ideas that seem to be directed to political leaders—yet in all cases I keep the average reader in mind. In other words, I seek the wisdom for <u>everyone,</u> not just for those in positions of government or business.*
>
> *I jot down a few notes, and for the next three days I think about what Lao-tzu is offering. I invite the Tao to be with me*

throughout the day in all my activities as a background to the title of this book. "Change your thoughts, Wayne," I tell myself, "and watch how your life changes." And my thoughts do change.

I feel the Tao with me, always there, always doing nothing, and always leaving absolutely nothing undone. As I'm now See-ing with a capital S, the landscape looks different. The people I See are godly creations who are ignoring their own nature, or even more poignantly, needily interfering in the affairs of others. I have a different perspective now: I feel more peaceful and patient. I keep being reminded of the cyclical nature of the world of the 10,000 things and have powerful insights that change what I see. I know that we humans are like the rest of the natural world and that sadness, fear, frustration, or any troubling feeling can-not last. Nature doesn't create a storm that never ends. Within misfortune, good fortune hides.

Following my days of thinking and then applying the wisdom of a particular verse, I look into the eyes of Lao-tzu's picture in the early morning, and I wonder, What did you mean? How does this apply here, today, to anyone who might want to live according to these majestic teachings?

What happens next is mind-blowing in that it simply comes. Through the ages, through the atmosphere, through my purple pen and onto the page, flows what I can only call automatic writ-ing. I know I don't own it. I know I can't touch it, feel it, see it, or even name it, but the words arrive in the world of the 10,000 things. I am grateful, bewildered, astonished, and overjoyed. The next day I begin another four-day adventure with this wisdom a Chinese master recorded 2,500 years ago, feeling so blessed, honored, and completely awestruck by the profound impact these words have on me.

It's my vision that in this 21st century, our world must recruit future leaders who are steeped in the importance of Lao-tzu's words. Our survival may depend on understanding that the concepts of "enemy" and "war" can cease to exist through living Tao-centered lives. Government will need to retreat from regulating our personal lives, overly taxing our income, and invading our privacy.

Yet the lessons and truths of the Tao must be discovered and applied by individuals. In this way, it can bring you to the enor-mous wonder of your own being—yes, you are the Tao at work. Your being came from, and will return to, nonbeing. So for maximum enjoyment and benefit, make reading this book a personal journey. First peruse one of the passages of the Tao Te Ching and the essay that follows it. Next, spend some time applying it, changing the way you've been conditioned to think and letting yourself open up to a new way of conceptualizing these ideas. Finally, individualize the verse by writing, recording, drawing, or expressing yourself in whatever way you're called to. And move on to the next verse with a rhythm that suits your nature.

The following is from *365 Tao: Daily Meditations* by Deng Ming-Dao, which I love to turn to each day. Read this excerpt and see the Tao coming alive in you:

> If you spend a long period of time in study and self-cultivation, you will enter Tao. By doing so, you also enter a world of extraordinary perceptions. You experience unimaginable things, receive thoughts and learning as if from nowhere, perceive things that could be classified as prescient. Yet if you try to communicate what you experience, there is no one to understand you, no one who will believe you. The more you walk this road, the farther you are from the ordinary ways of society. You may see the truth, but you will find that people would rather listen to politicians, performers, and charlatans.
>
> If you are known as a follower of Tao, people may seek you out, but they are seldom the ones who will truly understand Tao. They are people who would exploit Tao as a crutch. To speak to them of the wonders you have seen is often to engage in a futile bout of miscommunication. That is why it is said that those who know do not speak.
>
> Why not simply stay quiet? Enjoy Tao as you will. Let others think you are dumb. Inside yourself, you will know the joy of Tao's mysteries. If you meet someone who can profit by your experience, you should share. But if you are merely a wanderer in a crowd of strangers, it is wisdom to be silent.

Perhaps the overriding message of the Tao Te Ching is to learn how to luxuriate in the simplicity of what you're being told throughout this ancient sacred text. As you put its ideas into practice, you'll discover how profound it all is—but then you'll find yourself startled by its simplicity and naturalness. The advice of this ancient master is so easy to apply that you mustn't try to complicate it. Simply allow yourself to stay in harmony with your nature, which can be trusted if you just listen and act accordingly.

I hope that you'll feel joyously in love with Lao-tzu and his wondrous Tao Te Ching, and that you'll add *your* light and color to the Great Way. I offer you my love, along with my commitment to a Tao-centered world. I can think of no greater vision for you, for our planet, or for our universe.

— **Wayne W. Dyer**
Maui, Hawaii

(**Editor's note:** Lao-tzu's name has been spelled many different ways over the years, so in order to avoid confusion in this book, we'll be using the spelling preferred by *Merriam-Webster's Collegiate Dictionary, 11th Edition.*)

Of birds
I know that they
have wings to fly with,
of fish that they have fins to
swim with, of wild beasts that they
have feet to run with. For feet there are traps,
for fins nets, for wings arrows.
But who knows how dragons
surmount wind and cloud
into heaven? This day I have seen
[Lao-tzu] and he is a dragon.

— from *The Way of Life According to Lao Tzu,*
translated by Witter Bynner

(This quote is attributed to Confucius, after he visited the elder Lao-tzu
to seek advice on points of ceremonial etiquette.)

1st Verse

The Tao that can be told
is not the eternal Tao.
The name that can be named
is not the eternal name.

The Tao is both named and nameless.
As nameless it is the origin of all things;
as named it is the Mother of 10,000 things.

Ever desireless, one can see the mystery;
ever desiring, one sees only the manifestations.
And the mystery itself is the doorway
to all understanding.

$\mathcal{L}$iving the $\mathcal{M}$ystery

In this opening verse of the Tao Te Ching, Lao-tzu tells us that the "Tao is both named and nameless." This sounds paradoxical to our Western intellect—and it is! Paradoxical thinking is embedded in Eastern concepts such as yin *and* yang or the feminine *and* the masculine, and where things are comfortably described as both this *and* that. We in the West, by contrast, tend to view opposites as incompatible concepts that contradict each other. Yet this book is asking that we change our ingrained ways of thinking and see how our lives change as a result.

The Tao is an unknowable, unseeable realm where everything originates; while at the same time, the Tao is invisibly within everything. When we desire to see this invisibleness (mystery), we attempt to define it in terms of the outer world of form—what Lao-tzu calls "the 10,000 things." He counsels us that letting go of trying to see the mystery will actually allow us to see it. Or, as I like to think of it, "let go and let God." But how can we do that? One way is to permit ourselves to practice more paradoxical thinking by recognizing that desiring (wanting) and desireless (allowing) are different and the same . . . rather like the mysterious ends of a continuum.

Desiring is the physical expression of creating conditions that allow us to be receptive; that is, it's in-the-world preparation for receiving. According to Lao-tzu, wanting to know or see the mystery of the Tao will reveal evidence of it in a variety of manifestations, but not the mystery itself. But this isn't a dead end! From this ground of desiring, the flowering of the mysterious Tao grows. It's as if wanting transforms into effortless allowing. Desiring, one sees the manifestations; desireless, one can see the mystery itself.

When we tune in to what Lao-tzu is telling us, it becomes readily apparent that our world produces abundant examples of this paradoxical process. Think of gardening and desiring those luscious homegrown tomatoes or spring daffodils: *Allowing* them to grow is ultimately what happens. Now think of the things in life that involve *wanting* and how they differ from allowing: Wanting to go to sleep, for instance, rather than going to sleep. Wanting to diet, rather than dieting. Wanting to love, rather than loving. In this reference to the Tao, desireless means trusting, permitting, and allowing. Desire is both the beginning and the ground of desirelessness, yet wanting is also the beginning and the ground of allowing. They are the same, and they are different.

Pay attention to times when you can feel in your body where you are on the continuum between desiring and allowing (or trying and doing). *Trying* to play the piano, drive the car, or ride the bicycle is the same as, and different from, actually playing the piano, driving the car, and riding the bicycle. Once those outer-world activities are desired and learned, there's a time when allowing is what you do. The point here is to recognize the difference in your body between trying and allowing, and to then become aware of the effortless sensation of the latter. This practice will also lead to a greater awareness of the invisible mystery and the 10,000 things, which are the visible phenomena of our world.

The 10,000 things that Lao-tzu refers to represent the categorized, classified, and scientifically named objects of the earth, which help us communicate and identify what we're talking and thinking about. Yet for all our technological expertise and scientific categorization, we can never truly create a human eye or liver, or even a grain of wheat for that matter. Each of these things—along with the remainder that comprise the known or named world—emerge from the mystery, the eternal Tao. Just as the world is not its named parts, we're not exclusively the skin, bone, and rivers of fluids that we're

physically made of. We, too, are the eternal Tao, invisibly animating our tongues to speak, ears to hear, and eyes to see and experience the manifest and the mystery. Consciously allowing this nameless mystery is ultimately the way to practice the Tao.

Does that mean putting yourself in harm's way? Of course not. Does that mean trusting the mystery at the moment you're being mugged or mistreated? Probably not. Does it mean never trying to change things? No. It *does* mean cultivating a practice of being in the mystery and allowing it to flow through you unimpeded. It means permitting the paradox of being in form at the same time that you allow the mystery to unfold.

Do the Tao; find your personal ways of living in the mystery. As Lao-tzu says in this 1st verse, "And the mystery itself is the doorway to all understanding."

Here's my advice for translating this passage into daily practice in this 21st century:

First and foremost, enjoy the mystery!

Let the world unfold without always attempting to figure it all out. Let relationships just be, for example, since everything is going to stretch out in Divine order. Don't try so hard to make something work—simply allow. Don't always toil at trying to understand your mate, your children, your parents, your boss, or anyone else, because the Tao is working at all times. When expectations are shattered, practice allowing that to be the way it is. Relax, let go, allow, and recognize that some of your desires are about how you think your world *should* be, rather than how it *is* in that moment. Become an astute observer . . . judge less and listen more. Take time to open your mind to the fascinating mystery and uncertainty that we all experience.

Practice letting go of always naming and labeling.

The labeling process is what most of us were taught in school. We studied hard to be able to define things correctly in order to get what we called "high grades." Most educational institutions insisted on identifying everything, leading to a tag that distinguished us as graduates with knowledge of specific categories. Yet we know, without anyone telling us, that there is no title, degree, or distinguishing

5

label that truly defines us. In the same way that water is not the word *water*—any more than it is *agua, Wasser,* or H_2O—nothing in this universe is what it's named. In spite of our endless categorizations, each animal, flower, mineral, and human can never truly be described. In the same way, the Tao tells us that "the name that can be named is not the eternal name." We must bask in the magnificence of what is seen and sensed, instead of always memorizing and categorizing.

Do the Tao Now

At some point today, notice an instance of annoyance or irritation you have with another person or situation. Decide to do the Tao (or practice the Way) in that moment by turning inward with curiosity about where you are on the continuum between desire and allowing. Permit the paradox of wanting the irritant to vanish and allowing it to be what it is. Look inward for it in your thoughts and allow yourself to feel it wherever it is and however it moves in your body.

Turn all of your attention to becoming open-minded, allowing permissiveness to befriend the mystery within yourself. Notice how the feeling manifests itself: perhaps doing "loop-de-loops" in your stomach, giving a rigidity to your skeleton, making your heart pound, or tightening your throat. Wherever it is, allow it as an enigmatic messenger within you, and give it nonjudgmental attention. Notice the desire for the feeling to disappear, and allow it to be monitored compassionately by you. Accept whatever comes. Encounter the mystery within without labeling, explaining, or defending. It's a subtle distinction at first, which you must take personal responsibility for identifying. You alone can prepare the ground of your being for the experience of living the mystery.

2nd Verse

Under heaven all can see beauty as beauty,
only because there is ugliness.
All can know good as good only because there is evil.

Being and nonbeing produce each other.
The difficult is born in the easy.
Long is defined by short, the high by the low.
Before and after go along with each other.

So the sage lives openly with apparent duality
and paradoxical unity.
The sage can act without effort
and teach without words.
Nurturing things without possessing them,
he works, but not for rewards;
he competes, but not for results.

When the work is done, it is forgotten.
That is why it lasts forever.

*L*iving the *P*aradoxical *U*nity

The concept of something or someone being beautiful is grounded in a belief system that promotes duality and judgment. This way of thinking is prevalent and commonplace for just about everybody in our culture, perhaps even having some value in society. I encourage you to explore the concept of paradoxical unity in this 2nd verse of the Tao Te Ching. By changing your thoughts, you can change your life and truly live the bliss of oneness.

Has it ever occurred to you that beauty depends on something being identified as ugly? Therefore, the idea of beauty produces the idea of ugliness, and vice versa. Just think of how many concepts in this "duality belief system" depend on opposites: A person isn't tall unless there's a belief system that includes short. Our idea of life couldn't exist without that of death. Day is the opposite of night. Male is the antithesis of female.

What if you instead perceived all as a piece (or a glimpse) of the perfection of oneness? I think this is what Lao-tzu is suggesting with his description of the sage who "lives openly with apparent duality and paradoxical unity." Imagine the perfect oneness coexisting in the apparent duality, where opposites are simply judgments made by human minds in the world of 10,000 things. Surely the daffodil doesn't think that the daisy is prettier or uglier than it is, and the eagle and the mouse have no sense of the opposites we call life and death. The trees, flowers, and animals know not of ugliness or beauty; they simply *are* . . . in harmony with the eternal Tao, devoid of judgment.

As the sage lives openly with apparent duality, he synthesizes the origin with the manifestation without forming an opinion about it. Living without judgment and in perfect oneness is what Lao-tzu invites his readers to do. He invites our wisdom to combine perceived opposites and live a unified life. The perfection of the Tao is allowing apparent duality while seeing the unity that is reality. Life and death are identical. Virtue and sin are judgments, needing both to identify either. These are the paradoxes of a unified life; this is living within the eternal Tao. Once the dichotomies or pairs of opposites are transcended, or at least seen for what they are, they flow in and out of life like the tides.

Practice being a living, breathing paradox every moment of your life. The body has physical boundaries—it begins and ends and has material substance. Yet it also contains something that defies boundaries, has no substance, and is infinite and formless. You are both the Tao and the 10,000 things simultaneously. Let the contrasting and opposite ideas be within you at the same time. Allow yourself to hold those opposite thoughts without them canceling each other out. Believe strongly in your free will and ability to influence your surroundings, and simultaneously surrender to the energy within you. Know that good and evil are two aspects of a union. In other words, accept the duality of the material world while still remaining in constant contact with the oneness of the eternal Tao. The debilitating necessity to be right and make others wrong will diminish.

I believe that Lao-tzu would apply the Tao Te Ching to today's world by suggesting the following:

Live a unified life.

Enter the world of oneness with an awareness of the propensity to compartmentalize everything as good or bad, right or wrong. Beautiful or ugly are standards of the physical world, not the Tao.

Contemplate the insight that duality is a mind game. In other words, people look the way they look, period—criticism is not always necessary or helpful. See the unfolding of the Tao inside everyone, including yourself, and be at peace with what you observe.

Be a good animal and move freely, unencumbered with thoughts about where you *should* be and how you *should* be acting. For instance, imagine yourself as an otter just living your "otterness." You're not good or bad, beautiful or ugly, a hard worker or a slacker . . . you're simply an otter, moving through the water or on the land freely, peacefully, playfully, and without judgments. When it's time to leave your body, you do so, reclaiming your place in the pure mystery of oneness. This is what Lao-tzu means when he says, "When the work is done, it is forgotten. That is why it lasts forever."

In other words, you don't have to leave your body to experience forever; it's possible to know your eternal self even in the embodied condition. When duality and judgment crop up, allow them to be a part of the perfect unity. When other people create dichotomies, you can always know oneness by practicing the Tao.

Accomplish much by trying less.

Effort is one piece of the whole; another piece is non-effort. Fuse these dichotomies, and the result is effortless action without attachment to outcome. This is precisely how you dance with someone: You make an attempt, assume a position, listen to the music, and let go all at the same time, allowing yourself to easily move with your partner. Combine the so-called opposites into the oneness of being without judgment or fear. Labeling action as "a fine effort" implies a belief that trying hard is better than not trying. But trying itself only exists because of beliefs about not trying. Attempting to pick up a piece of trash is really just *not* picking up the trash. Once you've picked it up, then trying and not trying are irrelevant.

Understand that you can act without the implied judgment of words such as *effort* and *trying*. You can compete without being focused on outcome. Eliminating opposites paradoxically unifies them so that it is unnecessary to identify with one position. I imagine that in today's language, Lao-tzu would sum up this 2nd verse of the Tao Te Ching in these two simple words: *Just be.*

Do the Tao Now

Do the Tao today by noticing an opportunity to defend or explain yourself and choosing not to. Instead, turn within and sense the texture of misunderstanding, feeling it all the way through your physical system. Just be with what is, instead of opting to ease it by traversing the outer-world path of explaining and defending. Don't get caught up in the apparent duality of being right or wrong. Congratulate yourself for making a choice to be in paradoxical unity, a oneness where all of the spectrum simply is. Silently appreciate the opportunity, along with your willingness to practice your sageness!

3rd Verse

Putting a value on status
will create contentiousness.
If you overvalue possessions,
people begin to steal.
By not displaying what is desirable, you will
cause the people's hearts to remain undisturbed.

The sage governs
by emptying minds and hearts,
by weakening ambitions and strengthening bones.

Practice not doing. . . .
When action is pure and selfless,
everything settles into its own perfect place.

*L*iving *C*ontentment

This 3rd verse of the Tao Te Ching advises rearranging priorities to ensure contentment. Focusing on obtaining more objects of desire encourages external factors to have control over us. Pursuit of status, be it monetary or a position of power, blinds us to our relationship to the eternal Tao, along with the contented life that is available. Overvaluing possessions and accomplishments stems from our ego's fixation on getting *more*—wealth, belongings, status, power, or the like. The Tao recommends refraining from this kind of discontented way of life, which leads to thievery, contentiousness, and confusion. Rather than seeking more, the Tao practice of gratitude is what leads us to the contented life. We must replace personal desires with the Tao-centered question: *How may I serve?* By simply changing these kinds of thoughts, we will begin to see major changes taking place in our lives.

The advice to practice "not doing" and trusting that all will settle into a perfect place may sound like a prescription for laziness and a failed society, yet I don't think that's what Lao-tzu is offering here. He isn't saying to be slothful or inactive; rather, he's suggesting that trusting in the Tao is the way to be directed by the Source of your creation and to be guided by a higher principle than your ego-driven desires.

Ego-fixated wants can get in the way of Divine essence, so practice getting ego out of the way and be guided by the Tao in all that you do. In a state of frenzy? Trust in the Tao. Listen for what urges you onward, free from ego domination, and you'll paradoxically be more productive. Allow what's within to come forward by suspending worldly determination. In this way, it will no longer be just you who is conducting this orchestration that you call your life.

Much of this 3rd verse contains advice on how to govern. I view this not as political or administrative advice, but as it pertains to our own personal lives and those we're entrusted to guide—that is, our immediate family, and in a larger sense, the human family that comprises all of those with whom we're in contact on a daily basis.

Encourage your relatives to empty their minds of thoughts about status and acquisitions, and think instead about serving others and contributing to the health and strength of all. Model the harmony of this attitude; after all, everyone has a calling to be inspired. The Source of creation is not interested in material possessions or status. It will provide what is needed—it will guide, motivate, and influence you and everyone else. Ego (and its incessant inventory of desires) probably needs to be weakened so that the beauty of the Tao can be sensed. Demonstrate this to others by being a leader who removes the egocentric temptations that foster envy, anger, and competition.

If Lao-tzu were able to view our contemporary world from his 2,500-year-old perspective, I believe that he'd offer the following advice based upon this 3rd verse of the Tao Te Ching:

Remind yourself daily that there is no way to happiness; rather, happiness *is* the way.

You may have a long list of goals that you believe will provide you with contentment when they're achieved, yet if you examine your state of happiness in this moment, you'll notice that the fulfillment of some previous ambitions didn't create an enduring sense of joy. Desires can produce anxiety, stress, and competitiveness, and you need to recognize those that do. Bring happiness to every encounter in life, instead of expecting external events to produce joy. By staying in harmony on the path of the Tao, all the contentment you could ever dream of will begin to flow into your life—the right people, the means to finance where you're headed, and the necessary

factors will come together. "Stop pushing yourself," Lao-tzu would say, "and feel gratitude and awe for what is. Your life is controlled by something far bigger and more significant than the petty details of your lofty aspirations."

Trust the perfection of the eternal Tao, for it is the ultimate Source of the 10,000 things.

The Tao is working *for* and *with* you, so you needn't remind it of what you crave or what you think it has forgotten on your behalf. Trust the harmony of the Tao. It took care of everything that you needed in your creation as well as your first nine months of life without any assistance from you, and totally independent of any desires you may have had. The Tao will continue to do so if you just trust it and practice not doing.

Inventory your desires and then turn them over to the unnameable. Yes, turn them over and do nothing but trust. At the same time, listen and watch for guidance, and then connect yourself to the perfect energy that sends whatever is necessary into your life. You (meaning your ego) don't need to do anything. Instead, allow the eternal perfection of the Tao to work through you. This is Lao-tzu's message for our world now.

Henry David Thoreau made the following observation in the middle of the 19th century as he wrote at Walden Pond, and I feel that it personifies this 3rd verse of the Tao Te Ching:

> Let us spend one day as deliberately as Nature, and not be thrown off the track by every nutshell and mosquito's wing that falls on the rails. . . . If the engine whistles, let it whistle till it is hoarse for its pains. If the bell rings, why should we run? . . . I have always been regretting that I was not as wise as the day I was born.

Trust in your essential sageness. Don't let desires obscure your eternal connection to the Tao.

Do the Tao Now

Watch for an opportunity today to notice that you're planning on buying something. Choose to do the Tao and listen for guidance.

Be grateful that you have the choice to make the purchase, then practice listening to yourself and not doing. Through your feelings, the Tao will reveal the way for you in that moment. Trust it. You might be guided to buy the item and savor it with gratitude, donate it, procure one for you and one for someone else, give the money to a charity instead of getting the item, or refrain from obtaining it altogether.

Practice doing the Tao in everyday situations and you'll know contentment in a deeper sense. As this verse says, "When action is pure and selfless, everything settles into its own perfect place." Now that's my definition of contentment!

4th Verse

The Tao is empty
but inexhaustible,
bottomless,
the ancestor of it all.

Within it, the sharp edges become smooth;
the twisted knots loosen;
the sun is softened by a cloud;
the dust settles into place.

It is hidden but always present.
I do not know who gave birth to it.
It seems to be the common ancestor of all, the father of things.

Living Infinitely

The Tao is the Source of all life, yet it is empty and limitless and cannot be constrained, quantified, or measured. This life-giving energy of creation provides a profound Source of joy that's accessible at all times. If you live from an infinite perspective, you'll relinquish the idea that your only identity is the physical body in which you progress from birth to death. In your totality, you're an infinite being disguised as a person existing in the world of "sharp edges" and "twisted knots" that this verse refers to. Coalescing within and around you at all times is the invisible life-giving force of the Tao. It is inexhaustible. It is bottomless. It cannot be depleted.

This 4th verse of the Tao invites you to consider rearranging your thoughts about who you are. It seems to be saying that cultivating an awareness of the infinite aspect of yourself is the way to tap into the limitless Source of creative energy that flows through you. For example, you may want to help less fortunate people improve their day-to-day existence, but you don't believe that you have the time or energy to do so because of who you are and what you presently do. As you relax your hold on the idea of yourself as the job you do or the life you're living and seek to acquaint yourself with the limitless creative energy that's a part of you, the time and energy you require will appear.

Imagining yourself helping others, guided by the infinite aspect of yourself, will generate behavior and actions that complement your vision through the "common ancestor" of the Tao. Ultimately, you'll cultivate an absolute knowing that whatever assistance you need is right here and right now—in front of, in back of, above, and below you. It is empty, yet very much present. It is, as Lao-tzu reminds you, "inexhaustible, bottomless, the ancestor of it all."

Awareness of the omnipresence of the Tao means that thoughts of shortages or lack aren't prevalent. Beliefs such as "There's no way this will happen," "It's not my destiny," or "With my luck, things could never work out," cease to be entertained. Instead, you begin to expect that what you imagine for yourself is not only on its way—it's already here! This new self-portrait based on the cooperative presence of the invisible Tao elevates you to living an inspired life—that is, one of being "in spirit" or in unending touch with the Tao. When you live infinitely, the rewards are a sense of peaceful joy because you know that all is in order.

This is what I imagine Lao-tzu's ancient words mean in our modern era:

**Consider all things that seem to be a problem
from the perspective of the eternal Tao.**

Believing that there's a shortage of prosperity is a signal to think in terms of the inexhaustible Source: the Tao. Just like everything else on our planet, money is available in limitless quantities. Know this and connect to the bottomless supply. Do it first in your thoughts by affirming: *Everything I need now is here.* Prosperity thoughts are energetic instructions to access your infinite self, so actions will follow them.

Take this same approach—staying in harmony with the Tao—to all of your problems, for there's an all-encompassing supply of well-being to partner with. So rather than giving energy to illness and perceived misfortunes, stay with the Tao. Stay with what can never be used up. Stay with that which is the father of all things, the creative Source of all. It will work *with* and *for* you, as you have it in your thoughts, then in your feelings, and finally in your actions.

Be an infinite observer.

When acknowledged as a sign of change, worry is transitory—it's simply part of the world of the changing. If you view your life from the vantage point of an infinite observer, concerns, anxieties, and struggles blend into the eternal mix. From this ageless perspective, picture how important the things you feel depressed about now will be in a hundred, a thousand, a million, or an uncountable number of years. Remember that you, like the infinite Tao from which you originated, are part of an eternal reality.

Rearrange your thoughts to practice thinking in alignment with the Tao. With the assistance of the eternal Tao, all of the sharp edges of life smooth out, the knots loosen, and the dust settles. Try it!

Do the Tao Now

Pick a situation today (any situation will work), and instead of verbally responding, be silent and listen to your thoughts. For example, in a social gathering or business meeting, choose to seek the emptiness found in silence in order to be aware of your infinite self. Invite it to let you know when or whether to respond. If you find your worldly ego interpreting or judging, then just observe that without criticizing or changing it. You'll begin to find more and more situations where it feels peaceful and joyful to be without response . . . just to be in the infinity that's hidden but always present.

You might want to duplicate this advice of my teacher Nisargadatta Maharaj and post it conspicuously so that you can read it daily:

> *Wisdom is knowing I am nothing,*
> *love is knowing I am everything,*
> *and between the two my life moves.*

And while you're living, stay as close to love as you can.

5th Verse

Heaven and earth are impartial;
they see the 10,000 things as straw dogs.
The sage is not sentimental;
he treats all his people as straw dogs.

The sage is like heaven and earth:
To him none are especially dear,
nor is there anyone he disfavors.
He gives and gives, without condition,
offering his treasures to everyone.

Between heaven and earth
is a space like a bellows;
empty and inexhaustible,
the more it is used, the more it produces.

Hold on to the center.
Man was made to sit quietly and find
the truth within.

Living Impartially

The Tao does not discriminate—period! Like heaven and earth, it is impartial. The Tao is the Source of all, the great invisible provider. It doesn't show preference by giving energy to some while depriving others; rather, the basic life-sustaining components of air, sunshine, atmosphere, and rain are provided for *all* on our planet. By choosing to harmonize our inner and outer consciousness with this powerful feature of the Tao, we can realize the true self that we are. The true self is our unsentimental sage aspect that lives harmoniously with the Tao. This aspect doesn't view life in one form as more deserving than another, and it refuses to play favorites. Or, as Lao-tzu states, "He treats all his people as straw dogs."

Lao-tzu uses this term to describe how the Tao (as well as the enlightened ones) treats the 10,000 things that comprise the world of the manifest. In Stephen Mitchell's translation of the Tao Te Ching, he explains that "straw dogs were ritual objects, venerated before the ceremony but afterward abandoned and trampled underfoot." In other words, Taoism reveres and respects existence impartially, as an ebb and flow that is to be revered and then released. With impartial awareness, the sage genuinely sees the sacredness within all the straw dogs in this ceremony we call life.

The 5th verse encourages us to be aware of this unbiased Source and, as a bonus, to enjoy the paradoxical nature of the Tao. The more rapport we have with the energy of the Tao and the more we're living from its all-creating perspective, the more it is available to us. It's impossible to use it up—if we consume more, we simply receive more. But if we attempt to hoard it, we'll experience shortages ourselves, along with the failure of having even a wisp of understanding. The Tao and its inexhaustible powers paradoxically disappear when we attempt to exclude anyone from its unprejudiced nature.

The varied forms of life are illusory as far as the Tao is concerned, so no one is special or better than anyone else. This sentiment is echoed in the Christian scriptures: "[God] sends rain on the righteous and the unrighteous" (Matt. 5:45).

Practicing impartiality is a way to incorporate the 5th verse of the Tao Te Ching into your life, and to practice its wisdom in today's world. To that end, this is what I believe Lao-tzu was trying to impart to us from his 2,500-year-old vantage point:

Stay in harmony with the impartial essence of the Tao in all of your thoughts and all of your behaviors.

When you have a thought that excludes others, you've elected to see yourself as "special" and therefore deserving of exceptional favor from your Source of being. The moment you've promoted yourself to this category, you've elevated your self-importance above those whom you've decided are less deserving. Thinking this way will cause you to lose the all-encompassing power of the Tao. Organizations—including religious groups—that designate some members as "favored" aren't centered in the Tao. No matter how much they attempt to convince themselves and others of their spiritual connection, the act of exclusion and partiality eliminates their functioning from their true self. In other words, if a thought or behavior divides us, it is not of God; if it unites us, it *is* of God. Stay centered on this Tao that resides within you, Lao-tzu advises, and you'll never have a thought that isn't in harmony with spirit.

Offer your treasures to *everyone*.

This is what the Tao is doing at every moment—offering to all, the entire spectrum of creation. Think of this as a simple three-step process:

1. Eliminate as many judgments of others in your thoughts as possible. The simplest, most natural way to accomplish this is to see yourself in everyone. Remember that you and those you judge share one thing in common—the Tao! So rather than viewing appearances, which are really nothing more than straw dogs, see the unfolding of the Tao in those you encounter, and your criticisms and labels will dissolve.

2. Remove the word *special* from your vocabulary when you refer to yourself or others. If anyone is special, then we all are. And if we're all exceptional, then we don't need a word like that to define us, since it clearly implies that some are more favored than others!

3. Finally, implement the third step of this process by extending generosity through living the Tao impartially and connecting with the inner space of being the Tao. In this space you'll be able to be unbiased about your possessions, recognizing that they're not exclusively yours but are rather a part of the entirety. By unconditionally sharing and giving, you'll thrill at the experience of living the Tao and being unprejudiced. The Tao is your truth; it resides within you. Quietly be in the peace and joy of connecting with the inexhaustible Tao.

Do the Tao Now

As many times as possible today, decide to approach interactions or situations involving other people with a completely fair mind-set, which you allow and trust to guide your responses. Do this as often as you can for an entire day with individuals, groups, friends, family members, or strangers. Create a short sentence that you silently repeat to continually remind yourself that you're approaching this situation with an unbiased attitude, such as *Guide me right now, Tao; Holy Spirit, guide me now;* or *Holy Spirit, help us now.* Keeping this brief sentence on a loop in your mind will prevent judgment from habitually surfacing—but even more appealing is the feeling of relaxation and openness to whatever wants to happen in those moments of impartiality.

6th Verse

The spirit that never dies
is called the mysterious feminine.
Although she becomes the whole universe,
her immaculate purity is never lost.
Although she assumes countless forms,
her true identity remains intact.

The gateway to the mysterious female
is called the root of creation.

Listen to her voice,
hear it echo through creation.
Without fail, she reveals her presence.
Without fail, she brings us to our own perfection.
Although it is invisible, it endures;
it will never end.

Living Creatively

In this 6th verse, Lao-tzu refers to an eternal and indescribable force of creation that continuously gives birth to new life. He tells us that this "mysterious female" energy continually reveals itself in perfection, and he invites us to an awareness of that voice of creation echoing throughout life in myriad ways. "Living creatively" is how I describe existing with a conscious awareness of the presence of this feminine principle.

This mysterious female is always birthing, and the Tao Te Ching speaks of the gateway to her as the "root of creation." It's telling us that we have the ability to tap into this unlimited field and co-create, or as I've said, live creatively through the Tao. The never-dying formative energy is both our heritage and our destiny, functioning whether we're conscious of it or not. What awareness accomplishes, through practicing the Tao, is to let us participate in the process—which in turn leads us toward the wholeness that is our ultimate earthbound task.

Although his writings are almost 3,000 years old, Lao-tzu is offering 21st-century advice here, with a message that's as timeless and never-ending as the Tao itself. Words may change, but be assured that the feminine energy can and will bring you to your own perfection. If you choose to be aware of the inherent creativity that resonates deep within you, where the invisible Tao sings the loudest,

you'll assist the birthing of new ideas, new accomplishments, new projects, and new ways of understanding your life.

In Deng Ming-Dao's *365 Tao: Daily Meditations,* the Divine feminine energy is equated with the sound of birds soaring and gliding over a vast landscape:

> You can feel this in your life: Events will take on a perfect momentum, a glorious cadence. You can feel it in your body: The energy will rise up in you in a thrilling crescendo, setting your very nerves aglow. You can feel it in your spirit: You will enter a state of such perfect grace that you will resound over the landscape of reality like ephemeral bird song.
>
> When Tao comes to you in this way, ride it for all that you are worth. Don't interfere. Don't stop. . . . Don't try to direct it. Let it flow and follow it. . . . As long as the song lasts, follow. Just follow.

Here are some thoughts for living creatively:

Know that you are a Divine creation birthed, not by your parents, but by the great spiritual Divine Mother, the Tao.

When you're in touch with the energy of your origin, you offer the world your authentic intelligence, talents, and behaviors. You're co-creating with the you that originated in the Tao, with the very measure of your essence.

The Tao is not confused about what to create and how to go about it, as this is your legacy from the mysterious feminine. Listen to your inner callings, ignore how others might want to direct your life energies, and allow yourself to radiate outward what you feel so profoundly and deeply within you. There is a reservoir of talent, ability, and intelligence inside of you that's as endless and inexhaustible as the Tao itself. It must be that way, because you are what you came from, and where you came from is this all-encompassing, endlessly creative Divine Mother, the mysterious feminine of the Tao.

Whatever you feel within you as your calling—whatever makes you feel alive—know in your heart that this excitement is all the evidence you need to have your inner passion become reality. This is precisely how creation works . . . and it's that energy that harmonizes with the Tao.

**Be creative—in your thoughts, in your feelings,
and in all of your actions. Apply your own uniqueness
to everything you undertake.**

Whatever you feel compelled to do—be it write music, design software, do floral arrangements, clean teeth, or drive a taxi—do it with your unique flair. Being creative means trusting your inner calling, ignoring criticism or judgment, and releasing resistance to your natural talents. Reread this 6th verse, paying particular attention to these words: "Without fail, she reveals her presence. Without fail, she brings us to our own perfection." Then choose to let go of the doubt and fear you've harbored within you regarding your capacity to harmonize with the creative power—a power that's not only greater than your individual life, but *is* life itself.

As the great 14th-century Sufi poet Hafiz reminds all of us:

*Just sit there right now
Don't do a thing
Just rest.*

*For your separation from God,
From love,*

*Is the hardest work
In this
World.*

When you reconnect to your Divine Mother, you'll be living creatively. You will, in fact, be living the Tao!

Do the Tao Now

Today, notice babies and small children. Look for the mysterious feminine nature in little boys and girls who haven't yet become so attuned to cultural and societal demands that their true selves are hidden. Can you see some whose inherent nature is intact? Notice what seems to be their natural character, or their gift from the

31

Tao. Then try to recall yourself as a child, when the natural, Tao-given self was unaware of the ego-self—the time before you believed that acquisitions or power were important. Who were you? Who *are* you?

Yes, today spend a few moments with a young child and contemplate his or her connection to the Tao and how it unfolds perfectly without any interference.

7th Verse

Heaven is eternal—the earth endures.
Why do heaven and earth last forever?
They do not live for themselves only.
This is the secret of their durability.

For this reason the sage puts himself last
and so ends up ahead.
He stays a witness to life,
so he endures.

Serve the needs of others,
and all your own needs will be fulfilled.
Through selfless action, fulfillment is attained.

Living Beyond Ego

The opening line of this 7th verse of the Tao Te Ching is a reminder that the Tao, the Source of heaven and earth, is eternal. By extension, the original nature of life is everlasting and enduring. There is a quality that supports this durability, however, and that quality responds when we live from our Tao center, rather than from our worldly ego center. Identifying exclusively with the physicality of life—and basing our existence on acquiring and achieving things—disregards our infinite nature and limits our awareness of Taoness. In such a finite system, it therefore seems logical to strive for possessions and accomplishments.

Being civilized in most cultures primarily constitutes being consumed with attaining "success" in the acquisition of *power* and *things,* which supposedly will provide happiness and prevent unhappiness. The primary idea is of a self who's a separate being in a separate body, with a name, and with cultural and biological data that are similar in values and patriotism to others. The Tao, particularly in this 7th verse, is suggesting that we update those notions and choose to exist for more than ourselves or our tribe—that is, to radically change our thoughts in order to change our lives.

Lao-tzu says the secret of the ineffable nature of the eternal Tao is that it isn't identified with possessions or in asking anything of its endless creations. The Tao is a giving machine that never runs out

35

of gifts to offer, yet it asks nothing in return. Because of this natural tendency to live for others, the Tao teaches that it can never die. Giving and immortality then go hand in hand.

The sage who grasps the everlasting nature of the Tao has gone beyond false identification with the ego, and instead has a living connection to the Tao. This person puts others first, asks nothing in return, and wholeheartedly serves. In this way, the sage lives the ultimate paradox of the Tao—by giving without asking, he attracts everything that he's capable of handling or needing. By putting himself last, the sage ends up ahead. By putting others before himself, he endures just like the Tao. The sage emulates the natural philanthropy of the Tao, and all of his needs are fulfilled in the process.

The ego is a demanding force that's never satisfied: It constantly requires that we seek more money, power, acquisitions, glory, and prestige to provide the fuel it thinks it must have. Living a Tao-centered life rather than an ego-centered one removes us from that rat race, as it offers inner peace and satisfying fulfillment.

This is what I believe the wisdom of this verse of the Tao Te Ching is saying for the 21st century:

> **Make an attempt to reverse ego's hold on you**
> **by practicing the Tao's teaching to**
> **"serve the needs of others, and all your own**
> **needs will be fulfilled."**

Generously thinking of and serving others will lead to matching your behaviors with the perpetual rhythm of the Tao—then its power will flow freely, leading to a fulfilling life. Ego wants the opposite, however, as it tells you to think of yourself first and "get yours" before someone else beats you to it. The main problem with listening to ego is that you're always caught in the trap of striving and never arriving. Thus, you can never feel complete.

As you reach out in thoughts and behaviors, you activate loving energy, which is synonymous with giving. Put others ahead of you in as many ways as possible by affirming: *I see the sacred invisible Source of all in its eternal state of giving and asking nothing in return. I vow to be this, too, in my thoughts and behaviors.*

When you're tempted to focus on your personal successes and defeats, shift your attention in that very moment to a less fortunate individual. You'll feel more connected to life, as well as more satisfied than when you're dwelling on your own circumstances. Imagine what it would be like if you dismissed ego's hold on you. Serve others and watch how all that you give returns to you tenfold.

The poet Hafiz expresses this attitude perfectly:

> *Everyone*
> *Is God speaking.*
> *Why not be polite and*
> *Listen to*
> *Him?*

Stop the chase and be a witness.

The more you pursue desires, the more they'll elude you. Try letting life come to you and begin to notice the clues that what you crave is on its way. You're in a constant state of receiving because of the ceaseless generosity of the eternal Tao. The air you breathe, the water you drink, the food you eat, the sunshine that warms you, the nutrients that keep your body alive, and even the thoughts that fill your mind are all gifts from the eternal Tao. Stay appreciative of all that you receive, knowing that it flows from an all-providing Source. Stop the chase and become a witness—soothe your demanding habits by refusing to continue running after more. By letting go, you let God; and even more significantly, you become more like God and less like the ego, with its lifetime practice of edging God out.

Do the Tao Now

Be on the lookout for ego demands for an entire day. Decide to defuse as many of them as you can comfortably, perhaps by assigning them an "intensity grade." Living beyond ego situations that are easy to accomplish get a low number, while those requests that are difficult to quell get a higher number.

For example, let's say that your spouse is driving a car in which you are a passenger. You see the perfect parking space, but your mate drives right on by; or you watch him or her take a different route than you ordinarily do. Silently witness the degree of discomfort with your decision not to say anything. Did ego let you know its preference?

Or if you have a conversational opportunity to display your specialized knowledge or describe a situation wherein you were the recipient of honor or success, note how uncomfortable your decision to remain quiet felt. Again, did ego let you know its preference? As Lao-tzu says in this verse, "Through selfless action, fulfillment is attained." By holding back ego's demands, even for a few moments, you will feel more and more fulfilled.

8th Verse

The supreme good is like water,
which nourishes all things without trying to.
It flows to low places loathed by all men.
Therefore, it is like the Tao.

Live in accordance with the nature of things.
In dwelling, be close to the land.
In meditation, go deep in the heart.
In dealing with others, be gentle and kind.
Stand by your word.
Govern with equity.
Be timely in choosing the right moment.

One who lives in accordance with nature
does not go against the way of things.
He moves in harmony with the present moment,
always knowing the truth of just what to do.

*L*iving in the *F*low

The Tao and water are synonymous according to the teachings of Lao-tzu. You are water; water is you. Think about the first nine months of your life after conception: You lived in, and were nourished by, amniotic fluid, which is truly unconditional love flowing into you . . . flowing *as* you. You are now 75 percent water (and your brain is 85 percent), and the rest is simply muscled water.

Think about the mysterious magical nature of this liquid energy that we take for granted. Try to squeeze it, and it eludes us; relax our hands into it, and we experience it readily. If it stays stationary, it will become stagnant; if it is allowed to flow, it will stay pure. It does not seek the high spots to be above it all, but settles for the lowest places. It gathers into rivers, lakes, and streams; courses to the sea; and then evaporates to fall again as rain. It maps out nothing and it plays no favorites: It doesn't *intend* to provide sustenance to the animals and plants. It has no *plans* to irrigate the fields; to slake our thirst; or to provide the opportunity to swim, sail, ski, and scuba dive. These are some of the benefits that come naturally from water simply doing what it does and being what it is.

The Tao asks you to clearly see the parallels between you and this naturally flowing substance that allows life to sustain itself. Live as water lives, since you *are* water. Become as contented as is the fluid that animates and supports you. Let your thoughts and behaviors move smoothly in accordance with the nature of all things. It is natural for you to be gentle, to allow others to be free to go where they're inclined to go, and to be as they need to be without interference from you. It is natural to trust in the eternal flow, be true to your inner inclinations, and stick to your word. It is natural to treat everyone as an equal. All of these lessons can be derived by observing how water, which sustains all life, behaves. It simply moves, and the benefits it provides occur from it being what it is, in harmony with the present moment and knowing the truth of precisely how to behave.

What follows is what Lao-tzu might say to you, based upon his writing of the 8th verse of the Tao Te Ching:

When you're free to flow as water, you're free to communicate naturally—information is exchanged, and knowledge advances in a way that benefits everyone.

Be careful not to assign yourself a place of importance above anyone else. Be receptive to everyone, particularly those who may not routinely receive respect, such as the uneducated, homeless, or troubled members of our society. Go to the "low places loathed by all men," and have an open mind when you're there. Look for the Tao in everyone you encounter; and make a special effort to have acceptance, gentleness, and kindness course through you to others.

By not being irritating, you'll be received with respect. By making every effort to avoid controlling the lives of others, you'll be in peaceful harmony with the natural order of the Tao. This is the way you nourish others without trying. Be like water—which creates opportunities for swimming, fishing, surfing, drinking, wading, sprinkling, floating, and an endless list of benefits—by not trying to do anything other than simply flow.

Let your thoughts float freely.

Forget about fighting life or trying to be something else; rather, allow yourself to be like the material compound that comprises every aspect of your physical being. In *The Hidden Messages in Water*, Masaru Emoto explains that we are water, and water wants to be free. The author has thoroughly explored the ways in which this compound reacts, noting that by respecting and loving it, we can

literally change its crystallization process. If kept in a container with the words *love, thank you,* or *you're beautiful* imprinted on it, water becomes beautiful radiant crystals. Yet if the words on the container are *you fool, Satan,* or *I will kill you,* the crystals break apart, are distorted, and seem confused.

The implications of Emoto's work are stupendous. Since consciousness is located within us and we're essentially water, then if we're out of balance in our intentions, it's within the realm of possibility that our intentions can impact the entire planet (and beyond) in a destructive way. As our creator, the eternal Tao, might put it, "Water of life am I, poured forth for thirsty men."

Do the Tao Now

Drink water silently today, while reminding yourself with each sip to nourish others in the same life-flourishing way that streams give to the animals and rain delivers to the plants. Note how many places water is there for you—serving you by flowing naturally. Say a prayer of gratitude for this life-sustaining, always-flowing substance.

9th Verse

To keep on filling
is not as good as stopping.
Overfilled, the cupped hands drip,
better to stop pouring.

Sharpen a blade too much
and its edge will soon be lost.
Fill your house with jade and gold
and it brings insecurity.
Puff yourself with honor and pride
and no one can save you from a fall.

Retire when the work is done;
this is the way of heaven.

$\mathcal{L}$iving $\mathcal{H}$umility

As the eternal Tao is in a continuous state of creating, it knows precisely when enough is enough. Deep within ourselves, we sense that this organizing principle of unconditional supply knows when to stop, so we don't need to question the quantities that the Tao brings forth. The creative Source is beautifully balanced in the principle of humility elucidated in this 9th verse of the Tao Te Ching.

The Tao has the capability to generate everything in amounts that would stupefy an observer, yet its gentle humility seems to know when there are enough trees, flowers, bees, hippos, and every other living thing. Excess is eschewed by the Tao. It doesn't need to show off its unlimited capacity for creating—it knows exactly when to stop. This verse invites us to be in spiritual rapport with this characteristic of the Tao.

Cramming life with possessions, pleasures, pride, and activities when we've obviously reached a point where more is less indicates being in harmony with ego, not the Tao! Living humility knows when to just stop, let go, and enjoy the fruits of our labor. This verse clearly analogizes that the pursuit of more status, more money, more power, more approval, more *stuff*, is as foolish as honing a carving knife after it has reached its zenith of sharpness. Obviously, to continue would just create dullness, and it is obvious that a keen edge represents perfection.

Lao-tzu advises us to be careful about amassing great wealth and storing it away. This practice contributes to a life spent keeping our fortune safe and insured, while at the same time always feeling the need to pursue more. He counsels us to be satisfied at a level that fosters living with humility. If wealth and fame are desired, we must know when to retire from the treadmill and be like the Tao. This is the way of heaven, as opposed to the world that we live in, which is addicted to *more*.

We can heighten our awareness that advertising is primarily designed to sell products and services by convincing us that we need something in order to be happy. Analysts might tell us that the economy is failing if it isn't continuously growing, but we can realize that excessive growth, like cancer, will ultimately destroy itself. We can witness the results of overproduction in the gridlock on most highways: It now takes longer to go from one side of London to the other than it did before the invention of the automobile! We also see this principle at work whenever we shop. I call it "choice overload"—pain pills for backaches, menstrual cramps, headaches, joint pains, in the morning or at night, in a capsule or liquid or powder? And this is true whether we're purchasing toilet paper, orange juice, or anything else.

I believe that Lao-tzu sends the following modern advice from his ancient perspective:

Come to grips with the radical concept of "enough is enough"!

Make this commitment even though you live in a world addicted to the idea that one can never have enough of anything. To paraphrase Lao-tzu, do your work and then step back. Practice humility rather than ostentation and uncontrolled consumption. The obesity crisis in the Western world, particularly in America, is a direct result of not understanding (and living) the simple wisdom of the 9th verse of the Tao Te Ching. Eat, but stop when you're full—to continue stuffing food into a satiated body is to be trapped in believing that more of something is the cause of your happiness. And this is true of overly filling yourself with any artificial symbol of success. Think instead of the infinite wisdom of the Tao, which says, "To keep on filling is not as good as stopping." Enough is not only enough, it is in alignment with the perfection of the eternal Tao.

**Seek the joy in your activities rather
than focusing on ego's agenda.**

Ego wants you to gather more and more rewards for your actions. If you're in a state of loving appreciation in each of your present moments, you're letting go of the absurd idea that you're here to accumulate rewards and merit badges for your efforts. Seek the pleasure in what you're doing, rather than in how it might ultimately benefit you. Begin to trust in that infinite wisdom that birthed you into this material world. After all, it knew the exact timing of your arrival here. It didn't say, "If nine months will create such a beautiful baby, I'll extend the gestation period to five years. Now we'll have an even more perfect creation!" Nope, the Tao says that nine months is perfect—that's what you get, and you don't need any more time.

The next time you're mired in a desire for more, stop and think of the Tao. This creation principle fully grasps the idea that when the work is done, then for God's sake, it's time to stop! As Lao-tzu advises, "This is the way of heaven." Why ever choose to be in conflict with that?

Do the Tao Now

At your next meal, practice portion control by asking yourself after several bites if you're still famished. If not, just stop and wait. If no hunger appears, call it complete. At this one meal, you'll have practiced the last sentence of the 9th verse of the Tao Te Ching: "Retire when the [eating] is done; this is the way of heaven."

47

10th Verse

Carrying body and soul
and embracing the one,
can you avoid separation?

Can you let your body become
as supple as a newborn child's?
In the opening and shutting of heaven's gate,
can you play the feminine part?

Can you love your people
and govern your domain
without self-importance?

Giving birth and nourishing;
having, yet not possessing;
working, yet not taking credit;
leading without controlling or dominating.

One who heeds this power
brings the Tao to this very earth.
This is the primal virtue.

$\mathcal{L}$iving $\mathcal{O}$neness

This verse of the Tao Te Ching examines the paradoxical nature of life on Earth. Lao-tzu encourages the attainment of comfort with the seemingly incompatible opposites of body and soul, which form the basis of our daily life. We are connected to the power of the eternal Tao, while simultaneously being in a mortal physique. As we take on this seemingly ambiguous stance, we begin to see the world revealed as flawless. Everything that seems to be absolute is an opportunity to recognize its paradoxical reality.

This teaching takes the form of a series of questions: *Can an adult body with all of the conditions inherent in the aging process—such as stiffness, soreness, limitations caused by aching joints, and so on—be as supple as a newborn's? Is it possible to be someone who works and struggles and still be the feminine spirit, birthing creation? Can one succeed in these and similar ways and still be free of feelings of self-importance? Is it possible to stay true to the Tao without allowing ego to dominate, yet successfully function in an ego-dominated world?*

This 10th verse promotes a way of living that is guided by the power of "embracing the one" when the illusion of duality appears more powerful. Read Hafiz's writing on this subject thousands of years after the Tao Te Ching was written:

Only

That Illumined
One

Who keeps
Seducing the formless into form

Had the charm to win my
Heart.

Only a Perfect One

Who is always
Laughing at the word
<u>*Two*</u>

Can make you know

Of

Love.

Our origin cannot be split, yet we're in a world that all too often seems to reject the perfect oneness that is the Tao. We can personally live the Tao by suspending our belief in opposites and reactivating our awareness of its unity—that is, we can surrender ego and be *in* this world, without being *of* it.

This is my interpretation of Lao-tzu's advice from his 2,500-year-old perspective:

Embrace oneness by seeing yourself
in everyone you encounter.

Rather than having judgmental thoughts about those whom you regard as separate or different, view others as an extension of yourself. This will diminish self-importance and unite you with what Lao-tzu calls "the primal virtue." Letting go of ego-dominated thoughts lets you sense the oneness that you share with others; thus, you give yourself the opportunity to feel a part of the all-embracing Tao.

Practice inner awareness whenever you feel yourself about to criticize anyone or any group. News reports designed to encourage your sense of separateness or superiority in relation to others can be a perfect time to do this: Find yourself as one of them. In situations where you're expected to hate an assumed enemy, stop yourself from these judgments and walk an imaginary mile (or two) in their shoes. Do so with all forms of life, even the plant world. See yourself in everyone and all creations, noting the Tao in this simple observation: *We are the world.*

Take pleasure from what you possess without being attached to these things.

Let go of your identification with your stuff and with your accomplishments. Try instead to enjoy what you do and all that flows into your life simply for the pleasure of doing and observing the flow itself. You literally own nothing and no one: All that is composed will decompose; all that is yours will leave and become someone else's. So step back a bit and allow yourself to be an observer of this world of form. Becoming a detached witness will put you into a state of bliss, while loosening your tight grip on all of your possessions. It is in this releasing process that you'll gain the freedom to live out what the Tao is always teaching by example.

Do the Tao Now

Today, practice seeing oneness where you've previously seen "twoness" (separation). Feel the invisible energy that beats your heart, and then notice it beating the heart of every living creature all at once. Now feel the invisible energy that allows you to think, and sense it doing the same for every being currently alive.

Contemplate these words from the Gospel of Thomas: "His disciples said to him, 'When will the Kingdom come?' Jesus said, 'It will not come by looking outward. It will not say "Behold, this side" or "Behold, that one." Rather, the Kingdom of the Father is spread out upon the earth, and men do not see it.'" Today, know that practicing oneness thinking will help you see that Kingdom.

11th Verse

Thirty spokes converge upon a single hub;
it is on the hole in the center that
the use of the cart hinges.

Shape clay into a vessel;
it is the space within that makes it useful.
Carve fine doors and windows,
but the room is useful in its emptiness.

The usefulness of what is
depends on what is not.

Living from the Void

In this thought-provoking 11th verse of the Tao Te Ching, Lao-tzu cites the value of an emptiness that often goes unnoticed. He explains this idea with images of the hole in the center of a hub, the space within a clay vessel, and the interior area of a room, concluding that "the usefulness of what is depends on what is not." In other words, separated parts lack the usefulness that the center contributes. This passage invites us to live from the invisible void that's at the core of our being; that is, to change how we think about it.

Consider the paradoxical term *nonbeing* as you ponder your own beingness. You're comprised of bones, organs, and rivers of fluids that are encapsulated by a huge sheet of skin molded to hold you together. There's definitely a distinctive quality of beingness that is "you" in this arrangement of bodily parts—yet if it were possible to disassemble you and lay all of your still-functioning physical components on a blanket, there would be no you. Although all of the parts would be there, their usefulness depends on a nonbeingness, or in Lao-tzu's words, "what is not."

Imagine lining up the walls of the room you're presently in, with all of the elements present: Without the space of the center, it's no longer a room, even though everything else is the same. A clay pot is not a pot without the emptiness that the clay encapsulates. A house is not a house if there is no inner space for the exterior to enclose.

A composer once told me that the silence from which each note emerges is more important than the note itself. He said that it's the empty space between the notes that literally allows the music to be music—if there's no void, there's only continuous sound. You can apply this subtle awareness to everything that you experience in your daily life. Ask yourself what makes a tree, a tree. The bark? The branches? The roots? The leaves? All of these things are *what is*. And all of them do not constitute a tree. What's needed to have a tree is *what is not*—an imperceptible, invisible life force that eludes your five senses. You can cut and carve and search the cells of a tree endlessly and you'll never capture it.

In the first line of this verse, that hole in the center that's necessary for the movement of the wheel can be likened to the void that's vital for you to move through in your life. You have an inner state of nonbeing at your center, so take note of what is visible (your body) as well as the invisible essence that your existence depends upon . . . the Tao part of you.

The following is what I hear Lao-tzu saying to you regarding this concept of living in the void in today's world:

Your imperceptible center is your vital essence.

Take the time to shift your attention to the so-called nothingness that is your essence. What does it beckon you toward? The space emanates from the invisibleness that's responsible for all of creation, and the thoughts that emerge from your inner self are pure love and kindness.

Your inner nonbeingness isn't a separate part of you, so seek that mysterious center and explore it. Perhaps think of it as a space contained by your physical self, from which all of your thoughts and perceptions flow into the world. Rather than trying to have positive, loving notions, simply be sensitive to the essence of your beingness. The way of the Tao is to *allow* rather than to *try*. Thus, allow that essential center of pure love to activate your unique usefulness. Allow thoughts that emerge to enter your physical self and then leave. Allow and let go, just like your breathing. And vow to spend some time each day just being attentive to the awesome power of your imperceptible vital essence.

Practice the power of silence every day.

There are many individual ways of doing this. For example, meditation is a wonderful tool to help you feel the bliss that accompanies your connection to your inner void, that place where you experience the way of the Tao. Vow to be more aware of the "placeless place" within you, where all of your thoughts flow outward. Find your way to enter the space within you that is clean, pure, and in harmony with love.

The difference between saints and the rest of us isn't that they have loving, pure beliefs and we don't; rather, they function solely from their essence, where the way of the Tao flows invisibly through their physical being. This is the primary purpose of learning to meditate, or to be in the silence, inviting your essence to reveal itself and allowing you to live in the void.

Do the Tao Now

Spend at least 15 minutes today living in the void that is you. Ignore your body and your surroundings; let go of your material identifications such as your name, age, ethnicity, job title, and so on; and just be in that space between—that void which is absolutely crucial to your very existence. Look out at your world from "what is not" and appreciate that your very usefulness as a material being is completely dependent upon this void. Work today on befriending this "what is not" part of you.

12th Verse

The five colors blind the eye.
The five tones deafen the ear.
The five flavors dull the taste.
The chase and the hunt craze people's minds.

Wasting energy to obtain rare objects
only impedes one's growth.

The master observes the world
but trusts his inner vision.
He allows things to come and go.
He prefers what is within to what is without.

*L*iving with
*I*nner *C*onviction

In this passage of the Tao Te Ching, Lao-tzu reminds us that far too much attention is given to the pleasures and experiences of the senses at the expense of our inner vision. Focusing exclusively on sensory data creates a world of appearances, which are ultimately illusions. Since everything comes and goes, the nature of the material world is obviously restricted to transitory status. When our eyes see only the colors before them, they're destined to become blind to what lies beyond the world of appearances. We cannot know the creator if we're focused exclusively on what's been created. In the same way, we lose our own creativity when we're unaware of what's behind all acts of creation.

Sight, scent, sound, touch, and taste are the domains of the senses. If you're locked into a belief that the pursuit of sensory satisfaction is the focus of life, you'll be consumed by what Lao-tzu calls "the chase." This quest for adoration, money, and power is a waste of energy because there's never enough, so striving for more defines your daily regimen. You can't arrive at a place of peace and inner satisfaction when your entire existence is motivated by not having enough. In fact, Lao-tzu states that the relentless chase is a formula for craziness.

The person who lives according to the way of the Tao is referred to as a sage or a master, an enlightened being observing the world but not identifying exclusively with what's visible; being *in* the world, while simultaneously aware of not being *of* this world. The master goes within, where inner convictions replace the chase. In silence, sustenance is enjoyed beyond the dictates of the palate. From an inner perspective, nothing more is needed. Aware of his or her infinite nature, the sage has the realization that this is a temporary world of physical appearances, which includes the body that he or she arrived in and will leave in. The master sees the folly of appearances and avoids the seductive lure of acquisitions and fame.

I believe that our ancient friend and teacher Lao-tzu wanted to convey these simple truths when he dictated the 12th verse of the Tao Te Ching:

Extend your perspective beyond the sensory level.

Your inner conviction knows that a rose is more than a flower, as it offers a pleasant fragrance and velvety petals. Use that knowing to perceive the creative, invisible force that brings an intricate blooming miracle from *nowhere* to *now here*. Experience the essence of the creator who allowed this blossoming masterpiece to emerge from a tiny seed. Note that the seed arrived from what we can only refer to as the world of formless nothingness or spirit. See that spirit animating the colors, scents, and textures; and look at all of life from a transcendent perspective. You'll be less inclined to join the chase and more inclined to live from the inner conviction that your true essence is not of this world.

**Discontinue pressuring yourself to
perpetually accumulate *more*.**

Let others be consumed with the chase if they choose to, while you learn to relax. Rather than focusing outward, turn inward. Cultivate awe and appreciation as inner touchstones, rather than an outer determination for more adoration and accumulation. When you see a beautiful sight, hear an enchanting sound, or taste a mouthwatering delicacy, allow yourself to think of the miracle within these sensory pleasures. Be like the master who "prefers what is within to what is without." Allow things to come and go without any urgency to become attached to this ephemeral world of comings and goings.

Do the Tao Now

Plant a seed and cultivate it, observing its inner nature throughout its lifetime. Journal what's within the bud, and gaze in awe at what's in that seed that will one day create a flower. Then extend the same awe to yourself and the seed that had *you* contained inside as well. Use this as a reminder of your invisible inner self, which is the Tao at work.

13th Verse

Favor and disgrace seem alarming.
High status greatly afflicts your person.

Why are favor and disgrace alarming?
Seeking favor is degrading:
alarming when it is gotten,
alarming when it is lost.

Why does high status greatly afflict your person?
The reason we have a lot of trouble
is that we have selves.
If we had no selves,
what trouble would we have?

Man's true self is eternal,
yet he thinks, I am this body and will soon die.
If we have no body, what calamities can we have?
One who sees himself as everything
is fit to be guardian of the world.
One who loves himself as everyone
is fit to be teacher of the world.

*L*iving with an *I*ndependent *M*ind

The essential message of this 13th verse of the Tao Te Ching seems to be that it's crucial to remain independent of both the positive and negative opinions of other people. Regardless of whether they love or despise us, if we make their assessments more important than our own, we'll be greatly afflicted.

Seeking the favor of others isn't the way of the Tao. Pursuing status stops the natural flow of Divine energy to your independent mind. You have a basic nature that is uniquely yours—learn to trust that Tao nature and be free of other people's opinions. Allow yourself to be guided by your essential beingness, the "natural you" that nourishes your independent mind. By contrast, chasing after favored status or lofty titles to display self-importance are examples of living from a mind that depends on external signals rather than the natural inner voice.

The Tao doesn't force or interfere with things; it lets them work in their own way to produce results naturally. Whatever approval is supposed to come your way will do so in perfect alignment. Whatever disfavor shows up is also a part of this perfect alignment. Lao-tzu wryly points out that pursuing favor is alarming, regardless of the outcome. If you gain approval, you'll become a slave to outside messages of praise—someone else's opinion will be directing your life. If you gain disfavor, you'll push even harder to change *their* minds, and you'll still be directed by forces outside of yourself. Both outcomes result in the dependent mind dominating, as opposed to the way of the Tao, in which the independent mind flows freely.

This 13th verse insists that ego and the need for importance are troublemakers that are energized by your in-the-world self. The way of the Tao is to be aware of your eternal nature and step outside of your *self* or body. No ego means no trouble; big ego equals big trouble. The Tao Te Ching rhetorically inquires, "If we have no body, what calamities can we have?" If you ask *yourself* this question, you'll discover a Divine, invisible soul that's independent of the opinions of all the afflicted seekers populating the world. In the spirit of the Tao, your true nature will replace the pursuit of external favor with the awareness that what others think of you is really none of your business!

Practice the following principles in Lao-tzu's message and gain immeasurable inner peace. You'll be in balance with the natural law of the universe, living with an independent mind in the spirit of the Tao:

Practice trusting your own inner nature.

Every passionate thought that you have regarding how you want to conduct your life is evidence that you're in harmony with your own unique nature—your fervent belief is all you need. If you're tempted to feel insecure because others disagree with you, recall that Lao-tzu counseled that "seeking favor is degrading" and will lead you out of touch with your true self.

Give yourself permission to remember that you're not only your body, and that others' opinions about what you should or shouldn't be doing probably aren't taking into account your true, eternal being. Those other people are also not only their bodies, so seeking their approval doubles the illusion that the physical is all we are.

Your worldly self isn't your true identity, so trust your eternal self to communicate with you. It will do so through your inner nature, where you'll honor it through an independent mind. Respect your vision and trust your natural, passionate thoughts that are aligned with the loving essence of the Tao.

**Practice being the person Lao-tzu
describe in this 13th verse.**

Affirm the following: *I am a guardian of the world* and *I am fit to
be the teacher of the world.* Why? Because you recognize your connection to everyone and everything through an independent mind
whose Source is love. By living from your eternal self, you'll become
a mystical teacher and guardian. The approval that your worldly self
sought will be felt as what it was—the dependent mind's struggle to
engage life as if it depended on external approval.

Do the Tao Now

Ask yourself right now, *What's my own nature if I have no outside
forces telling me who or what I should be?* Then work at living one day
in complete harmony with your own nature, ignoring pressures to
be otherwise. If your inner nature is one of peace, love, and harmony as a musical genius, for instance, then act on just that today.

14th Verse

That which cannot be seen is called invisible.
That which cannot be heard is called inaudible.
That which cannot be held is called intangible.
These three cannot be defined;
therefore, they are merged as one.

Each of these three is subtle for description.
By intuition you can see it,
hear it,
and feel it.
Then the unseen,
unheard,
and untouched
are present as one.

Its rising brings no dawn,
its setting no darkness;
it goes on and on, unnameable,
returning into nothingness.

Approach it and there is no beginning;
follow it and there is no end.
You cannot know it, but you can be it,
at ease in your own life.

Discovering how things have always been
brings one into harmony with the Way.

*L*iving *B*eyond *F*orm

Try to imagine the idea of forever: that which has never changed, that which has no beginning or end. It cannot be seen, heard, or touched . . . but you know it is and always has been. Think of that which even now, in this very moment as you read these words, is the very understanding that's within you—that essence that permeates you and everything else, yet always eludes your grasp.

This primordial principle has ruled—and still rules—all beings; all that is or has ever been is a result of its unfolding. Lao-tzu insists that you become aware of this amorphous precept by not relying upon your senses to experience this oneness. In the opening of this verse, you're urged to see without eyes, hear without ears, and hold without touching; these three ways of living beyond form need to be a part of your awareness. These shapeless realms merge into the one world of spirit (the Tao), which creates and rules all life. You're being encouraged to live with a total awareness of this all-encompassing principle.

Some scholars have singled out this 14th verse of the Tao Te Ching as the most significant of all its 81 offerings because it stresses the significance of the single principle that's the underpinning of all existence. Tapping into this invisible, untouchable, immeasurable force will enable you to gain the harmony that comes with being connected to the oneness, and harmony is your ultimate objective in deciding to live an "in-Spirited" life. You want to learn to abandon your ego—which identifies with the world of things, possessions, and achievements—and reenter the placeless place from which you and all others originated. By doing so you regain the mystical, almost magical powers of your eternal Source of being. Here, you live beyond the world of form.

When you live exclusively "in-form," you concentrate on accumulating "in-form-ation." This 14th verse of the Tao calls for you to immerse yourself in inspiration rather than information, to become at one with that which has always been. And as this verse of the Tao concludes so insightfully, "Discovering how things have always been brings one into harmony with the Way."

The Way has no conflict in it. How could it? There is only the oneness that is a blend of the invisible, inaudible, and intangible. Imagine a world where conflict is impossible, where Lao-tzu says that there is no darkness or light. The nameless Source that has always been gives only the peace and harmony you desire, so recognize this infinite oneness and keep it in your awareness. You'll know that the Way is simply the Way when you stop questioning why things have been as they have! Free of the fears that attend sole identification with this world of form, you can embrace your infinite nature. That is, you can love your foreverness, rather than dread that life ends with the death of your body. You, your body, and all of life are the result of the unwinding of this eternity.

Here's what Lao-tzu is relating in this 14th verse of the Tao Te Ching from his 2,500-year-old perspective:

Use the technique of walking meditation to obtain knowledge of the absolute.

Stay in a persistent state of awareness of the eternal principle that animates all of life. By seeing the unfolding of God in everyone you encounter—and in all of your identification with your ego-based world—you'll come to be more like Him, and less like that which has tarnished your link to Him. This is the alignment that will bring you back into balance and restore the harmony that is your true egoless nature.

**Improve your vision by looking
beyond what your eyes see.**

Whatever you gaze upon, ask yourself, *What is the true essence of what my eyes reveal to me?* Wonder about that magical something that awakens a tree in the springtime and places blossoms where frozen limbs existed only a few weeks before. Inquire, *What is the energy behind the creation of that mosquito—or behind my every thought, for that matter?* Do the same thing with everything you hear as well. Those sounds emerge from, and return to, a silent world—improve your hearing by listening for the "quiet sounds."

Awe and gratitude will grow when you embrace this forever principle. But even greater than this, you'll awaken to new possibilities that include your own Divine magnificence. Your mind will free itself from a false identification with the transitory world, and you'll see the eternal in all things. Yes, Lao-tzu tells you, you'll transform your life by being in-Spirit. It is here that you will recognize what Rumi poetically offered some 1,500 years after Lao-tzu's powerful words:

> *Every tree and plant in the meadow seemed to be dancing,
> those which average eyes would see as fixed and still.*

I urge you to see the dance of "how things have always been" in the unseen, unheard, and untouched present.

Do the Tao Now

Take note of as much invisibleness as you can when gazing at a tree, a distant star, a mountain, a cloud, or anything else in the natural world. Embrace the principle that allows it to be, and then turn it inward and do the same for your own physical existence. It is the principle that expands your lungs, beats your heart, and grows your fingernails—live in this principle for ten minutes today and take note of how you feel connected to your Source of Being.

15th Verse

The ancient masters were profound and subtle.
Their wisdom was unfathomable.
There is no way to describe it.
One can only describe them vaguely by their appearance.

Watchful, like men crossing a winter stream.
Alert, like men aware of danger.
Simple as uncarved wood.
Hollow like caves.
Yielding, like ice about to melt.
Amorphous, like muddy water.

But the muddiest water clears
as it is stilled.
And out of that stillness
life arises.

He who keeps the Tao does not want to be full.
But precisely because he is never full,
he can remain like a hidden sprout
and does not rush to early ripening.

*L*iving an *U*nhurried *L*ife

This 15th verse speaks of ancient masters who enjoyed an indescribably profound level of cooperation with their world. Lao-tzu uses similes to dramatize the flexible and peaceful lives of these sages: Imagine crossing an icy winter stream that might crack at any moment, remaining cautious and watchful while at the same time alert to imminent danger. These descriptors paint a picture of those who live unhurriedly but are also in a profoundly aware state.

Consider the two ways of being presented in this verse of the Tao Te Ching: first to meld into, and therefore become at one with, your immediate surroundings; and to then simultaneously stay so relaxed that your stillness allows all things around you to settle, resulting in a deep clarity. Keep alert and subtly aware, yet at the same time stay still within—not rushing or demanding, but totally in charge of your inner world. This passage of the Tao reminds me of these words of the Bible: "Be still, and know that I am God" (Ps. 46:10).

The place of your origination is stillness, from which all of creation comes. Stay in a creative, simple state, which Lao-tzu describes as "uncarved wood," symbolizing beginner's mind and unlimited potential. Have a mind that's willing to flow with life and be shaped by the eternal forces of the Tao. See yourself as all of these things mentioned in this 15th verse of the Tao: watchful, yet relaxed and peaceful; alert, yet unhurried and confident; yielding, yet willing to be still and wait for the waters to become clear.

This verse reminds you that through nature, everything ultimately becomes clear. Your purpose is to stay in harmony with nature like the sprout hidden beneath the surface of the ground, waiting unhurriedly to emerge and fulfill its destiny. It cannot be rushed, nor can anything in nature. Creation takes place on its own timetable. The metaphor is clear here for you as well: You are unfolding in Divine order. All that you require will be provided in an unhurried fashion. Let go of your demands and trust in the perfect unfolding of the Tao. Be in a state of watchful gratitude and align with the Way.

In attempting to access the mind and intentions of Lao-tzu through meditation and research on the Tao Te Ching, here's what I believe he would say to us today:

Stop chasing your dreams.

Allow them to come to you in perfect order with unquestioned timing. Slow down your frantic pace and practice being hollow like the cave and open to all possibilities like the uncarved wood. Make stillness a regular part of your daily practice. Imagine all that you'd like to experience in life and then let go. Trust the Tao to work in Divine perfection, as it does with everything on the planet. You don't really need to rush or force anything. Be an observer and receiver rather than the pushy director of your life. It is through this unhurried unfolding that you master your existence in the way of the Tao.

Get in the flow of life and allow yourself to proceed gently down its stream.

Give up struggling and start trusting in the wisdom of the Tao. What is yours will come to you when you aren't trying to push the river. You've probably been encouraged to actively direct and go after your desires all of your life . . . now it's time to trust in the eternal wisdom that flows through you.

The Way of Life According to Lao Tzu, translated by Witter Bynner in 1944, poetically sums up the 15th verse of the Tao in this way:

> *How can a man's life keep its course*
> *If he will not let it flow?*
> *Those who flow as life flows know*
> *They need no other force:*
> *They feel no wear, they feel no tear,*
> *They need no mending, no repair.*

Great advice for living an unhurried life.

Do the Tao Now

Set this book down right now. Take ten minutes to sit quietly while contemplating all that you have and all that is flowing into your life on a Divinely orchestrated timetable. Be at peace and give thanks for what is allowing your life to unfold so perfectly. Let go of all other hurried thoughts.

16th Verse

Become totally empty.
Let your heart be at peace.
Amidst the rush of worldly comings and goings,
observe how endings become beginnings.

Things flourish, each by each,
only to return to the Source . . .
to what is and what is to be.

To return to the root is to find peace.
To find peace is to fulfill one's destiny.
To fulfill one's destiny is to be constant.
To know the constant is called insight.
Not knowing this cycle
leads to eternal disaster.

Knowing the constant gives perspective.
This perspective is impartial.
Impartiality is the highest nobility;
the highest nobility is Divine.

Being Divine, you will be at one with the Tao.
Being at one with the Tao is eternal.
This way is everlasting,
not endangered by physical death.

Living with Constancy

The 16th verse of the Tao Te Ching describes the value of being supremely conscious of the constant cycle of all. Rather than viewing change as a disruptive, unwanted occurrence, you can choose to view the variances in your world as valuable influences in the cycle of a Tao-centered existence.

When you see change as the only constant there really is, you start to recognize it as an expression of ongoing life that's a welcome clue to your own purpose and meaning. In this way, you're returned to the experience of your Source and the peace of an impartial perspective. Begin this process by altering your ego-based thoughts and letting yourself feel the bliss of being at one with the Tao. Then become an acute observer of how your world really works, and allow yourself to be in harmony with the cyclical nature of all living things.

There's an immutable cycle of "no life, life, no life" that we're part of. All things come, and then they go. Life materializes in a variety of forms—it's here, and then at some point it ends in what we call death. This coming and going might seem to be a temporary condition, but it's actually the ultimate constant because it never ceases. Embrace this nature of cyclical change and you'll thrive.

An ending may feel like a reason to mourn, whether it be the closing of a phase in your life, the completion of a project, the termination of a relationship, or death itself. But Lao-tzu invites you to realize that after things flourish, they "return to the Source . . . to what is and what is to be." The constancy of the cycles of life is an opportunity to return to your root, where what is and what is to be are located. The ultimate place of peace and enlightenment is in this continuous return to the nameless, placeless site of your origination.

Lao-tzu tells you that a sense of inner peace comes with returning to the Source, where all cycles begin and end. This is the fulfillment of your own personal destiny; that is, you're here to know and be the Tao, the constant beyond the comings and goings of life. You've been in many bodies already, and you're in a new one every day. You've been in and out of many relationships, yet the eternal you survives despite transitions from beginnings back into endings. You're now being urged to know yourself as a physical creation *and* as a piece of the everlasting Tao.

The Tao that animates all existences, including your own, is totally impartial. It plays no favorites: It brings winter regardless of whether you want it or not. It sends those you love on to other people and then back, irrespective of your desires to have it otherwise. All of life must return to it; there are no exceptions or apologies.

When you're unaware of this steadying influence, you attach to one element of one cycle in life, leading to what Lao-tzu calls "eternal disaster." When one person leaves you, it feels like the end of the world. When a business venture fails, you flunk out of school, or you have a painful illness or injury, you feel depressed. If you get trapped in these emotional endings, you're not permitting them to also be a natural part of life, leading you to feel disconnected from your Source. You become stuck in the "rush of worldly comings and goings," unable to remember the constancy where "endings become beginnings."

The reality is that beginnings are often disguised as painful endings. So when you know that there's a constant beyond the present moment's disappointment, you can sense that "this too shall pass"—it always has and always will. When you change the way you look at things, the things you look at change!

This is what Lao-tzu seems to be telling you in this 16th chapter of the Tao Te Ching:

**Take time to be an impartial observer of life,
particularly when an ending is causing despair.**

Remind yourself that your Source is at work within this event, and then make a decision to connect to that Source with your thoughts. All endings are part of the cyclical process; you're merely returning to a life of constancy, which Lao-tzu taught in this passage. You don't have to learn anything new, change any behavior, or adopt any new strategies—just think about the word *return,* and take comfort in the ever-constant Tao, which brings peace to despair. The Tao never leaves or disappoints, and it is always impartial. Wherever you are in the emotional cycle, you're not being judged. Rather, you're learning to be in all phases, free of judgment and living with constancy.

Write these words and post them in a conspicuous place in your living environment: *This too shall pass.*

This phrase will remind you that change is the only constant in life. Everything you notice is in a cycle of coming and going. Everything! There are no exceptions. Know this and let your thoughts flow in the constancy of change. This is the root, the Source of all cyclical happenings. It is perfect. It is Divine. It is something you can totally rely upon. It brings spring flowers, it brings the aging process, it brings rebirth, it brings new relationships—it is the Tao and it is constant. Return to it and experience your eternal essence here and now, in the temporary container you call your body and all of its dramas. *This too shall pass . . .* you can count on it!

Do the Tao Now

Dedicate a day to consciously seeking situations to practice impartially observing endings as beginnings, challenging yourself to find a specific number by noon. Begin in the morning by being aware that the end of asleep is the beginning of awake. Break your waking time into sections, noticing without judging the endings that make space for beginnings. Start to consciously live with constancy by opening your mind to the fact that change is the only certain thing. Remember to include all of your feelings in its cycle—impartially observing *sad,* for instance, permits its natural ending to transform to a beginning. You're doing the Tao!

17th Verse

With the greatest leader above them,
people barely know one exists.
Next comes one whom they love and praise.
Next comes one whom they fear.
Next comes one whom they despise and defy.

When a leader trusts no one,
no one trusts him.

The great leader speaks little.
He never speaks carelessly.
He works without self-interest
and leaves no trace.
When all is finished, the people say,
"We did it ourselves."

*L*iving as an *E*nlightened *L*eader

To reflect the lesson in this verse of the Tao Te Ching means changing how you see authority—which means viewing great or enlightened leaders as those who don't actually *lead* anyone! Through the perspective of the Tao, such individuals create an environment where everyone feels that they have a personal responsibility to, and are a part of, the process. By adopting this model of an enlightened leader, you'll be more than likely to alter the ways you criticize and admire captains of industry, government, or religion, as well as the way *you* guide others.

The advice in this 17th verse is directed toward leaders of all kinds; in fact, you can personalize it by substituting the words *parent* or *teacher* for *leader*. Examine the ways you view your own tactics, and then make the changes that are necessary in order to be someone who makes an enlightening difference in the lives of others. First, you must stay in the background and become an astute observer of what's taking place; then ask yourself how, without interfering, you can create an environment that will help everyone act responsibly.

The Tao advises making yourself as invisible as possible if you truly wish to be an effective leader. Thus, perhaps your best strategy would be to actually leave the room and allow everyone else to act without feeling that they need to impress you. Maybe you should offer a slight suggestion and then an immediate departure. A knowing smile or gesture that conveys to the group that you trust in its ability to figure things out might work best. Possibly what's needed is for you tell a quick story of how others have resolved similar issues. Or you could simply meditate and send positive conflict-resolving energy to all the individuals present.

Whatever your decision, you'll be well aware of the need to create an environment where everyone will be able to say, "We fixed it ourselves without the need for any interference from anyone—we really don't need a supervisor." This approach, of course, involves suspending your desire to be seen as a strong authority figure.

Truly inspiring leaders get results by their own example: They encourage others to be responsible and do the right thing, but not by proclaiming and bragging about their unimpeachable management. They create space for others to be inspired and to achieve their own greatness. When the time comes for receiving accolades, they dissolve in the background, wanting everyone else to feel that their accomplishments arose from their own leadership qualities. The supreme Taoist leader always leaves people to choose and pursue their own way of life, their own conception of the good. The view of a self-styled authoritarian is not the way enlightened leaders see themselves; rather, they raise the energy of an environment through a viewpoint that elevates lower inclinations.

In this verse, the Tao offers three other ways of choosing to be a leader. One option is to make a difference in the lives of others, resolving conflicts through love. By being an instrument of love and making an effort to praise others, this leader stays in harmony with the Tao. Those who are praised are inclined to become self-loving and act in a cooperative rather than competitive fashion. The drawback is that using the approval and affection of a leader for motivation means turning control of one's life over to that leader. But if you see that the choice is between love or fear, the Tao always sees love as superior.

The ineffectiveness of fear as a leadership style is obvious: If I can get you to do as I desire by using that weapon, then you'll only behave in these ways as long as I have the power to threaten you. When I leave, my influence over you departs as well. Studies have measured the effectiveness of teachers who were considered strict disciplinarians. Students in this setting were well behaved when the

feared individual was in the room, yet when he or she departed, the classroom turned chaotic.

The opposite was true of instructors who viewed education as an opportunity to praise and encourage students: Their presence or absence from the room had almost no noticeable impact. This is a great thing to keep in mind if you're a mother or father. That is, do you want your children to behave only when you're around, or do you want them to have the self-discipline to conduct themselves wisely whether you're there or not? I've always believed that parents are not for leaning upon, but rather exist to make leaning unnecessary.

The least effective means for managing others is to use tactics that will encourage them to despise you, for the moment they leave your sight, they'll defy all that you say and stand for. Dictators almost always find this out the hard way, when the people they've abused rise up to threaten them in the same intolerable fashion in which they've been treated. Children who despise a parent similarly tend to emulate the hateful tactics to which they were subjected, or they detach themselves completely from that dictatorial adult and spend years attempting to heal the scars from the terrible treatment.

The enlightened leader trusts those whom he or she is in a position to govern. This view results in trust, as he or she who has faith in the people will be trusted by them in turn. Consequently, they'll be able to say, "We did it ourselves." So raise your children to be self-sufficient, to make their own decisions as soon as they're able, and to feel pride in the decisions they do make. See yourself as an enlightened leader, and show the world a new type of leadership. Children who grow up with such a view will be the next generation of great leaders that Lao-tzu describes.

Here's what I believe the esteemed master Lao-tzu is offering you today:

**Instead of believing that you know what's best for others,
trust that they know what's best for themselves.**

Allow other people to share their thoughts about the path they see for themselves. Let your position be known, but also convey that you trust them to make the right choice. Then step back and peacefully believe that the way you look at this situation will change. Offer praise when those in your charge are making their own decisions, even when their behavior may conflict with yours. Trust yourself to give the best response by not seeing yourself as knowing what's right. Remember this phrase from the Tao Te Ching: "When a leader trusts no one, no one trusts him." The surest way to gain the faith of those you govern or supervise is to allow them to make as many decisions as possible.

Take pride in refusing to take credit
for the achievements of others.

If you look at others' accomplishments as a reason for *you* to be rewarded, promoted, or complimented, change your viewpoint. Let praise go to those who are the beneficiaries of your leadership. Speak less frequently and suspend your self-interest—instead, allow everyone in your care to speak for themselves. Change how you see their performance from being a credit to your skill to the thrill they exhibit over their accomplishment. You'll cease wanting credit, and alternatively feel the happiness and pride that they're experiencing.

This is how Hafiz described it in his 14th-century poetry:

Even
After
All this time
The sun never says to the earth,
"You owe
Me."

Look
What happens
With a love like that,
It lights the
Whole
Sky.

Love those you're entrusted to lead, just as the sun loves our planet. Simply be there to serve, never demanding anything in return.

Do the Tao Now

Choose some situations with your children (or anyone you've been designated to supervise) to become an active observer. Nod, smile, frown, or gesture without saying a thing, where you previously would have readily interfered. Notice how your active observing impacts those you've been assigned to lead.

18th Verse

When the greatness of the Tao is present,
action arises from one's own heart.
When the greatness of the Tao is absent,
action comes from the rules
of "kindness and justice."

If you need rules to be kind and just,
if you _act_ virtuous,
this is a sure sign that virtue is absent.
Thus we see the great hypocrisy.

When kinship falls into discord,
piety and rites of devotion arise.
When the country falls into chaos,
official loyalists will appear;
patriotism is born.

Living Without Rules

Picture yourself in a world where rules and laws don't exist, where everyone lives peacefully and harmoniously. There's no anarchy, thievery, hatred, or war; people simply live, work, love, and play without needing to be governed. Can you imagine a planet where the need for codes of conduct and edicts to govern the populace are simply unnecessary? This is the sort of idealistic mental meandering that led Lao-tzu to create this 18th verse of the Tao Te Ching, in which he's clearly stating that you don't need rules to be kind and just.

I'm suggesting that when you change the way you look at the underlying reason for regulation, the organizations controlling society, politics, and the criminal-justice system will eventually change. (Need I add "for the better"?) When you alter your viewpoint to a Tao-oriented one, you cease to see your dominant reason for being and doing as being dictated by your nation, city, school, religion, or even your condominium association! Laws or rules are seen by many as solely responsible for effective kindness, justice, and love—but you can choose to live from your heart, viewing these virtues as individual responsibilities that you adhere to without a statute or convention telling you to. This is what I mean by living without rules: You can choose to see yourself in harmony with the regulations and laws of your business, government, family, and religion rather than *because* of them. I promise you that when you adjust rule-based thinking to a heart-based attitude, your life will change!

In the Tao orientation, unlimited joy, kindness, abundance, and well-being flow through all; seeing life in this way makes rules irrelevant. You can act in accordance with this munificence and beneficence, which are the essence of the Tao. Make love the bedrock of your family's motivation to be loving, rather than just feeling obligated to be kind to others. This doesn't mean there isn't certain etiquette or behavior to follow—it means that the reason to do so is so that love and kindness flow through all individuals. And if there *is* any "crime," it's the stopping or hindering of that energy of the Tao.

You and your children can learn to change the way you look at edicts and laws. When harmony is lost, a rule may seem to be helpful, but make sure everyone in the family realizes that you're inviting them to learn to live without it! The existence of codes of conduct are proof that we aren't allowing the Tao to flow freely through our lives. Learning that it is each individual's personal responsibility to live without governing will ultimately demonstrate that when you change your thoughts, you change your life.

This idea extends further: Ask yourself if laws create a healthy society, and if patriotism is valuable. Or does it appear that when a country has fallen into chaos or some form of civil war, laws and codes concerning patriotism seem to need to be enforced? Rules are created to impose penalties to control or govern people who haven't learned their individual responsibility as a part of the wholeness of the group. Yet a national sense of unity needn't regulate a universal sense, for the Tao oneness is greater than any group on Earth.

So here we have a summary of what takes place when the Great Way is deserted: The need for justice arises. Falsity among the people creates a need for rules, and rulers are needed to restore order. Political ministers appear to bring light to the disorder and darkness. Knowing all of this, I believe it's essential to get back to that picture I asked you to envision a few paragraphs ago and apply what Lao-tzu is saying in this profound verse of the Tao Te Ching:

Let your actions arise from your Tao-centered heart.

When you're centered in the Tao, you don't need any rules, nor are you bound by what's declared to be legal or illegal. Your reason for not stealing from others isn't because it's against the law; rather, you assume personal responsibility for your actions. Your life isn't based on living by rules; your reason for not stealing is that you respect the rights of others to be free from pilfering because it resonates with the Tao. In the Tao there is no stealing because everything belongs to everyone. There is no ownership of land or property—there is only the willingness to love and respect everyone and all things. The laws making stealing, maiming, or fighting illegal arose because of disconnection from the Tao.

Don't act virtuous; *be* virtue.

Acting virtuous is not the same as *being* virtuous, so the Tao instructs you to be authentic in all of your interactions. Be pious because your own heart feels the piety that is the great Tao. Be spontaneously generous to others because your inner calling demands it, not because others in their code making have determined that this is how you should behave. Don't wait for chaos to erupt before you are generous and kind to others. A natural disaster may stimulate your desire to reach out and help your fellow humans—yet if you change the way you look at that natural disaster, you could also see it as a reminder to let the Tao be your guiding spirit at all times. This would inspire your patriotism to be for all of humanity, rather than confined to the land where you happened to be born.

Again, I'd like to remind you of the similar sentiment expressed by Hafiz, the great Sufi poet:

> *Everyone*
> *Is God speaking.*
> *Why not be polite and*
> *Listen to*
> *Him?*

And everyone really means *everyone*, not just those who are subject to your rules and your laws.

Do the Tao Now

Emphasize *why* you're obeying human-made edicts today. Spend some time connecting to the underlying reason for stopping at a red light, having a driver's license, wearing a seat belt, paying to enter a movie theater, or not drinking and driving. See if your ego enjoys "breaking" rules for its purposes by listing all the rules and laws you obey or disobey in one day, and then identify your most important "heart rules."

19th Verse

Give up sainthood, renounce wisdom,
and it will be a hundred times better for everyone.
Throw away morality and justice
and people will do the right thing.
Throw away industry and profit
and there will be no thieves.

All of these are outward forms alone;
they are not sufficient in themselves.

It is more important
to see the simplicity,
to realize one's true nature,
to cast off selfishness
and temper desire.

$\mathcal{L}$iving $\mathcal{W}$ithout $\mathcal{A}$ttachment

Upon first reading this 19th verse of the Tao Te Ching, it appears that Lao-tzu is encouraging us to abandon the highest principles of the Tao. Renounce sainthood, wisdom, morality, justice, industry, and profit, says the great sage, and all will be well. Lao-tzu tells us that "all of these are outward forms alone" and are insufficient for living according to the highest Way.

The first of these categories represents education and the way you look at your sources of learning. This verse advises you to alter your concept of being saintly just because you follow the teachings of an organized religion, and to change your view of self-importance because of degrees you've received from an educational institution. Lao-tzu gently informs you that it's far more valuable to cultivate your true nature.

As with virtually all of the teachings of the Tao, the greatest trust is placed in your accessing the sacred Tao center of yourself. Within you lies a piece of God that instinctively knows what to do and how to be. Trust yourself, Lao-tzu advises, and reevaluate the ultimate importance of educational and religious institutions. When you modify how you see them, you'll notice that the true essence of you is "a hundred times better for everyone." Lao-tzu might say that a truth is a truth until you organize it, and then it becomes a lie. Why? Because the purposes of the organization begin to take precedence over that which it first attempted to keep in order.

"Throw away morality and justice," this verse urges, "and people will do the right thing." Here, in the second of the outward forms, Lao-tzu reveals a legal system that takes precedence over your natural internal integrity. When you know that you emerged from an impeccable Source of honor and equality, you don't have to rely on a system of justice. Lao-tzu reminds you that it's very important not to view yourself as relegated to an inferior position because laws of morality tell you who you "really" are. See yourself centered with the perfection of the Tao, which is your nature, rather than needing to consult a law book, a courtroom, or a judge to determine your ethical standing. These labyrinthine systems designed to determine all issues of right and wrong are evidence of our drift away from the simplicity of our inborn nature.

The last of the outward forms is the whole world of business. "Renounce profit seeking, give up ingenuity, and discard record keeping, and thieves will disappear altogether," could be one interpretation. Lao-tzu advises you to stay centered within the all-encompassing integrity of the Tao and to release your view of profits and monetary gain as indicators of your level of success. When you see your life through the perspective of the Tao teaching, you'll have no need to hoard large sums of money. Instead, you'll discover the pleasure of serving others in a spirit of endless generosity. Or, as this translation of the Tao Te Ching puts it, you'll "cast off selfishness and temper desire."

These, then, are the three outward forms: education, justice, and business. You're being encouraged to update how you see the reasons for, the methods used by, and the way well-meaning people have taught to value those arenas of life. When you change how you see them, you'll note the simplicity and sacredness of a higher principle, which will enrich those institutions with the free-flowing Tao. You'll realize your own true nature, cast off selfishness, and temper your desire. Be *in* the world of education, justice, and business—but not *of* it—and you'll see the inner world where you're centered in the Tao.

This is what Lao-tzu is saying to you, through me, from his 2,500-year-old perch:

Observe your relationship to systems of education, justice, and business.

Notice attempts to compartmentalize you: Are you dependent on a system of reward and punishment for approval? Do the rules and codes of conduct you follow come from a heart-centered space, or are they designed to create a label of "specialness"? Don't fight these institutional pressures or even the fact that they exist—simply let go of all attachments to them. You are not saintly (a good person) because an organization says so, but rather because you stay connected to the divinity of your origination. You are not intelligent because of a transcript; you are intelligence itself, which needs no external confirmation. You are not moral because you obey the laws; you are morality itself because you are the same as what you came from.

Choose to see the outward forms as poor substitutions for your true nature and you'll begin to live without attachment to those forms. You'll see your own inner laws, which never require codifying; you'll live with freedom and simplicity. Trust first and foremost in yourself.

Live without attachment by being generous.

Let go of evaluating yourself on the basis of how much you've accumulated and what is in your financial portfolio. Stop putting a dollar value on all that you have and do. Let go of your need to get a "good deal" and choose instead to be a being of sharing. You'll be happily surprised by how nice it feels to simply change your belief that you're only successful if you're making money. The less you focus on making a profit—instead shifting your energy to living your purpose in harmony with everyone else—the more money will flow to you and the more opportunities for generosity will be available to you.

The world of institutional pressures is built on an endless list of human-made do's and don'ts. Lao-tzu advocates that you discover your heart's true desire, all the while remembering that no one else can tell you what it is.

Do the Tao Now

Post the following affirmation for your constant attention: *I am moral, profitable, and a genius extraordinaire, regardless of what any institutional transcript or bank statement says.* Repeat this mantra until it becomes your way of being. You will feel a sense of inner peace as you release the hold that outer forms have on you.

20th Verse

Give up learning and you will be free
from all your cares.
What is the difference between yes and no?
What is the difference between good and evil?

Must I fear what others fear?
Should I fear desolation
when there is abundance?
Should I fear darkness
when that light is shining everywhere?

In spring, some go to the park and climb the terrace,
but I alone am drifting, not knowing where I am.
Like a newborn babe before it learns to smile,
I am alone, without a place to go.

Most people have too much;
I alone seem to be missing something.
Mine is indeed the mind of an ignoramus
in its unadulterated simplicity.
I am but a guest in this world.
While others rush about to get things done,
I accept what is offered.
I alone seem foolish,
earning little, spending less.

Other people strive for fame;
I avoid the limelight,
preferring to be left alone.
Indeed, I seem like an idiot:
no mind, no worries.

I drift like a wave on the ocean.
I blow as aimless as the wind.

All men settle down in their grooves;
I alone am stubborn and remain outside.
But wherein I am most different from others is
in knowing to take sustenance from the great Mother!

Living Without Striving

In this verse of the Tao Te Ching, you're encouraged to experience your life free of worldly striving. Lao-tzu advises you to slow down your incessant demands for more, and to relax your efforts to fill up every moment in anticipation of being somewhere else. You're invited to experience life in a way that can be summarized in the title of Ram Dass's book *Be Here Now*.

Be here in your mind as well as in your body, in a state of appreciation and an absence of longing. Let go of wondering about doing the right thing. Release the what-ifs and all of your goals for the future, replacing them with the power of this instant. Be here, and remember to do it now, for thinking about being someplace else uses up your precious present moments. The enlightened sage makes a practice of immersing himself completely in the current "nowness" of his life.

Being here now is accomplished by adopting an acceptance of life as it is presented by the great Mother, or the Tao. It's a surrendering process, if you will—simply allowing this great all-creating, all-nourishing Source to take you where it will. You give up the idea of having to get more or to be in another place in the future, and instead see yourself as whole and complete just as you are. This surrendering process allows you to bear witness to the unlimited abundance and eternal light that is always present. You retrain yourself to give up your beliefs about lacks and shortages; you instead trust in the great Source to provide what you need, as it has always done for all beings.

Lao-tzu emphasizes that this wasn't a socially accepted standard even 2,500 years ago, as he refers to himself as an outsider who is unlike most people. Striving for satisfaction was viewed at that time as a proper role in life, just as it is today. The narrator of this verse admits that he is drifting, not knowing where he is, yet his tone is ironic. It's as if he's saying, "No one really knows where they are in this endless universe with no beginning and no ending, so why not admit it and allow yourself to be moved by the Tao that brought you here from nowhere?"

You're being encouraged to simplify your life by not seeking another thing. Yes, others might judge you as unmotivated and call you an ignoramus, but your reward will be the strong sense of inner peace that comes from a direct knowing that you're here as a guest who's always being provided for. Yes, you may seem to be missing something, but the something is really only an illusion. You're no longer living inside of yourself with a desire to be someone else or to gain something that seems to be omnipresent in all of those around you—you've traded in *striving* for *arriving*.

"I accept what is offered," says the narrator of this provocative verse in the Tao Te Ching. He continues to express that this may seem foolish, perhaps echoing your thoughts as you contemplate letting go of striving. Lao-tzu is telling you to change how you see what's here now in your life, for then it will become exactly what you need in order to be happy. In other words, you can change how you look at striving and have contentment without anxiety and fear.

When you live by the tenets explained in this verse, you begin to have a worry-free existence. Imagine that! No concerns or fears—only a sense of being connected to the Source of all, knowing that all will be handled for you by the same force that's always handling everything. Lao-tzu is teaching you to free your mind from its persistent nagging. The world and everything in it are already taken care of by the Tao . . . it has always done so and always will.

Your mind continually urges you to strive in spite of the all-providing perfection of the Tao; it prompts you to pursue fame, to look for a groove or purpose. Lao-tzu encourages you to do precisely the opposite: Stay outside the rat race and let your mind be in peaceful harmony with the Tao rather than worrying and fighting. The concluding line of this passage of the Tao Te Ching says it all, instructing you to change how you look at your life by "knowing to take sustenance from the great Mother!"

The following are suggestions coming from Lao-tzu to you in the 20th verse of the Tao:

Practice letting go of thoughts about what's not here now.

Just allow yourself to meld into the perfection of the universe you live in. You don't need another thing to be happy; it's all being provided for you right here, right now. Be in this moment, and free yourself of striving for something more or someone else. This is a mind exercise that will put you in touch with the peace of the Tao. Affirm: *It is all perfect. God's love is everywhere and forgets no one. I trust in this force to guide me, and I am not allowing ego to enter now.* Notice how free you feel when you relax into this no-fears, no-worries attitude.

Take time to "let go and let God," every single day.

Say the words over and over to yourself until you can actually tell what the difference feels like. Letting go is a markedly distinct physical and psychological experience, much different from striving. Let go of your demands, along with your beliefs that you can't be happy because of what is supposedly missing in your life. Insisting that you need what you don't have is insane! The fact that you're okay without what you think you need is the change you want to see. Then you can note that you already have everything you need to be peaceful, happy, and content right here and right now! Relax into this knowing, and affirm again and again: *I am letting go and letting God. I am a glorious infant nursing at the great all-providing Mother's breast.*

Do the Tao Now

Begin to notice the situations where you're not in the moment because you're striving to complete or attain something for a future benefit. You may not realize how often you endeavor to accomplish all sorts of things with the idea that once you do, you'll finally have the time to do what you *really* want. This is one of the most pernicious ways that many of us unconsciously prevent (or perpetually postpone) a life free of striving. It's a tough one to become aware of, and may be easiest to see when your free time becomes hijacked by family members or business emergencies.

Here's an example: You've put in extra hours at work all week in order to have a deliciously imagined free day to [fill in the blank], when you learn that your spouse has invited a friend of a friend who's never been to this part of the country before—and whom you've never met—to stay at your home.

There are two opportunities to practice living without striving in this situation. The first, of course, is to catch yourself wrapped up in striving for future benefit, notice what you're doing, and focus on the now. The second comes after the example above, which is a difficult but incredibly rewarding exercise. Do the Tao now by accepting what is offered—that is, know that this situation, in some way that your striving ego rejects, is actually sustenance from the Great Mother.

21st Verse

The greatest virtue is to follow the Tao and the Tao alone.

The Tao is elusive and intangible.
Although formless and intangible,
it gives rise to form.
Although vague and elusive,
it gives rise to shapes.
Although dark and obscure,
it is the spirit, the essence,
the life breath of all things.

Throughout the ages, its name has been preserved
in order to recall the beginning of all things.
How do I know the ways of all things at the beginning?
I look inside myself and see what is within me.

*L*iving the
*E*lusive *P*aradox

Here in this 21st verse of the Tao Te Ching, Lao-tzu takes us back to the book's very first premise: living the mystery. He has returned to the idea's definition and virtue and reaffirmed it with greater clarity and precision. In this lesson, he not only asks us to become conscious of the elusive nature of the Tao, a principle that simply cannot be pinned down or experienced with the senses, but to also validate this awareness by recognizing ourselves as examples of this elusive paradox.

Reread the concluding lines of this important verse: "How do I know the ways of all things at the beginning? I look inside myself and see what is within me." Now go all the way back to your own beginning—how did you get here? I don't mean from a droplet or particle of human protoplasm; go even before that. Quantum physics teaches that particles emerge from an invisible and formless energy field. So all creation, including your own, is a function of motion: from formless energy to form, from spirit to body, from the nameless Tao to a named object. The process of creation, along with the theme of understanding eternal namelessness, runs throughout the Tao Te Ching. This is the elusive paradox that you're invited to contemplate, allow, and experience. You can know it by examining your own nature and recognizing that the same principle that creates everything is animating your every thought and action.

Right now make a simple decision to move your index finger. Now wiggle your toes. Next, lift your arm. Finally, ask yourself, *What is it that allows me to make these movements?* In other words, what is it that allows you to see shapes and colors? What force behind your eyes invisibly signals you to process the sky as blue or a tree as tall? What is the formless energy that tweaks a vibration somewhere in your ear to give rise to sound?

What it all is, is formless and nameless. Yes, it is vague. Yes, it is obscure. And when you begin to see the world in this manner, you begin knowing that aspect of yourself. This is what Lao-tzu describes as "the life breath of all things," and it needn't remain a mystery. You have the same eternal Tao inside of you, and you apply it a million times a day. It is within you . . . it *is* you.

This far-reaching verse of the Tao Te Ching asks you to let go of seeking results in money, accomplishments, acquisitions, fame, and so on. Instead, shift your attention to the energy in the beginning of all things—the elusive and intangible Tao. The greatest virtue is to find this nameless, formless force within yourself. Know it by looking within and seeing it at work in all of your thoughts and actions.

This is what Lao-tzu was conveying to you more than 2,500 years before your birth:

Have an unquenchable thirst for the intangible and enigmatic force that supports all life.

Communicate with the Source regularly: Ask for its guidance, and meditate on its sacredness. The more you practice benevolent reverence for the invisible Tao, the more you'll feel connected to it. The presence of a known connection with the Tao will release you from the worry, stress, and anxiety that are ego's way of looking at the world. While others around you may stay focused on their pursuit of wealth, fame, and power, you'll notice it and smile compassionately as you practice being in a state of appreciation for "the life breath of all things," including yourself. You'll feel safe and secure knowing that you're in a Divine partnership with the all-knowing, all-providing Tao.

I suggest that you simply take a moment or two several times a day to say aloud, "Thank You, God, for everything." Make this your own personal respectful ritual. In fact, just a moment ago I said

these very words: "Thank You, God, for allowing these words to appear, supposedly from my pen. I know that the Source of everything, including these words, is the elusive and intangible Tao."

**Memorize the final two lines of this verse and silently
recite them when needed.**

Repeat these two sentences: "How do I know the ways of all things at the beginning? I look inside myself and see what is within me." Doing so will remind you that the Tao comes from the truth that's inside of you at all times. Give up trying to persuade anyone else of the correctness of your vision—when they're ready, their own teachers will surely appear.

Here's a concluding thought on the elusive nature of the Tao, written by Hafiz many centuries after the death of Lao-tzu:

> *If you think that the Truth can be known
> From words,*
>
> *If you think that the Sun and the Ocean
> Can pass through that tiny opening called the mouth.*
>
> *O someone should start laughing!
> Someone should start wildly laughing—
> Now!*

Do the Tao Now

Today, become conscious of the force that allows your every movement. For five minutes in your meditation, stay in "the gap" between your thoughts and notice the elusive but omnipresent invisible Source that allows you to speak, hear, touch, and move. (I've created a meditation that can assist you in this process, and it's included in my book *Getting in the Gap*.)

22nd Verse

The flexible are preserved unbroken.
The bent become straight.
The empty are filled.
The exhausted become renewed.
The poor are enriched.
The rich are confounded.

Therefore the sage embraces the one.
Because he doesn't display himself,
people can see his light.
Because he has nothing to prove,
people can trust his words.
Because he doesn't know who he is,
people recognize themselves in him.
Because he has no goal in mind,
everything he does succeeds.

The old saying that the flexible are preserved unbroken is surely right!
If you have truly attained wholeness,
everything will flock to you.

Living with Flexibility

Having lived by the ocean for many years, I've observed the beauty and majesty of the tall palm trees that grow at the water's edge, often measuring 30 or 40 feet in height. These stately giants are able to withstand the enormous pressure that hurricane-force winds bring as they blow at speeds up to 200 miles per hour. Thousands of other trees in the huge storms' paths are uprooted and destroyed, while the stately palms remain fixed in their rooted selves, proudly holding sway over their otherwise decimated domain. So what is the palm trees' secret to staying in one piece? The answer is flexibility. They bend almost down to the ground at times, and it's that very ability that allows them to remain unbroken.

In this 22nd verse of the Tao Te Ching, Lao-tzu invites you to embrace a similar quality of elasticity. Begin to sense the oneness that is the Tao supplying your resiliency and grounding, helping you withstand the storms of your life as pliantly as the supple palm tree. When destructive energy comes along, allow yourself to resist brokenness by bending. Look for times you can make the choice to weather a storm by allowing it to blow through without resistance. By not fighting, but instead relaxing and going with all that confronts you, you enter "the Tao time."

This verse implies an added benefit of wholeness, which attracts everything to you. That is, if you want abundance, knowledge, health, love, and all the other attributes that personify the Tao, you need to be receptive to them. Lao-tzu instructs that you must be empty in order to become filled, for attachments keep you so restricted that nothing can enter your already-filled self. Being empty in this sense means not being full of beliefs, possessions, or ego-driven ideas, but rather remaining open to *all* possibilities. This is in keeping with the nameless Tao: It doesn't restrict itself to a particular point of view or a singular way of doing things; it animates all. Similarly, the flexible person is open to all possibilities—there's nothing for him or her to prove because the Tao, not ego, is in charge.

Awareness of the Tao nurtures flexibility, and removing your rigidity creates an atmosphere of trust. When you live from the perspective of being able to say, "I don't know for certain, but I'm willing to listen," you become a person whom others identify with. Why? Because your flexibility lets them see that their point of view is welcome. By being open to all possibilities, everyone who encounters you feels their ideas are valuable and there's no need for conflict.

As you connect more and more to your Tao nature, you begin noticing that this principle is perpetually present, available in every moment. In other words, the Tao isn't trying to get someplace other than where it is. It has no goals, no desire, no judgments; it flows everywhere because it is the energy of creation. To be in harmony with the Tao is to be free of goals, immersed in all that you're doing without concern about the outcome—just noticing in each moment and allowing yourself to flow with the creative Source that's energizing everything and everyone in the universe. When you live in this way, failure becomes an impossibility. How can you fail at being yourself and trusting completely in the wisdom of the Source of everything? With failure removed from your life, you understand what Lao-tzu means when he says that "everything he does succeeds."

Following are the messages from Lao-tzu as he wrote out this 22nd verse of the Tao Te Ching two-and-a-half millennia ago:

Change the way you see the storms of your life.

Work at removing ego as the dominant influence over you. Release the need for the attention of others and witness how people become drawn to you naturally. Let go of having to win an argument and being right by changing the atmosphere with a statement such as "You're very likely correct. Thanks for giving me a new perspective." This kind of a proclamation gives everyone permission to relax their rigidity because you have no need to prove yourself or make others wrong. If you change the way you think, the life you're living will change, so be willing to say, "I don't know" or "I'm uncertain as to why I even did what I did." As Lao-tzu reminds you, when you suspend your pomposity and rigidity, others recognize themselves in your flexible nature, and they'll trust you.

Imagine yourself as a tall, stately palm tree.

Be an organism without goals and objectives—instead, stand strong and successful, capable of adjusting to the forces of nature. Be willing to adapt to whatever may come your way by initially allowing yourself to experience that energy, much like the bending tree in hurricane-force winds. When criticism comes, listen. When powerful forces push you in any direction, bow rather than fight, lean rather than break, and allow yourself to be free from a rigid set of rules—in so doing, you'll be preserved and unbroken. Keep an inner vision of the wind symbolizing difficult situations as you affirm: *I have no rigidity within me. I can bend to any wind and remain unbroken. I will use the strength of the wind to make me even stronger and better preserved.*

This simple teaching is so pleasant that you'll wonder why you didn't realize it before. In the Tao time, acknowledge the "storm" and then allow it to be felt in your body—observe it without judgment, just like the tree bends in the wind. As rigidity reappears, notice that as well, allowing the winds to blow as you exercise the Tao in place of ego! Seek to uncover the root of your stiffness and achieve greater flexibility in the storms of life. When seen as this kind of opportunity to open to the Tao energy, storminess can be transformed into exhilarating events that uncover more of your true nature of love.

Do the Tao Now

Listen to someone express an opinion that's the opposite of yours today. It could be on any of a variety of topics, such as politics, the environment, religion, drugs, war, the death penalty, or what have you. Refuse to impose your position, and instead remark, "I've never considered that point of view. Thank you for sharing your ideas with me." By allowing a contrary position to be heard, you'll dismiss ego's attitude and welcome the flexibility of the Tao.

23rd Verse

To talk little is natural:
Fierce winds do not blow all morning;
a downpour of rain does not last the day.
Who does this? Heaven and earth.

But these are exaggerated, forced effects,
and that is why they cannot be sustained.
If heaven and earth cannot sustain a forced action,
how much less is man able to do?

Those who follow the Way
become one with the Way.
Those who follow goodness
become one with goodness.
Those who stray from the Way and goodness
become one with failure.

If you conform to the Way,
its power flows through you.
Your actions become those of nature,
your ways those of heaven.

Open yourself to the Tao
and trust your natural responses . . .
then everything will fall into place.

Living Naturally

Every *thing* that composes ultimately decomposes. Notice that I put the emphasis on the word *thing*—that's because all things on Earth are temporary and in a constant state of change. Since you're on this planet, you too are a part of this always-changing and always-decomposing principle. In this 23rd verse of the Tao Te Ching, you're asked to observe the ways of nature and then make the choice to live harmoniously with them.

Nature doesn't have to insist, push, or force anything; after all, storms don't last forever. Winds blow hard, but then they subside. The Tao creates from an eternal perspective, but everything is on its return trip home the moment it comes into being. So Lao-tzu instructs that if you live harmoniously with this simple principle, you'll be in tune with nature. Let go of a desire to force anyone or anything, and choose instead to consciously be part of the cyclical pattern of nature. Lao-tzu reminds you that not even heaven can sustain a forced action. In its inherent beingness, all action has a temporary existence and returns to a calmer state. In contemporary language, we'd say that "everything blows over."

The teachings of this passage invite you to pause in the midst of strife or tension and remember that serenity and peace are on the way. This verse emphatically points out that you always have a choice! In every single situation, you can choose to observe exaggerated and forced energy. It might be verbally attempting to control a situation or cursing how life's events are unfolding; regardless, these moments can be invitations to open to the Tao even while in the midst of chaos and angst. This is how to "follow the Way": Remember how nature blows hard and then returns to calm. Follow the goodness of the Tao and you become goodness. Stray from goodness and you become one with failure.

You are part of the law of form in time and space, composing and decomposing. Everything in nature is returning to its Source. . . . The question is, do you wish to participate consciously with this natural goodness, or would you rather spend your moments in anxiety and failure? The Tao response to this crucial question isn't within your ego, for it strongly believes in your ability to force things, to make things happen, or to be the person in charge. The Tao points out that the Way is responsible for everything, with a naturalness about it that isn't forced. It reminds you that what seems so devastating in the moment is benevolent perfection in another moment. When you conform to the naturalness of the universe, you cooperate with this all-creating power that flows through you. Suspend ego-driven plans and instead participate in the power that created you—allow *it* to be the guiding force in your life.

Here's what Lao-tzu says to you, through me, from his 2,500-year-old perspective in this verse of the Tao Te Ching:

Change your life by actively observing nature's way.

See how thunderstorms or fierce winds are temporary conditions that pass, instead of thinking of them as destructive or inconvenient events. When what seems like a forceful, uncomfortable situation arises, seek the natural cycle. Affirm: *This is a temporary setback. I am going to release myself from having to be the person in control.* Then observe what you're feeling, with openness to what is, in this moment. Remember that this is nature's method. Center your mind in a natural way, in perfect rapport with the patience of the universal Tao.

Change your life by trusting your ability to respond naturally to the circumstances in your life.

At first this may involve observing yourself in a friendly way instead of responding immediately. When you feel your inclination to make your opinion known, let this urge silently tell you what it *truly* wants. Your body knows how to be at peace and wait out the storms of life, but you need to allow it to feel that you're welcoming its signals. Be still and allow yourself to be in harmony with the creative Tao, opening yourself to its power.

T. S. Eliot evokes the natural cycle in his poem "Ash-Wednesday":

> *Because I know that time is always time*
> *And place is always and only place*
> *And what is actual is actual only for one time*
> *And only for one place*
> *I rejoice that things are as they are . . .*

That's the idea: *Rejoice* in the stillness of the Tao.

Do the Tao Now

Spend an entire day noticing nature and the countless instances that it cycles organically. Seek at least three ways that you'd like to be more natural in your response to life. The cat curling languidly in the sun might symbolize how you'd like to be. Or perhaps it's the dawn slowly illuminating the dark without rushing. Maybe you prefer to focus on the tide comfortably coming in and out, apparently without judgment. Find your symbolic images, whatever they may be, and invite their counterparts in the Tao to blossom within you.

24th Verse

If you stand on tiptoe, you cannot stand firmly.
If you take long steps, you cannot walk far.

Showing off does not reveal enlightenment.
Boasting will not produce accomplishment.
He who is self-righteous is not respected.
He who brags will not endure.

All these ways of acting are odious, distasteful.
They are superfluous excesses.
They are like a pain in the stomach,
a tumor in the body.

When walking the path of the Tao,
this is the very stuff that must be
uprooted, thrown out, and left behind.

Living Without Excess

In this verse, Lao-tzu advises that the path of the Tao needs to be cleared of any weeds of excessive personal importance. After all, accomplishments derive from the all-creating Source that Lao-tzu calls "the Tao." Everything that you see, touch, or own is a gift from the Tao; thus, it is your duty to suspend your ego and seek an attitude of gratitude and generosity for the Tao's creativity. In this way, you walk the path of the Tao by becoming like it is, which is always existing in a state of unlimited giving. It is to this state that the 24th verse of the Tao Te Ching urges you to return.

Notice how the natural flow of the Tao operates: It asks nothing of you as it provides you and everyone else with unlimited supplies of food, air, water, sunshine, land, and beauty. It is always creating for the benefit of all, and it has no need for prideful boasting or demanding something in return.

This poem by Hafiz bears repeating here to illustrate this point:

Even
After
All this time
The sun never says to the earth,

"You owe
Me."

113

Look
What happens
With a love like that,
It lights the
Whole
Sky.

The sun symbolizes the Tao at work: It offers its warmth, light, and life-giving energy to all, illuminating the globe without any demand for recognition. Imagine if the sun needed attention and demanded accolades for its efforts—it would shine only where it felt most appreciated or when it received payment for that life-giving energy! Soon the world would be partially shut off from the sun's magnificence, and ultimately the entire planet would be covered in darkness as wars erupted over ways of appeasing the "sun god." It's easy to see why Lao-tzu refers to such inclinations to be boastful and self-righteous as "odious" and akin to "a tumor in the body."

Walk the path of the Tao by being a giver rather than a taker, providing for others and asking nothing in return. Then view your desires to brag and seek approval as weeds appearing on your journey. Seeing yourself as important and special because of your artistic talent, for instance, is walking the path of ego. Walking the path of the Tao means that you express appreciation for the hands that allow you to create a sculpture.

This is how Lao-tzu advises you to walk the path of the Tao, free of your ego-driven desires to be recognized for all of your efforts and accomplishments:

Change your life by consciously choosing
to be in a state of gratitude.

The journey of your life will change when you emphasize gratitude for all that you are, all that you accomplish, and all that you receive. Practice silently repeating *I thank You* throughout your waking hours, and as you fall asleep and awaken. It really doesn't matter whether you're thanking God, Spirit, Allah, the Tao, Krishna, Buddha, the Source, or self, because all those names represent the great wisdom traditions. Give thanks for the sunshine, the rain, and your body, including all of its components. Have a brain-, heart-, liver-, and even a toenail-appreciation day! Your practice of gratitude helps

you focus on the real Source of everything, as well as notice when you're letting ego dominate. Make this a silent daily practice: Give thanks for the bed, the sheets, the pillows, and the room you sleep in at night; and in the morning, say *I thank You* for what lies ahead. Then begin the beautiful day doing something kind for another human being someplace on the planet.

**Change your life by examining your urge
to boast and be self-righteous.**

When you're about to brag to others about your credentials or accomplishments, momentarily sense the urge and recall Lao-tzu's advice that "this is the very stuff that must be uprooted, thrown out, and left behind." On the Tao path, inner approval is healthy and pure, while self-righteous boasting is simply superfluous. When you notice your gloating habit, you can choose to get back on the Tao path by remembering this 24th verse of the Tao Te Ching. Pomposity and self-inflating comments can then be seen as weeds you really have no need for. By returning to radical humility and seeing the greatness within everyone, you've then cleared your life of excessive self-importance . . . and this is the way of the Tao.

Do the Tao Now

Tomorrow morning, do something expressing your kindness to someone who will be totally surprised by your actions. E-mail someone, expressing your love and appreciation. Call a grandparent who may be feeling lonely in an assisted-living facility. Send flowers to a loved one who's alone, or even a stranger if necessary. Note how your gratitude for another truly nurtures your Tao path, not that of your ego.

25th Verse

There was something formless and perfect
before the universe was born.
It is serene. Empty.
Solitary. Unchanging.
Infinite. Eternally present.
It is the Mother of the universe.
For lack of a better name,
I call it the Tao.

I call it great.
Great is boundless;
boundless is eternally flowing;
ever flowing, it is constantly returning.

Therefore, the Way is great,
heaven is great,
earth is great,
people are great.

Thus, to know humanity,
understand earth.
To know earth,
understand heaven.
To know heaven,
understand the Way.
To know the Way,
understand the great within yourself.

*L*iving from *G*reatness

Many of the scholars who have written about the Tao Te Ching over the centuries consider this 25th verse to be one of the most significant lessons in the entire manuscript. In my research, all the translations of this passage actually include the word *great* to describe it.

This verse tells the story that even before the beginning there existed "something formless and perfect." It goes on to say that this formless perfection is the "Mother of the universe." Even though it's nameless, it's called the "Tao," and it's synonymous with what is great. That is, there's nothing within the Tao that is the opposite of great—there's nothing that's puny, insignificant, weak, unimportant, or even average.

The story appears to want the reader to realize there's a pure, timeless energy that's within everything on the planet and that remains uncontaminated by the solid appearance of form. The conclusion is a directive to the student, who is you, the reader. To know this formless perfection, you must "understand the great within yourself." You're the central character in this wonderful saga!

Since you're animated by the eternal Tao, this tale's message of greatness invites you to change the way you live and to see the life you're living change. You can begin to do so by examining thoughts and ideas that are inconsistent with this phenomenal observation made by Lao-tzu, which has been echoed by others throughout history. In her book *The Journey,* which was published in 1954, Lillian Smith describes it like this:

> The need that one feels every day of one's life, even though one does not acknowledge it. To be related to something bigger than one's self, something more alive than one's self, something older and something not yet born, that will endure through time.

That enduring "something" confirms your greatness, your absolute connection to the infinite. There's a sense of being permanently aligned with a sort of senior partner that is greatness itself.

Lao-tzu advises you to notice the planet, its people, and the heavens and see greatness. Next, look at yourself and see that you're a component of them all. That is, befriend what appears to be the great mystery of creation by discovering the greatness within you, then bask in the joy of noting the greatness you share with heaven, Earth, and all of its people. By persistently hanging on to your own "greatness heritage," you ensure that the always-present Tao is consciously available. From a perspective of greatness, only greatness can emerge from you; from an inner perspective of inferiority, you only attract events that align with those beliefs.

Your greatness won't be found in a classroom; an apprenticeship; a teacher; or flattering comments from well-meaning family members, friends, or lovers. It is within you. It's crucial for you to become conscious of the greatness that constantly flows through you—to do so, meet it in meditative moments of gratitude, and cease to be influenced by contrary points of view.

In particular, watch and listen for the critical comments that originate from your own inner dialogue. When such thoughts emerge in your mind, let them tell you what they want. If you allow those not-so-great notions to speak, you'll always discover that what they really want is to feel good. Give them the time they need to trust that there's no payoff for their existence, and they will happily merge into the greatness within you. Accessing this quality allows you to participate in the greater whole, where the power of the Tao flows unimpeded by fearful self-judgment. Change the way you live by tapping into this greatness, and the life you're living will literally change.

Following are the thoughts that Lao-tzu would have you adopt as he wrote out this verse of the Tao Te Ching some 25 centuries ago:

Trust in your own greatness.

You are not this body you occupy, which is temporary and on its way back to the nowhere from which it came. You are pure greatness . . . precisely the very same greatness that creates all of life. Keep this thought uppermost in your mind and you'll attract to yourself these same powers of creation: The right people will appear. The exact events that you desire will transpire. The financing will show up. That's because greatness attracts more of its own self *to* itself, just as thoughts of inadequacy act upon a belief that ensures that deficiency will become your reality. Affirm the following to yourself over and over until it becomes your automatic inner response to the world: *I come from greatness. I attract greatness. I am greatness.*

Look for beliefs that contradict your status as a being of greatness.

Catch yourself in the midst of any utterance that reflects your belief that you're average. Silently speak warmly to that belief and ask it what it wants. It may think it has to protect you from disappointment or pain, as it probably did earlier in your existence. But with continued accepting attention, the feeling will always eventually admit that it wants to feel great. So let it! You're good enough to withstand the passing disappointments and pain that afflict life on this planet—but trying to protect yourself by believing that you don't embody greatness is overkill.

Look for these misbeliefs and give them the chance to transform to what they (and you) really want. Whatever you desire to become or to attract to yourself, make the internal shift from *It probably won't happen for me* to *It is on its way!* Then begin the process of looking for even minute evidence that what you desire is indeed on its way. It's crucial to keep this ancient axiom in mind: *I get what I think about, whether I want it or not.* So think about how fortunate you are to have greatness located within yourself. Now you can live the ultimate paradox: You can be greatness and be nobody, simultaneously.

Do the Tao Now

Copy the following words and apply them to yourself: *I came from greatness. I must be like what I came from. I will never abandon my belief in my greatness and the greatness of others.* Read these words daily, perhaps by posting them conspicuously where you can see them. They will serve to remind you of the truth of your own greatness. Meditate for ten minutes today, focusing on your inner greatness.

26th Verse

The heavy is the root of the light.
The still is the master of unrest.

Realizing this,
the successful person is
poised and centered
in the midst of all activities;
although surrounded by opulence,
he is not swayed.

Why should the lord of the country
flit about like a fool?
If you let yourself be blown to and fro,
you lose touch with your root.
To be restless is to lose one's self-mastery.

*L*iving *C*almly

In this chapter of the Tao Te Ching, you're being advised to maintain a sense of serenity regardless of what you may see taking place around you. Moreover, you're being told that the true master knows that the ability to stay calm is always located within. From this perspective, there's no need to assign responsibility to others for how you feel. Even though you may live in a world where blame and faultfinding are endemic, you will own your feelings and actions. You will know that circumstances don't determine your state of mind, for that power rests with you. When you maintain a peaceful inner posture, even in the midst of chaos, you change your life.

The wisdom of this verse of the Tao Te Ching prompts you to know that you have a choice. Do you want to be in a state of confusion or to have a tranquil inner landscape? It's up to you! Armed with this insight, the Tao master doesn't allow an external event to be a disturbance. Lao-tzu tells you that assigning blame for your lack of calmness will never bring you to the state of being that you're striving to attain. Self-mastery only blossoms when you practice being aware of, and responsible for, what you're feeling.

This particular part of the Tao Te Ching is one that you'll probably want to immerse yourself in repeatedly. After all, what could be better than the freedom of going through life without feeling that people and circumstances control you without your permission?

Are you depressed? Irritated? Frustrated? Exhilarated? Ecstatically in love? Whatever your current state, if you believe that a changing economic picture or a tapestry of events taking place around you is responsible—and you then use these external factors to explain your inner state of mind—you've lost touch with your root. Why? Because you're allowing yourself to be "blown to and fro" by the shifting winds of circumstance.

The solution for a life of unrest is choosing stillness. The quiet of the Tao is oblivious to any turmoil in the world of the 10,000 things. Be like the Tao, advises Lao-tzu: "The still is the master of unrest." You have a choice in every moment, so you can decide to be a *host* to God and carry around with you the calmness that is the Tao, or you can be a *hostage* to your ego, which insists that you can't really help feeling disorderly when you're in circumstances that resemble pandemonium.

Here's what Lao-tzu offers to you in this profoundly simple passage, from the profoundly simple life he chose 2,500 years before yours:

**Vow to seek a calm inner response
to the circumstances of your life.**

In the midst of any kind of unrest—be it an argument, a traffic jam, a monetary crisis, or anything at all—make the immediate decision that you will find the calm center of yourself. By not thinking of what is taking place, and instead taking a few deep breaths in which you opt to empty your mind of judgments, it becomes impossible to mentally "flit about like a fool." You have the innate ability to choose calmness in the face of situations that drive others to madness. Your willingness to do so, especially when chaos and anger have been your previous choices, puts you in touch with "the master of unrest." There was a time when I thought this was impossible. Now I know that even in the most troublesome of times, my reaction is to choose stillness . . . the way of the Tao.

Don't lose touch with your root.

With a written declaration or picture placed strategically in your home and workplace, remind yourself that no one can make you

lose touch with your root without your consent. Affirm the following often: *I have the ability to stay poised and centered, regardless of what goes before me.* Then vow to put this new way of being into practice the next time a situation of unrest crops up. Do the mental work in advance and you'll achieve the self-mastery that Lao-tzu refers to in this verse. More significantly, you'll be in harmony with the Tao, which is your ultimate calling.

Do the Tao Now

Sit in a quiet place and picture the one person with whom you have some kind of long-standing conflict sitting there before you. Now say out loud, directly to him or her, "I forgive you. I surround you with love and light, and I do the same for myself." This will put the message of the 26th verse of the Tao Te Ching to work for you by bringing about a sense of calm.

27th Verse

A knower of the truth
travels without leaving a trace,
speaks without causing harm,
gives without keeping an account.
The door he shuts, though having no lock,
cannot be opened.
The knot he ties, though using no cord,
cannot be undone.

Be wise and help all beings impartially,
abandoning none.
Waste no opportunities.
This is called following the light.

What is a good man but a bad man's teacher?
What is a bad man but a good man's job?
If the teacher is not respected
and the student not cared for,
confusion will arise, however clever one is.
This is the great secret.

Living by Your Inner Light

For just a moment, imagine your most valuable possessions, including a large cache of money, on a table in your bedroom and in full view of anyone who might come in. Now further imagine that your pile of precious jewelry, cash, and important documents is completely safe—there's no need for insurance, and no one could ever possibly steal your treasure. Is this state of complete trust possible? I think so, especially since it's encouraged in this 27th verse of the Tao Te Ching: "The door . . . though having no lock, cannot be opened."

The "knower of the truth" lives by an inner light. This illumination shines on the fact that stealing isn't the way of truth, so it's unnecessary to lock anything up. Possessions are safe among those who live by an inner light, which reflects the perfection of the Tao. It's the Source you're encouraged to always carry with you and to consult when you feel the need for assistance or direction.

Lao-tzu advises you to give without keeping an account or expecting something in return, for this is the nature of the Tao, and you are of the Tao. Giving is synonymous with receiving when you live by this illumination. Trust the inner light to guide you, for it is your heritage. Your origin is more from the Tao than from parents, culture, or country.

It's also important that you live more spontaneously—you don't need to neatly wrap up each detail of your life. Understand this and you can travel without being attached to a plan that covers every possible scenario. Your inner light is more trustworthy than any guidebook, and it will point you in the direction that's most beneficial to you and everyone you encounter. When you develop a trust in the Tao, you'll change the way you look at life. You'll marvel at the brilliance and clarity of what you begin to see: Fear, anxiety, stress, and unrest will simply become facets of yourself seen in the glow of the Tao, like candles marking your way and helping you love everyone as a piece of yourself.

Lao-tzu advises you to "be wise and help all beings impartially, abandoning none"—that is, you don't need anyone else's rules in order to reach out to others. Giving of yourself becomes your natural response because you're following the inner light of the Tao. You and giving are one; you and receiving are one. In such an arrangement, there is no one who is not you.

The most revealing lines of this verse remind you that a good man is but a bad man's teacher, and a bad man is but a good man's job. This is an extremely empowering way to see life and eliminate stress and anger: If you perceive yourself to be a "good" person, then those whom you call "bad"—including convicted felons or enemies on the other side of the world—are your job! Try on the view that you're here to teach yourself and others in some way, and that the work is to raise the collective energy of our entire universe. Cultivate your awareness of the inner light that's within all. *Be* the Tao!

Virtually every translation of the Tao Te Ching I've examined refers to all of us being one, and all of us needing to be there for each other. The great secret is this: Waste no opportunity, abandon no one, respect the teachers, and care for the student. Twenty-five hundred years later, the Tao remains elusive to most of us because it's so infrequently practiced. Nevertheless, it must be instilled within us if we're to ever truly walk in the luminosity of the Great Way.

Become "a knower of the truth," as Lao-tzu advises, by forgetting the locks, chains, maps, and plans. Travel without leaving a trace, trust in the goodness that is the root of all, and rather than curse the darkness that seems so rampant, reach out with that inner light and let it shine on those who aren't seeing their own legacy in the Tao.

From his ancient spiritual throne, Lao-tzu is telling you to practice in these new ways:

Trust in yourself.

Develop an inner code of conduct that's based exclusively on your irreversible connection to the Tao. When you trust this wisdom that created you, you're trusting yourself. Know that nothing could ever dissuade you from your internal code of honesty, and live by this standard. If you encounter an easy opportunity to cheat, perhaps because you've been handed too much change by a hurried cashier, make the decision to be down-to-the-penny honest. Furthermore, have faith in yourself to go on a trip with a minimal amount of planning. Allow yourself to trust in the energy of the Tao to guide you, rather than relying upon fixed plans arranged by someone else.

Don't judge yourself or others.

Don't criticize the behavior or appearance of those you've assessed to be "bad people." Instead, switch your thoughts to something along these lines: *I am my own student and have this opportunity to learn that I'm instructing rather than judging. I will now cease critiquing myself or any other, and teach by being the Tao.* If the entire world of the 10,000 things knew the simple truth that we are all one, then in my opinion war, hostilities, confusion, and even illness would cease to exist.

Why not be one individual who chooses to respect yourself and all others as teachers *and* as students? When you see the world as full of opportunities to help, one thought and one action at a time, you'll be living by your inner light.

The great Sufi poet Hafiz speaks of this in his poem "No More Leaving":

At
Some point
Your relationship
With God
Will
Become like this:

Next time you meet Him in the forest
Or on a crowded city street

There won't be anymore

"Leaving."

That is,

God will climb into
Your pocket.

You will simply just take

Yourself

Along!

Do the Tao Now

Find one person labeled "bad," and use that opportunity to do your job. Be a teacher by reaching out and sending a loving message to him or her—perhaps you could pass along a book, write an e-mail or letter, or make a phone call. Just do one thing as a "good" person today, even if it's for a stranger living in a prison cell. He or she is your assignment right now.

28th Verse

Know the strength of man,
but keep a woman's care!
Be a valley under heaven;
if you do, the constant virtue
will not fade away.
One will become like a child again.

Know the white,
keep to the black,
and be the pattern of the world.
To be the pattern of the world is
to move constantly in the path of virtue
without erring a single step,
and to return again to the infinite.

One who understands splendor
while holding to humility
acts in accord with eternal power.
To be the fountain of the world is
to live the abundant life of virtue.

When the unformed is formed into objects,
its original qualities are lost.
If you preserve your original qualities,
you can govern anything.
Truly, the best governor governs least.

$\mathcal{L}$iving $\mathcal{V}$irtuously

In this verse, the word *virtue* is synonymous with "nature" or "the Tao." By being one with nature, the sage is in concert with the Tao and is a virtuous person in daily life. Here, Lao-tzu speaks about your personal path, and also a Tao-oriented way of governing others. These others could be your family members, fellow employees, business associates, friends, and even the entire process of government if you're in a political position. In fact, much of the Tao Te Ching is focused on teaching all of us how to create an administration that is in accord with these highest principles of the Tao. It is my most fervent intention to spread these teachings throughout the world in such a way as to facilitate a transformation of all those who call themselves "leaders" and are destined for, or presently in, positions of power.

Every person has the inherent capacity to spark massive changes that can lead to the tranquility, harmony, and peace that are our heritage. Lao-tzu calls this preserving our "original qualities." Such qualities require the least amount of government, so it seems natural to see that we rule best by allowing our Tao nature, which rules the least, to flourish!

Living virtuously is what you do when you're permitting the Tao to guide you. The advice Lao-tzu gives for doing this is contained in four distinct images in this verse:

1. "Be a valley under heaven" is number one. Let the river of life flow through you. As a valley beneath heaven, you're a fertile place of grace where everything is received and allowed. You might see it as the lowest area in the spectrum of the 10,000 things, or as the point where you can see all things flowing above you. In this place of humility, the constant virtue of the Tao will never fade away. For me, this means living from radical humility. So get down (if you can) to the eye level of a small child. Looking up, see if "original qualities" are more visible. Be like the valley under heaven, ready to embrace and tend the seeds that blow your way.

2. "Be the pattern of the world" is the second image that invites you to live virtuously. See nature unspoiled by culture, as in the perfection of the uncarved block of wood. The pattern of the world, untouched by humans, is a design of the Tao. So rather than insisting on changing or resisting, you're encouraged to row your boat, and your life, gently *down* the stream. Trust the perfection of the Tao to take you merrily back to your perfect place of origination. Lao-tzu is basically saying to let go and let the Tao. Dismiss ego, which you've created, and allow yourself to be *in* the world by changing how you look *at* the world.

3. "[Act] in accord with eternal power" is the third image for living virtuously. Just contemplate for a moment the idea of a fountain of the world, which never fades, never ends, and is there beyond the comings and goings of the 10,000 things. This kind of power is the one to create and then retreat, to form and then to render formless. It is always there, an endless geyser gushing forth the abundant life of virtue.

You are in accord with eternal power when you suspend your ego and become conscious of the Tao flowing in this fountain of you. Picture yourself pouring forth, not from your ideas of self-importance and your need for external power over others, but from a ceaseless Source of good and virtue that's in harmony with your infinite nature. Change the image of yourself to a being who's in accord with eternal power, and the virtuous life you want to see will be visible.

4. "Preserve your original qualities" is the fourth image of living virtuously, and one that I happen to love. Your original qualities are those that were you before there *was* a you! This is what Jesus meant by "And now, Father, glorify me in your presence with the glory I had with you before the world began" (John 17:5). Imagine if you can what is meant by "before the world began." The original qualities Lao-tzu speaks of are the love, kindness, and beauty that defined your essence before you were formed into a particle and then a human being. In other words, living virtuously has nothing to do with obeying laws, being a good citizen, or fulfilling some externally inspired idea of who you're meant to become.

This insightful verse of the Tao Te Ching tells you how to live virtuously. Be a valley under heaven by being humble and allowing seeming opposites to flow through you. Be the pattern of the world by *seeing* the pattern of your world and living in harmony without imposing ego on others. In accord with eternal power, be a fountain of the planet by consciously pouring forth from the endless ocean of goodness and virtue that's your birthright. Preserve your original qualities by reclaiming and reacquainting yourself with the Tao's essence, which preceded your birth into form and is your original quality.

Here's what Lao-tzu offers you from his 2,500-year-old perspective in this 28th verse of the Tao Te Ching:

Entertain the exact opposite of what you've been conditioned to believe.

Instead of striving to see yourself as superior to others, perhaps choose the self-image of a valley. From this grounded, fertile, and receptive position, be willing to hear and receive. Listen intently when you're inclined to offer advice. Be a humble earth source rather than a lofty ego-inspired person. In the last line of the 28th verse, Lao-tzu is clear on this: "Truly, the best governor governs least." This isn't advice to lower your opinion of yourself, but rather to see yourself as so strongly connected to your Source of being that you know and trust that you're a piece of it.

Replace all negativity with love.

Kahlil Gibran, the spiritual Lebanese poet, once advised that "if you cannot work with love but only with distaste, it is better that you should leave your work and sit at the gate of the temple and take alms of those who work with joy." Actively begin the process of preserving your original qualities by being an instrument of Spirit, particularly in places where you find it easy to forget your own true virtuous self.

Do the Tao Now

Be childlike at least once a day. Deliberately select a typically stressful situation and become a valley of heaven. Play rather than work, even while you're at your job! Giggle rather than maintaining a solemn air. Be in awe for a moment or two. For example, find a spider-web and just gaze at the miracle before you: a tiny little creature spinning a perfect net bigger than it is in order to catch airborne bugs for dinner . . . wow!

29th Verse

Do you think you can take over the universe and improve it?
I do not believe it can be done.

Everything under heaven is a sacred vessel and cannot be controlled.
Trying to control leads to ruin.
Trying to grasp, we lose.

Allow your life to unfold naturally.
Know that it too is a vessel of perfection.
Just as you breathe in and breathe out,
there is a time for being ahead
and a time for being behind;
a time for being in motion
and a time for being at rest;
a time for being vigorous
and a time for being exhausted;
a time for being safe
and a time for being in danger.

To the sage
all of life is a movement toward perfection,
so what need has he
for the excessive, the extravagant, or the extreme?

Living by Natural Law

This verse speaks of a natural law that's unaffected by ego. The message? You're not in charge—you never have been, and you never will be. So you're advised to let go of any ideas you have about controlling anything or anyone, including yourself. It's a difficult lesson for most of us to learn. As Lao-tzu puts it in the beginning of this verse, "I do not believe it can be done."

Nevertheless, here's one of the world's most famous scientific minds, Albert Einstein, commenting on this law:

> [The scientist's] religious feeling takes the form of a rapturous amazement at the harmony of natural law, which reveals an intelligence of such superiority that, compared with it, all the systematic thinking and acting of human beings is an utterly insignificant reflection. This feeling is the guiding principle of his life and work . . .

It is to this feeling that I urge you to turn as you put into practice the wisdom of the 29th verse of the Tao Te Ching. Tuning in to this rapturous feeling of amazement at the sacred perfection of the world helps you release your desire to control anything or anyone. Doing so will allow you to live in the "harmony of natural law," as Einstein describes it.

Lao-tzu reminds you that "everything under heaven is a sacred vessel," needing no input from you. Since you're also a part of everything, you may need to change the way you look at your life and all that has transpired in it, as well as your vision of the future. Whether you agree or disagree, whether you like it or not, all of it is outside of your ego's domain. It's all unfolding according to the same natural law that causes the seasons to follow one another, the moon to look as if it rises and falls, the whales to traverse oceans, and the birds to migrate and return without benefit of a map or human-made guidance system. When you look at your life in this way, you'll begin to see it unfolding organically.

The Tao is a natural law, not some controlling force that's manipulating you. In *The Tao of Philosophy,* Alan Watts reminds us that Lao-tzu once said, "The Great Tao flows everywhere, both to the left and to the right. It loves and nourishes all things but does not lord it over them." The Tao is the informing principle of God, not nature's lord and master. A power-hungry and ego-dominated control freak it's not! Feeling superior is a human creation. The Tao doesn't act as boss, forcing itself on you or anyone. It simply allows all of creation to reveal itself with perfect timing . . . and all that is revealed is sacred because it's a piece of the ego-free Tao.

I suggest that you create some quiet time to reread this verse and reflect on the sacred nature of everything in your life. Include past experiences that you've blamed for preventing you from having the abundance, health, or happiness that you've wanted and even expected. Ponder the advice that there's a time for it all: Just as you must breathe in to breathe out, you may experience what it is to be ahead by also having a "being-behind experience." All of those times that you felt betrayed, abandoned, abused, frightened, anxious, or incomplete—they all came about according to a natural law that also led you to feel cared for, protected, loved, comforted, and whole. There's a time for everything, including what you're experiencing today.

Begin recognizing that every moment of your life is in accordance with the Divine Tao. By doing so, you'll shift from judgment (and perhaps anger) to gratefulness for being able to feel both exhausted and rested, scared and safe, unloved and cared for. All of it is a part of the natural law. Your "ego-mind" tries to protect you from pain by insisting that you can learn to eliminate some aspects

of your life. However, the sage within you desires to be more harmonious with the perfection of the Tao. How do you allow this? Lao-tzu urges you to avoid the extremes, the excesses, and the extravagant, and know that all is unfolding perfectly, even if your thoughts tell you that it's imperfect. Those thoughts must also have their own time, and in the natural flow, they'll be replaced by new ones . . . which will show up on time as well.

Here's what I believe this verse from Lao-tzu offers you from its 2,500-year-old perspective:

Give up needing to control.

Begin a conscious program of surrendering, and allowing your world and everyone in it to do as they are ordained to do. Surrendering is a mental process: It involves taking a split second to stop yourself in your mode of judgment or frustration and have a brief talk with yourself on the spot. Just remind yourself to step back and be a witness rather than a protagonist, which you can do by providing a sanctuary for the feeling you're judging. Invite Divine natural order in by simply allowing what you're experiencing to go forward without criticism or control; in this way, you move to the center. Think of the need to control as a signal to allow the Tao to flow freely through your life. At first your ego-mind may loudly scoff at the idea of the Tao being responsible for the perfect unfolding of everything. It's up to you to recognize that your belief that ego can control life is an illusion.

Practice recognizing that there's a time for everything.

When you're in the middle of a tough moment, repeat the lines given to you by Lao-tzu. I do this in yoga practice when I feel exhausted holding a position for what seems like a too-lengthy period. I remind myself, *There's a time for being exhausted, and there's a time for being vigorous.* This frees me immediately from my demanding ego, which is saying, *You shouldn't be feeling this tired.* You can do the same in any moment in your life. Experiences of pain, loss, fear, anger, and even hatred seem to vanish when you remember that this is a part of the perfect blossoming of natural law; and there will soon be a time for comfort, peace, and love.

Apply this verse of the Tao Te Ching by creating your personalized statement when you observe things such as crime, AIDS, hunger, and war. Try something like, *Yes, there seems to be a time for such things, and I choose not to remain in extremes of resentment and anger. But there is also my desire to do something about these circumstances—that feeling is also a part of the natural law unfolding. I choose to act on my inner desire to rectify these conditions. By remaining internally peaceful and avoiding the extremes, I will impact the world in the same loving way that the Tao eternally manifests from love and kindness.*

It's not what you see around you that keeps you connected to the Tao; it's understanding how this eternal flow works. As Ralph Waldo Emerson put it, "By atoms, by trifles, by sots, heaven operates. The needles are nothing, the magnetism is all."

Do the Tao Now

Find a place where control is all-consuming and relinquish it today. Stifle your inclination to interfere, reminding yourself as you do so that there's a time for everything and you're becoming more adept at observing peacefully rather than taking over.

Post this poem by Naomi Long Madgett where you can read it, and be constantly reminded of your desire to live naturally:

Woman with Flower

I wouldn't coax the plant if I were you.
Such watchful nurturing may do it harm.
Let the soil rest from so much digging
And wait until it's dry before you water it.
The leaf's inclined to find its own direction;
Give it a chance to seek the sunlight for itself.

Much growth is stunted by too careful prodding,
Too eager tenderness.
The things we love we have to learn to leave alone.

30th Verse

One who would guide a leader of men in the uses of life
will warn him against the use of arms for conquest.
Weapons often turn upon the wielder.

Where armies settle,
nature offers nothing but briars and thorns.
After a great battle has been fought,
the land is cursed, the crops fail,
the earth lies stripped of its Motherhood.

After you have attained your purpose,
you must not parade your success,
you must not boast of your ability,
you must not feel proud;
you must rather regret that you had not been
able to prevent the war.

You must never think of conquering others by force.
Whatever strains with force
will soon decay.
It is not attuned to the Way.
Not being attuned to the Way,
its end comes all too soon.

*L*iving *W*ithout *F*orce

If you were to explicitly follow the advice offered in this 30th verse of the Tao Te Ching, you'd be in a position to have a conflict-free existence. Imagine that! If our entire global population understood and lived the directives of this chapter of the Tao Te Ching, we'd finally be free of battle-related stress, along with the ravages that war has spread across our planet since we began keeping historical records. As the 29th verse wisely instructed, there's a time for everything—could *this* be the time for living without force?

Here's my impression of what's being offered to you in this verse: Force creates a counterforce, and this exchange goes on and on until an all-out war is in progress. Once war has begun, decimation and famine result because the land cannot produce crops. Now when you create war in your personal life, it produces a dearth of love, kindness, and joy, which leaves you and everyone around you stripped of Divine Motherhood. Lao-tzu is encouraging you to look for an alternative to force for settling disputes. If you can find no other option, then you're encouraged to abandon any reference to yourself as winning or conquering.

Force includes any use of physical or mental abuse in which the weapons of hatred and intolerance are applied. There will always be a counterforce, and what you've opted to do isn't "attuned to the Way." This means that you'll ultimately lose—especially when you consider that Martin Luther King, Jr., once observed that the only way to convert an enemy to a friend is through love.

Unfortunately, whenever force is used, resentment and ultimately revenge become the means for responding. If we're thinking in war-zone terms, the killing of a large group of people designated as enemies leaves their sons and daughters growing up hating the vanquishers. Ultimately, those survivors take up weapons to exact revenge on the children of those who vanquished them. The use of force propels entire generations of people into a continuation of war. Or as Lao-tzu puts it, "Weapons often turn upon the wielder."

Thinking in alignment with the Tao applies to any conflict you may experience. When you resort to force, then disputes with your spouse, your children, your business partners, and even your neighbors will continue to intensify. That's because the Great Way of Tao is that of cooperation, not competition.

The all-creating Source is always providing, asking nothing in return, and coming from a place of sharing its inherent love. It knows that all are part of the 10,000 things, and they must cooperate with each other because they share the same origin. So whenever you're in a mode that propels you in the direction of using force, you've lost sight of your connection to the Tao. Moreover, any collection of people (such as communities or countries) who resort to weapons to get their points across are unattuned to the Way. They'll leave the earth and the hearts of the people uninhabitable, except to "briars and thorns." Your choice concerning your commitment to practicing the Tao includes refusing to participate in any manner, be it mental or physical, in anything that violates your understanding of the advice offered in this powerful passage of the Tao Te Ching.

Perhaps the easiest lesson presented here is the reminder to eschew the behaviors of boastfulness and pomposity for anything achieved by force. Remember that whatever is accomplished in such a way creates a counterforce that will ultimately result in your victory turning to a defeat. If you somehow feel that you had no other choice than to use violence to protect yourself and those you love, immediately retreat to a position that doesn't allow for bragging and self-congratulation. Vow to work on restoring a balance of love where hatred previously resided, and do all that you can to make amends for any damage that resulted from your use of force. This is the Way. It has also been called *wu-wei,* or "not forcing," which means to take the line of least resistance in all of one's actions, and by doing so, create more strength.

Here's what I believe you can learn and practice from Lao-tzu's advice in this 30th verse of the Tao Te Ching:

Eliminate verbal and/or physical force in all situations.

Examine the relationships in which you experience conflict. Make a concerted decision to use less harsh language and to completely veer away from becoming physical in the resolution of any altercation. Practice stopping thoughts of violence by shifting right in the moment to a stance of listening. Bite your tongue! Stifle yourself! Hold back any response at all for the time being.

These are great reminders to you to become attuned to the Way. Remember, any act of force will definitely produce a counterforce, so if you insist on escalating devastation, your weapons will be turned back upon you.

Refuse to participate in violent actions in any way.

Create distance between any form of violence and yourself. This includes listening to TV or radio reports or even perusing newspaper articles about the uses of force taking place all over the planet. See if you're justifying hearing or reading about hostile activities as a need to be "fully informed." Once you know that force is being applied anywhere in the name of subjugating others, you'll realize that the constant repetition of that news makes you a participant in the violence. By refusing to allow such energy into your life, even as a passive observer, you keep yourself attuned to the Way.

Eventually, when enough of us are unwilling to tolerate such behavior in any form, we'll be closer to bringing an end to the use of force on our planet. Remember that every use of force, even the smallest, creates a counterforce.

Here's what a great 16th-century poet, Saint John of the Cross, advises:

You might quiet the whole world for a second
if you pray.

And if you love, if you
really love,

our guns will
wilt.

Do the Tao Now

In line with altering the way you look at the world, today change every television channel and radio station that presents an image or audio of the use of force or violence. Then increase that "no tolerance" policy to include movies, videos, and games that have beatings, homicides, and chase scenes.

31st Verse

Weapons are the tools of violence;
all decent men detest them.
Therefore, followers of the Tao never use them.

Arms serve evil.
They are the tools of those who oppose wise rule.
Use them only as a last resort.
For peace and quiet are dearest to the decent man's heart,
and to him even a victory is no cause for rejoicing.

He who thinks triumph beautiful
is one with a will to kill,
and one with a will to kill
shall never prevail upon the world.

It is a good sign when man's higher nature
comes forward.
A bad sign when his lower nature comes forward.

With the slaughter of multitudes,
we have grief and sorrow.
Every victory is a funeral;
when you win a war,
you celebrate by mourning.

Living Without Weapons

The 31st verse of the Tao Te Ching unequivocally states that implements of violence serve evil. Lao-tzu clearly knew that weapons designed to kill are tools of futility and should be avoided if you choose to live according to the principles of the Tao. This includes the design, production, marketing, distribution, and of course, the use of weapons in the business of killing. The Tao is about life; weapons are about death. The Tao is a creative force; weapons are about destruction. Humanity has failed to learn this profound teaching of the Tao Te Ching, which was written when weapons consisted mainly of bows and arrows, spears, hatchets, and the like.

From his position as an observer and a being of Divine wisdom, Lao-tzu recognized that there's no victory in any activity where killing takes place. Why? Because all people, regardless of their geographic location or belief system, are connected to each other by their originating spirit. We all come from, retain, and return to the Tao. When we destroy each other, we're destroying our opportunity to allow the Tao to inform us, to flow freely in and through the form we're in. What appears to our ego to be a victory to celebrate is really a funeral, a time to mourn. Lao-tzu reminds us that taking pleasure in winning a battle is aligned with an ego will to kill. The Tao has only a creative, nurturing, and loving will. On this physical plane, our highest nature expresses itself through the precepts of the Tao, while our lowest nature expresses itself by engaging in the business of killing.

The written history of humankind involves wars as far back as it can go, and we measure our supposed march toward civilization by the sophistication of our weapons. We've advanced from simple spears used in close individual combat to bows and arrows that kill from a short distance, rifles and explosive devices that execute from farther away, and bombs that decimate when dropped from the air. We've reached the level where we have to invent terms like *mega-death* and *weapons of mass destruction* to describe our current ability to annihilate millions of people and other life-forms with one nuclear blast.

The current level of presumably enlightened sophistication means that we have the capacity to destroy all life on our planet with the weapons we've amassed. This perilous state has emerged because we've ignored the basic tenet of the Tao Te Ching, particularly as stressed in the infinite wisdom of this verse: "Arms serve evil. They are the tools of those who oppose wise rule."

I believe that Lao-tzu was not only speaking about physical weapons, but also nonphysical behaviors that are just as destructive. These include violent words, gestures, and threats that aren't a part of humankind's higher nature. If you change the way you look at your world, you must include noticing your language and your demeanor. Do you demonstrate that you're a person who values life in all of its costumes? Are you someone who wouldn't take up any type of arms—be they physical or not—against another, unless alternative means had been exhausted? And then, if forced to injure another, are you able to feel compassion for your so-called enemy? Weapons designed to kill are inconsistent with the very essence of the Tao. Thus, you must make every effort to be peaceful and harmonious with its life-giving energy.

The massive proliferation of guns in our modern society is a giant step away from humankind's highest nature. So replace defending the right to own and use weapons with the Tao consciousness. Seek instead to aspire to a time when our collective human energy is elevated to such a high status that even the contemplation of killing is impossible. You can begin to do so by changing the way you look at the necessity for weapons. It begins with each and every one

of us, and we can start by taking heed of what the Tao Te Ching teaches us. By making this verse your personal calling, you have the ability to save our planet from becoming a lifeless one.

This is what I believe Lao-tzu is saying to you personally from his 2,500-year-old perspective:

Begin to see the use of physical or verbal weapons as unwanted responses.

Change your need to defend yourself to a stance of realizing that this is evidence you're ignoring the teachings of your Source of being. Refuse to consider using weapons of violence in any form by noticing your language and abolishing hatred from your vocabulary. Replace defending your right to possess and use arms with an attitude that all deaths from such instruments are signals of detachment from the wisdom of the Tao. When enough of us reach a critical mass in our thinking so that it disallows the existence of weapons, we'll be moving the direction of our world. No longer will we be able to evaluate the planet's level of civilization by the sophistication of our weapons; instead, the measurement will be on the Tao scale of how well we're able to feed and love each other. Then being civil will authenticate the root word found in *civilization*.

Discontinue celebrating death or violence in any form.

Distance yourself from as many images of death as possible, including watching movies or TV shows that depict killing as a form of entertainment, along with news reports that emphasize the extinguishing of life. Teach your kids, and any children you can, to sanctify life. Encourage them not to take pleasure in the demise of so-called enemies, terrorists, or insurgents—all of these kinds of death, be they on a battlefield or an urban street, are evidence of our collective will to kill. And don't demonstrate hatred and outrage; rather, teach yourself and others that every victory accomplished with weapons is a funeral that should be mourned.

Here are some sensitive lines from Saint Thomas Aquinas, a holy man who attempted to teach us what Lao-tzu offered in this verse of the Tao Te Ching:

How is it they live for eons in such harmony—
the billions of stars—

when most men can barely go a minute
without declaring war in their mind against someone they know.

There are wars where no one marches with a flag,
though that does not keep casualties
from mounting.

Our hearts irrigate this earth.
We are fields before
each other.

How can we live in harmony?
First we need to
know

we are all madly in love
with the same
God.

Do the Tao Now

Say a private prayer today for every person you read or hear about who's a victim of killing by a weapon, no matter how distant.

32nd Verse

The eternal Tao has no name.
Although simple and subtle,
no one in the world can master it.

If kings and lords could harness them,
the 10,000 things would naturally obey.
Heaven and earth would rejoice
with the dripping of sweet dew.
Everyone would live in harmony,
not by official decree,
but by their own goodness.

Once the whole is divided, the parts need names.
There are already enough names;
know when to stop.
Know when reason sets limits
to avoid peril.

Rivers and streams are born of the ocean,
and all creation is born of the Tao.
Just as all water flows back to become the ocean,
all creation flows back to become the Tao.

Living the Perfect Goodness of the Tao

In this verse, Lao-tzu describes the ecstasy of being truly on the same page as your Source. What you might describe as openheartedness or joy is the "simple and subtle" flow of the Tao energy that's responsible for all of life . . . and no effort on your part is necessary.

Lao-tzu opens this verse with a reminder that no one—not you, me, or even the most powerful king or dictator—can rein in or master this force known as the Tao. If it were under our control, then all of nature and its 10,000 things would celebrate because we'd live in peace and harmony. When we're able to live and breathe the perfect goodness that is the Tao, wars, famine, conflict, and other negative human creations cease to exist. The challenge presented in this 32nd verse of the Tao Te Ching is how to live in our physical world in unison with the eternal, always-molding and always-creating Tao.

Look at what you desire to bring into your life; then, in the context of this sweet verse, feel grateful for everything you encounter. Express gratitude by riding the flow of your existence and allowing it to be your ally. You can steer while still enjoying this glorious ride, but if you elect to fight it, you'll ultimately get pulled under by its current. This is true for every aspect of your life: The more you push against it, the more resistance you create.

Be aware of anything that's directing you toward activities that truly ignite your passion. If events seem to be taking you in a new direction in your work, for instance, or signs point to changing your job or location, pay attention! Don't get pulled under by refusing to budge and continuing a familiar frustrating routine, and then justifying your fear of change. Recognize the Tao energy coursing through your life and quit fighting your calling.

I watch my young son on a surfboard each day of the summer here on Maui. He loves the thrilling ride as he accelerates by going with the wave—he's not attempting to control it by prolonging it or forcing it to move in a different direction. I use this as a metaphor for my life, for I write in the flow. I allow thoughts and ideas to come in and move onto the page. I allow myself to be carried by the great wave of the Tao in all of my decisions, which brings me peace. That's because I trust in the perfect goodness of the Tao to guide me, direct me, and take me where it will.

You and I are like the rivers and streams that Lao-tzu mentions in this verse. We were born of the Tao, our Source of being, and we're returning to the Tao. The return trip is inevitable—it can't be stopped. So watch your body as it goes through its changes, noting that it does so in the same way that the rivers head down to the ocean to reemerge and become one with it.

Lao-tzu urges you to know when to stop driving yourself, advising you to instead jump into the oneness and avoid all manner of difficulties that he calls your "peril." Flow with the Tao in everything you do. Give up the need to be in charge, which is just your ego working overtime. You cannot force the Tao . . . let it carry you by relaxing into it with trust and faith.

As you ride this glorious wave of the Tao, consider this advice from Alan Watts in *Tao: The Watercourse Way:*

> Let your ears hear whatever they want to hear; let your eyes see whatever they want to see; let your mind think whatever it wants to think; let your lungs breathe in their own rhythm. Do not expect any special result, for in this wordless and idealess state, where can there be past or future, and where any notion of purpose?

Stop, look, and listen right now before you go on reading. Yes, get in the perfect goodness of the Tao right now—in your business, in your relationships, in your career, in your everything! Stop, listen for your passion, and then allow yourself be taken there by the ceaseless tide of all creation, which continues in spite of your ego's opinions.

Here's what Lao-tzu seems to be saying to you, through me, about implementing the idea of this 32nd verse of the Tao Te Ching:

Pay attention to the flow of your life.

Remind yourself that you don't have to be in charge—that, in fact, it's *impossible* for you to be in charge. The nameless force, which Lao-tzu calls the Tao, moves everything, so your continual argument with it only causes dissatisfaction. Each day, practice letting go and seeing where you're directed. Take note of who shows up and when. Observe the "strange coincidences" that seem to collaborate with fate and in some way steer you in a new direction. Keep track of situations that occur spontaneously or out of the realm of your control.

Look for a new, joyous feeling within you.

As you move in the direction of "loosening the leash," so to speak, you'll become keenly aware of the exhilaration of the Tao flowing through you. Begin to see what passions are stirred up as you allow the ride to be directed by your Source rather than ego. These joyous feelings are clues that you're beginning to harmonize with what Lao-tzu calls "[your] own goodness." Your enthusiastic inner receptivity is your reminder that all is perfect, so trust that energy.

Do the Tao Now

Pick a time today, perhaps between noon and 4 P.M., to consciously free your mind from attempting to control the events of your life. Go for a walk and simply let yourself be carried along: Let your feet go where they will. Observe everything in your line of vision. Notice your breath, the sounds you hear, the wind, the cloud formations, the humidity, the temperature—everything. Simply let yourself be immersed and transported, and notice how it feels to just go with the flow. Now decide to let freedom be your guide. Realize that traffic, the people in your life, the stock exchange, the weather, the tides . . . all of it is taking place at its own pace in its own way. You can move with the eternal, perfect Tao as well. *Be it . . .* now.

33rd Verse

One who understands others has knowledge;
one who understands himself has wisdom.
Mastering others requires force;
mastering the self needs strength.

If you realize that you have enough,
you are truly rich.

One who gives himself to his position
surely lives long.
One who gives himself to the Tao
surely lives forever.

$\mathcal{L}$iving $\mathcal{S}$elf-$\mathcal{M}$astery

In our contemporary world, an educated person is generally thought of as someone with several diplomas who's in a position to intelligently discuss all manner of topics, particularly in the academic field. In addition to amassing scholastic credits, highly learned people often understand and reach out to help others. In fact, they seem to possess the ability to effectively "read" other people. These individuals' power and status tends to increase in proportion to the number of men and women they oversee, such as with the president of a university, a CEO of a business, or a general of an army.

In this 33rd verse of the Tao Te Ching, Lao-tzu is asking you to change the way you look at these twin ideas of *knowledge* and *power*. You're invited to evaluate your level of self-mastery by turning your gaze inward and seeing the world, and your place in it, in a new light. A Tao-oriented life focuses on understanding yourself, rather than on the thinking and behaviors of others. You shift from the acquisition of information and the pursuit of status symbols to understanding and mastering yourself in any and all situations. Power over others is replaced with an inner strength that empowers you to behave from a wisdom that is inherently the Tao.

As you modify your thinking, your world will undergo pleasantly dramatic changes. For example, as you realize that you are responsible for your reactions in any given moment, others will cease to have any power or control over you. Rather than worrying, *Why is that person behaving that way and making me feel so upset?* you can see the situation as an invitation to explore yourself from a new attitude of self-mastery. Your inward exploration allows you to permit the flow of inner responses, examining them with tolerance directed toward yourself. By seeking *your* stream of thoughts and simply going with them, the conduct of that other person instantly loses its potency. You begin seeing your world suffused with the harmony of the Tao eternally (and *in*ternally!) flowing through you.

In any situation—whether it be under the heading of "family," "work," or "social"; or even just seeing the atrocities reported on the evening news—you'll become aware that there's no "they" who have power over you. By refusing to turn the controls of your existence over to anyone or any set of circumstances, you're exercising personal strength instead of force. You are indeed experiencing self-mastery, and this new state of internal control has come about because you've elected to live in accordance with the Tao. You don't need the approval of others or another possession in order to be happy—you must merely understand yourself as a Divine piece of the eternal Tao, always connected to that infinite essence.

Lao-tzu equates the ability to look within for the Source of enlightenment and strength with eternal life. He reminds you that while externals such as knowledge and the power over others may provide a long life, shifting to being in charge of yourself offers imperishable wisdom and a ticket to immortality.

Here's what this great master wants you to take from this verse of the Tao Te Ching and apply to your world:

Focus on understanding yourself instead of blaming others.

Whenever you're anxious, in pain, or even mildly upset over the conduct of others, take the focus off those you're holding responsible for your inner distress. Shift your mental energy to allowing yourself to be with whatever you're feeling—let the Tao flow freely, without blaming others for your feelings. And don't blame yourself either! Just allow the Tao to unfold. . . . Tell yourself that no one has the power to make you uneasy without your consent, and that

you're unwilling to grant that authority to this person right now. But you *are* willing to freely experience your emotions without calling them "wrong" or needing to chase them away. Flow in the Tao now! In this way, with this simple exercise at the moment of your dis-ease, you've made a shift to self-mastery.

It's important to bypass blame and even your desire to understand the other person; instead, focus on understanding *yourself.* By taking responsibility for how you choose to respond to anything or anyone, you're aligning yourself with the Tao. Change the way you choose to perceive the power that others have over you and you will see a bright new world of unlimited potential for yourself.

Cultivate your desire for others to discover the Tao in their lives.

Dismiss any desire to extend power over others through the forceful nature of your actions and your personality. Ego believes that others are incapable of running their own lives and wants to control with force, so demonstrate your inner strength by abandoning such tactics. Catch yourself as you're about to tell others how they "should" be. Use the opportunity to practice allowing them to learn their own lessons without interference from you. Notice how often you attempt to use verbal force to convince others to listen to you. Remind yourself to remain quiet and send loving energy. Practice this kind of self-mastery even though it's rare in today's world. You are strong enough to trust the Tao.

When your judgments dominate, the flow of the Tao slows. See how the world truly changes right before your eyes when you sincerely desire that others follow their own life paths, which will lead them to realize the greatness of the Tao. All those formerly perceived as needing you to tell them what or how to live are also the same as you are in the Tao's wisdom and strength.

Do the Tao Now

Today, practice experiencing the unfolding of the Tao with someone who usually causes you distress. Consciously initiate a conversation with that in-law, ex-spouse, bullying co-worker, or family member, inviting the Tao to flow freely. Notice how, what, and

where you feel; remain warmly and tolerantly in touch with the sensations within your body. You've entered the space of self-mastery in this moment.

Here's what *A Course in Miracles* offers on this verse of the Tao Te Ching: "This is the only thing that you need to do for vision, happiness, release from pain. . . . Say only this, but mean it with no reservations . . . *I am responsible for what I see. I chose the feelings I experience . . .*"

34th Verse

The Great Way is universal;
it can apply to the left or the right.
All beings depend on it for life;
even so, it does not take possession of them.

It accomplishes its purpose,
but makes no claim for itself.
It covers all creatures like the sky,
but does not dominate them.

All things return to it as to their home,
but it does not lord it over them;
thus, it may be called "great."

The sage imitates this conduct:
By not claiming greatness,
the sage achieves greatness.

Living the Great Way

In this verse, Lao-tzu asks you to reevaluate your perception of greatness. Typical definitions tend to center around the amount of fame and fortune that an individual accumulates in his or her lifetime. As the previous verse emphasized, the power to dominate and control others can also be used as a benchmark of this quality: Commanders of huge armies and heads of state who attract worldwide attention are considered great. Yet great men or women are often thought of as having been instrumental in affecting the course of human events in a positive way, making the world a better place on either a local or global level. Greatness, then, is a claim made by or for individuals who stand out from the crowd.

Verse 34 of the Tao Te Ching describes greatness in an entirely different manner: Such a quality is the Tao, which is so all-encompassing that every plant, creature, and human originates and lives because of it, yet it doesn't seek to dominate anyone or anything. The Tao doesn't ask for recognition of any kind, for it has no interest in fame or being thanked for all that it provides. It is this indifference toward notoriety that makes true greatness.

When you change the way you think about this quality, you'll see your world in an entirely new way: You'll no longer be gauging appearances and accumulations, and you won't notice how much power you or anyone else uses to exact dominance or control over others. Rather, your new way of thinking will allow you to look for the unfolding of the Tao in everyone you see. Perhaps for the very first time, you'll notice greatness in others, as well as yourself, in terms of the Tao that includes all. You'll be able to look at the sky and see its grandness, which demands absolutely nothing in return.

As you change your enculturated view of greatness, you'll begin seeing a different world. You'll see the importance of everyone, including those individuals you've previously identified as difficult or unreasonable. You'll begin to see that the holiness that ferments the galaxies is working in you, in me, and in everyone. You'll begin to trust that greatness is every person's heritage. The Tao is everywhere; therefore, this quality will be visible in all things and people.

Here are my suggestions for applying the 34th verse of the Tao Te Ching to your everyday life:

Discontinue deciding what anyone else should or shouldn't be doing.

Avoid thoughts and activities that involve telling people who are perfectly capable of making their own choices what to do. In your family, remember that you do not own anyone. The poet Kahlil Gibran reminds you:

> *Your children are not your children.*
> *They are the sons and daughters of Life's longing for itself.*
> *They come through you but not from you . . .*

This is always true. In fact, disregard any inclination to dominate in *all* of your relationships. Listen rather than expound. Pay attention to yourself when you're having judgmental opinions and see where self-attention takes you. When you replace an ownership mentality with one of allowing, you'll begin to see the true unfolding of the Tao in yourself and other people. From that moment on, you'll be free of frustration with those who don't behave according to your ego-dominated expectations.

Discover a new definition of greatness.

Offer yourself a definition that doesn't use any standards of appearance or traditional external measures of success. Notice those who give much, boast little, nurture others, and decline recognition or credit, and put them in your greatness file. Encourage yourself to practice these same kinds of behaviors. Begin noticing how the Tao is always flowing in an all-providing, no-boasting, nondemanding, nonpossessing manner. Can you see how great that truly is? There are many people in your daily life doing just that. Seek them out and acknowledge them, while quietly emulating what they do. Remember that a great sage never claims ownership of greatness, so when you change your definition, you'll see that quality cropping up everywhere, especially within yourself.

Do the Tao Now

Make a decision to spend a day seeking out several people who fit the model of this verse of the Tao Te Ching. Silently convey to them that you sense their greatness as an unfolding of the Tao. Then notice how your interactions with them differ when you're not making judgments based on their age, sex, title, conduct, manner of dress, height, weight, skin color, religious affiliation, or political beliefs.

35th Verse

All men will come to him
who keeps to the one.
They flock to him and receive no harm,
for in him they find peace, security, and happiness.

Music and dining are passing pleasures,
yet they cause people to stop.
How bland and insipid are the things of this world
when one compares them to the Tao!

When you look for it, there is nothing to see.
When you listen for it, there is nothing to hear.
When you use it, it cannot be exhausted.

Living Beyond Worldly Pleasures

Take a few moments before reading this chapter and ask yourself the following questions: *When I think of pleasure, what activities readily come to mind? How do I distinguish between what I find enjoyable and what I don't?*

Generally, pleasure is described as something experienced by the senses and available here in the world of form. Perhaps you experience it in a sumptuous meal, in your favorite music, or on the golf course, but it's most certainly a welcome motivating force for you. Problems can occur, however, when such pursuits become the primary focus of life. In other words, an emphasis on worldly pleasures can quite easily create an imbalance in your system, leading to upset and disease. Obesity, eating disorders, drug and alcohol abuse, addictions of every description, and preoccupations with plastic surgery are just a few of the undesirable results.

Most everything defined as pleasurable is temporary, so if you need more and more of it, then it has a grip on you. What you desire so strongly has become your jailer, trapping you into believing that it will bring you peace, security, or happiness . . . but it never does. Worldly pleasures only seduce you into becoming dependent on them, and they leave you always wanting more. It's a craving that can never be satisfied: You need another great meal in order to have that pleasure again because it vanished almost immediately upon the completion of your dessert. You need to keep the music playing because when it stops, your enjoyment stops, too. All addictions scream out this depressing message: "You'll never, ever get enough of what you don't want."

Contrast this bleak picture of pleasure, which Lao-tzu calls "bland and insipid," with the ecstasy of the Tao. Just for a moment, imagine having the perspective of the Tao as you read this verse, and see if you can change the way you look at this idea of pleasure. The benefits of having a concept that harmonizes with the Tao are outlined in the opening lines: All people will flock to you, and they'll find peace, security, and happiness when they do. The reason why they'll discover these three jewels is because *you* exude such qualities. Your emphasis is on the Tao—it's who you are and therefore what you have to give away.

You are now changing the way you look at things, so your idea of pleasure shifts beyond the worldly nudges of your senses. You taste your food, but you're in awe of the magic that produced the delectables you're eating, as well as the perfection of this incredible cycle that continues in the elimination and reuse of what you've consumed. The constant behind this ever-changing world becomes your new Source of pleasure, expressed in the wonder and bewilderment you feel. Yes, of course you continue to enjoy your meals, but your pleasure is in being at one with what allows it all to transpire.

You know that you can't find, hear, see, or touch the Source, yet it's always available and can never be depleted. The music that you hear isn't the Tao; the Tao is the invisible energy that fills the empty spaces that give you so much joy. And that happiness you feel is the eternally available and longed-for pleasure of transcending the physical limitations of a human body. Touching the Tao is way beyond any of the sensory pleasures that we somehow believe will satisfy that longing for transcendence.

Addictions become impossible because you no longer try to get worldly pursuits to satisfy you. It's like realizing that you can fly when you've been walking faster and faster, but never getting enough speed or altitude—you kept trying to satisfy a natural longing to be aloft through the pleasure of rapid walking. Now you observe the way nature flows: You clearly see it never asking for more, never using up more, and absolutely never demanding that it be provided with more than is necessary to maintain a perfect balance. The realm of passing pleasures is no longer your central place of

self-identification. You're at peace, feeling secure and happy because you've changed your worldview to include the infinite Tao . . . how could addictions ever compare?

Imagine a heroin addict believing that peace, security, and happiness are available with an inexhaustible supply of opiates. That scenario is impossible because the pleasure that drugs bring lasts but a few seconds, and then the opposite of peace, security, and happiness clicks in. The addict keeps trying to fly by running faster— ultimately he comes to despise his life and destroy himself in the process. Such is the destiny of those who seek the pleasures of the world of the senses to fulfill their longing and natural ability to transcend the physical plane.

Here's what Lao-tzu is offering you in this profound verse of the Tao Te Ching:

Notice the eternal bliss that's always with you— even when the delicacies are out of sight!

Change your way of thinking of yourself as a totally physical being. Instead, recognize that worldly pleasures that tend to be overdone are attempts to transcend the physical, which isn't going to happen without tapping into your natural connection to the Tao. Stop equating sensory delight with the Tao-inspired bliss that's available to you. Enjoy all that you experience through the senses: Love your fine dining, bask in the melodies of your favorite music, and be appreciative of the excitement of sexual energy. But notice that this is all coming from your sensory self, which is happily adaptable to this world. Then seek your "Tao self," which transcends the physical, and explore *its* pleasures.

Reexamine what true, lasting, enjoyment is. Even though the effects of the Tao may initially have no appeal to your seeing, hearing, touching, tasting, and smelling faculties, they'll fulfill the longing you're trying to sate with worldly pursuits. When you're chasing any passing fancy, begin recognizing its value in the here and now, but stop trying to get it to satisfy a greater longing.

Introduce transcendent thankfulness to your everyday life.

Make it a daily practice to give thanks for the presence of the eternal Tao that's always with you. From an appreciative viewpoint, the world that you formerly desired will begin to look different. In the grateful Tao awareness, feelings of being incomplete when worldly pleasures are unavailable are replaced with a transcendent thankfulness. What used to be a need for a worldly delight is replaced with gratitude and contentment for being aware of the aspect of you that is the Tao, free of physical and earthly limitations and confinement. Living with conscious appreciation of the Tao will attract more people and experiences, enriching your balance of mortal and eternal awareness. Open yourself to the unlimited love and abundance of the Tao and you'll attract more of that same love and abundance to you. Your world has changed because you see the Tao where you previously only noticed your mortal self needing worldly pleasures.

Do the Tao Now

Go on a 24-hour fast. When you feel hunger pangs, switch your thoughts to gratitude for the eternal force that's always with you. Warmly let your physical self know that it will be fed when the fast is over, then switch to the Tao self that's unaware of hunger. Enjoy the different nature of the Tao self by concentrating on locating its energy flowing through your body. It will reveal itself—perhaps as contented, exhilarated, or blissful. Note the difference between how this feels compared with worldly pleasures.

36th Verse

Should you want to contain something,
you must deliberately let it expand.
Should you want to weaken something,
you must deliberately let it grow strong.
Should you want to eliminate something,
you must deliberately allow it to flourish.
Should you want to take something away,
you must deliberately grant it access.

The lesson here is called
the wisdom of obscurity.
The gentle outlasts the strong.
The obscure outlasts the obvious.

Fish cannot leave deep waters,
and a country's weapons should not be displayed.

$\mathcal{L}$iving in $\mathcal{O}$bscurity

A large part of your growing-up life lessons revolved around the words *Notice me!* You were taught that the more attention you received, particularly for being a "good little person," the more status and approval you'd get from your peers (as well as the adults you knew). Become number one, you were told, earn that gold star, win that championship, get the best grades, become valedictorian, attain that letter sweater, gather up trophies, and so on. Such lessons were all about rising to the top of the crowd and evaluating yourself based on how you stacked up competitively with everyone around you.

When you change the way you think about your place in the great scheme of things, you'll discover that "the wisdom of obscurity" allows you to eliminate competition from your life and retreat into quiet strength. In other words, Lao-tzu is asking you to take it easy and base your view on entirely new criteria. As you do, your world will begin to reflect a gentle, low-key soul who outlasts those who measure their strength by how much status they have compared to their peers.

This verse opens with the idea of understanding the dichotomous nature of the material world and then encourages you to become an astute observer of your life. Feeling belittled means that you must know what it's like to be important; the idea of being weak grows out of having known what it's like to feel strong. As one translation of the Tao Te Ching (*The Way of Life According to Lao Tzu,* translated by Witter Bynner) reminds us:

> *He who feels punctured*
> *Must once have been a bubble,*
> *He who feels unarmed*
> *Must have carried arms,*
> *He who feels deprived*
> *Must have had privilege . . .*

Avoid the pitfalls of feeling weak, unimportant, stressed, or fearful by transcending the thinking that got you there in the first place. Keep in mind that if you feel weak, you must have had the opposite perception of being strong at least once. If you experience stress, you have an idea of what being unstressed is like. By becoming independent of the need to compare yourself and fit in, you choose the path that Lao-tzu calls "the wisdom of obscurity"—that is, you release your need to be more *anything* in the eyes of others.

Lao-tzu concludes this elegant verse with the metaphor of fish leaving the deep water—when they try to examine the surface and see the "big world" beyond those depths, the little guys no longer endure because they're captured by a net. Hence, you find the great lesson of this 36th verse: Stay under the radar and you'll outlast all who strive to be recognized. When you shift to this viewpoint, your desire for obscurity will surpass your need to be seen as strong and above everyone else—and you won't end up all alone in your trophy room!

Here's what Lao-tzu offers you from 25 centuries ago, when he dictated this enduring tome of wisdom:

Strive to know oneness by seeking awareness of opposites.

Make every effort to stay in a state of oneness in your mind. For example, if you're tired, remind yourself that you know what being rested is like. Recognize the opposing feeling so that you can know both of them simultaneously. Do this with any sensation: If you're depressed, weak, jealous, unloved—anything—the antithesis of what you're going through is within your experiential framework. Seek the

opposite feeling right in the moment and be at one with it in your mind, for this will provide you with a balanced sense of being at peace within yourself. This is oneness, wherein you entertain extremes and use your mind to be like the Tao, which never divides anything. How can oneness be broken apart? It would no longer exist if you could split it up.

Withdraw yourself and allow others.

Monitor your inclinations to compare yourself to others or to stay within the "system." A system is designed to get you to behave just like everyone else, as it contrives to make comparisons determine your success or happiness. The Tao Te Ching urges you to seek obscurity: Draw little or no attention to yourself, and don't ask to be recognized. Instead, allow, allow, allow.

Let other people flourish, waxing on about their strength and popularity. As Lao-tzu says, you must deliberately grant others the right to expand, but take your own lesson from the fish that endure and stay in the deep waters of your Tao-directed soul.

Do the Tao Now

Give yourself an assignment to be as much in the background as you can for an entire day. Stifle inclinations to compare yourself to anyone else or to draw attention to yourself. You can accomplish this by making a commitment to be interested in others today, substituting the pronoun *I* for *you*. So instead of saying, "I did this kind of work for years; let me tell you how you should proceed," remark, "You seem to be doing so well with your new business." In the language of the Tao, stay soft and gentle and you will endure.

37th Verse

The Tao does nothing,
but leaves nothing undone.

If powerful men
could center themselves in it,
the whole world would be transformed
by itself, in its natural rhythms.

When life is simple,
pretenses fall away;
our essential natures shine through.

By not wanting, there is calm,
and the world will straighten itself.
When there is silence,
one finds the anchor of the universe within oneself.

Living in Simplicity

I call this the "Bite your tongue, zip your lips" verse of the Tao Te Ching. The paradox inherent in the two opening lines intrigues me enormously: "The Tao does nothing, but leaves nothing undone." Just imagine what we're being told to consider in this verse—do nothing and everything gets done. It obviously contradicts all that you and I have been taught. Doing nothing in our culture suggests a lazy, unsuccessful, and quite possibly worthless individual. So for a moment, let's modify the way we think about living simply and doing nothing.

Of all the troubles that are reported in the media—including wars, terrorism, famine, hatred, crime, and disease—how many are the result of interfering with the natural unfolding of creation? How much of the essential nature of ourselves and our planet is able to shine through? What would Earth be like if governments didn't meddle in everyone's lives? What if no one could be perceived as an enemy? Could there be a world where groups of people never got together to control others or to invade or conquer—how about where oceans, mountains, natural resources, air, plants, and animals were respected and allowed to flourish without any interference? Suppose that such a place of simplicity and lack of interference existed . . . it would be acting exactly as the Tao does, doing nothing and yet leaving nothing undone.

Now shift out of this highly imaginative scenario and begin to reconsider what's meant in this passage by the concept of powerful individuals transforming the world. When they're interfering with natural rhythms, they ultimately create difficulties that are inconsistent with the Tao. Try to visualize great leaders who are instead centered in the Tao—they bite their tongues and zip their lips rather than act in a hostile way, and they refuse to participate in activities that cause harm to anything on the planet. Yes, this may be a fantasy, but it's not an impossibility when you think like a sage and are centered in the Tao.

The 37th verse of the Tao Te Ching can also help you change the way you look at yourself. Let's say that you're accustomed to equating the idea of success with a take-charge kind of person. You believe that this individual allocates responsibilities to others because he or she is a leader who's willing and able to tell others what to do and how to do it. Well, this view is completely out of harmony with the Tao, which "does nothing" and "leaves nothing undone." As you alter the way you look at your own power and success, you'll begin to replace strong desires with calm contentment. When you start to allow your true nature—which is the anchor of the universe—to shine through, you'll recognize that the way you look at things has absolutely changed.

I've used this simplicity lesson in dealing with all of my children. When I step in and tell them "how," I create resistance. But when I bite my tongue, zip my lips, and retreat into silence, they not only figure it out themselves, but a calm energy replaces their frustration. I've learned that my kids know how to be: They too have the anchor of the universe within them. They too are centered in the do-nothing, get-everything-done Tao. They too have an essential nature that they're listening to. As I've gotten more adept at trusting this—not only for my children, but for everyone I encounter—I'm more peaceful. And guess what? More, not less, seems to get accomplished—on time and without problems that used to surface because of my interference.

Change the way you think about the entire idea of success and power, for this isn't the result of obsessive accomplishment and continually following directions. Start living in a world that you know

works far better with less meddling. You understand that not everyone will stop instructing others and just allow the Tao to unfold, but *you* can be an observer, watching others tap into their power by centering themselves.

Here's what Lao-tzu suggests for making this verse become your daily reality:

Cultivate your unique, natural self.

Practice allowing your essential nature to shine by not enforcing judgments on yourself that were imposed by others. Remind yourself that you don't have to do anything: You don't have to be better than anyone else. You don't have to win. You don't have to be number 1 or number 27 or any other number. Give yourself permission to just *be.* Stop interfering with your unique natural being. Lighten the burden you carry to be productive, wealthy, and successful in the eyes of others; and replace it with an inner assertion that allows you to access the Tao. Affirm: *I am centered in the Tao. I trust that I am able to straighten myself out, and so is the world. I retreat into silence, knowing that all is well.*

Expect to see the essential nature of others by remaining silent.

Deliberately bite your tongue and zip your lips at the precise moment that you're tempted to get involved in the lives of those around you. Become aware of your inclination to tell others, particularly your family members, how they should be conducting their lives. Even if you hold off for a few moments before you butt in to someone else's business, you're on your way to allowing those around you to find their anchor of the universe within themselves. This new discipline of resisting your habit to get involved by pausing before interfering will enable you to see how capable everyone truly is when they're in the energy field of someone who *allows* rather than *dictates.*

Do the Tao Now

Print or copy the first two lines of this 37th verse: "The Tao does nothing, but leaves nothing undone." Read the words repeatedly until you've committed them to memory; then go for a 30-minute walk and take note of their truth. The air, sky, clouds, grass, wind, and flowers . . . nothing natural that you see is undone, but nothing is taking place to work it all out. It is all accomplished by the truth of these words.

I'm reminded of a 13th-century poem by Rumi called "Nibble At Me," which applies perfectly to this section of the Tao Te Ching:

> *Nibble at me.*
> *Don't gulp me down.*
> *How often is it you have a guest in your house*
> *who can fix everything?*

Let your all-knowing guest fix things while you live naturally.

38th Verse

A truly good man is not aware of his goodness
and is therefore good.
A foolish man tries to be good
and is therefore not good.

The master does nothing,
yet he leaves nothing undone.
The ordinary man is always doing things,
yet many more are left to be done.

The highest virtue is to act without a sense of self.
The highest kindness is to give without condition.
The highest justice is to see without preference.

When the Tao is lost, there is goodness.
When goodness is lost, there is morality.
When morality is lost, there is ritual.
Ritual is the husk of true faith,
the beginning of chaos.

The great master follows his own nature
and not the trappings of life.
It is said:
"He stays with the fruit and not the fluff."
"He stays with the firm and not the flimsy."
"He stays with the true and not the false."

Living Within Your Own Nature

Here's the message behind this seemingly paradoxical verse of the Tao Te Ching: Your nature is to be good because you came from the Tao, which is goodness. But when you're *trying* to be good, your essential nature becomes inoperative. In your effort to be good, moral, or obedient, you lose touch with your Tao nature.

There's one sentence in this verse that I pondered for days before writing this short essay: "When the Tao is lost, there is goodness." I felt perplexed because it seemed so contradictory to what the Tao Te Ching was teaching. Finally, in a moment of contemplation while I meditated on a drawing of Lao-tzu, it became clear to me: *Nature is good without knowing it* were the exact words I heard in my meditation. I then understood what Lao-tzu seemed to want me to convey about this somewhat confusing (to me) 38th verse.

Live by your essential nature, the Tao, which is oneness; it has no polarity. Yet the moment that you know you're good, you introduce the polarity of "good" versus "bad," which causes you to lose your connection to the Tao. Then you introduce something new— you figure that if you can't be good, you'll try to be moral. And what is morality but standards of right and wrong that you *try* to uphold? As Lao-tzu seems to be saying to me, *The Tao is oneness; it has no standards for you to follow.* In other words, the Tao just *is;* it isn't doing anything, yet it leaves nothing undone. There's no morality; there

187

is only the unattached Tao. It isn't right and it isn't fair, but it *is* essential nature, and you're encouraged to be true to your own.

As morality is lost, the idea of ritual surfaces, so you try to live in accordance with rules and customs that have defined "your people" for centuries. But I could almost hear Lao-tzu saying: *The Tao is infinite and excludes no one.* Rituals keep you disconnected from the Tao, and you lose them by trying. So you rely upon laws, further dividing yourself and creating chaos for yourself. Again, the Tao just is its own true, essential nature—it has no laws, rituals, morality, or goodness. Observe it and live within its nature. In other words, act without being concerned for your own ego. Give as the Tao does, without condition or trying to be good, moral, or just. Just give to all without preference, as Lao-tzu advises.

I admit that living by this 38th verse may be the total opposite of what you've learned in this lifetime. It certainly represents both an intellectual and a behavioral challenge for me at times. You may appreciate knowing that many of the scholars whom I researched regarding this verse said that Lao-tzu wrote it (and the next one) in response to his opposition to Confucius, his contemporary who laid out specific edicts and codes of conduct for the people. What Lao-tzu seemed to be saying to me through meditation was: *Trust your own essential nature. Let go of all polarities and live in the indivisible oneness that is the Tao.* The dichotomies of good/bad, right/wrong, proper/improper, legal/illegal, and the like can be difficult—just remember that when they surface, the Tao is lost.

Here's some more advice for you, through me, from Lao-tzu:

Live in your essential nature by rejecting artificial principles.

These principles in descending order are goodness, fairness, rites, and laws. Artificial goodness is an attempt to live by not being "bad," so you allow others to decide where you fit in on a goodness scale. Affirm: *I am of the Tao, a piece of God, and I need no human-made device to confirm it. Goodness and God-ness are one, and I trust who I am and will act from this perspective. I am staying with this truth and not what is false.* Furthermore, see that the Tao isn't concerned with fairness—give of yourself knowing that this is an artificial contrivance that cannot exist from a perspective of oneness. You are from, and will return to, that oneness, regardless of your opinions about it. So open up generously without desiring to be treated fairly.

Abandon outmoded familial and cultural customs.

Relinquish rites that you feel compelled to follow simply because they've been that way in your lifetime, and particularly in your family. Peacefully affirm: *I am free to live, trusting in the eternal Tao. I do not have to be as my ancestors were. I relinquish ancient rituals that no longer work or that perpetuate separation or enmity.* Remind yourself that goodness isn't accessed by obeying laws; rather, it is what resonates with your essential nature. You don't need any sort of code to decide what is proper, good, moral, ethical, or legal. Trust yourself to be an instrument of love by surrendering to your highest nature rather than being seduced by mortal laws.

This poem from the 16th-century mystic Saint John of the Cross, titled "A Rabbit Noticed My Condition," beautifully describes this attitude:

> *I was sad one day and went for a walk;*
> *I sat in a field.*
>
> *A rabbit noticed my condition and came near.*
>
> *It often does not take more than that to help at times—*
>
> *to just be close to creatures who*
> *are so full of knowing,*
> *so full of love*
> *that they don't—*
> *chat,*
>
> *they just gaze with*
> *their marvelous understanding.*

Do the Tao Now

Spend a day consciously choosing to notice one of God's creatures, such as a dog, a butterfly, a moth, a spider, an ant, a fish, a cat, a deer, or whatever attracts you. You can learn a lot from them about trusting your inner nature. They are, as the poet says, "so full of knowing."

39th Verse

These things from ancient times arise from one:
The sky is whole and clear.
The earth is whole and firm.
The spirit is whole and full.
The 10,000 things are whole, and the country is upright.
All these are in virtue of wholeness.

When man interferes with the Tao,
the sky becomes filthy,
the earth becomes depleted,
the equilibrium crumbles,
creatures become extinct.

Therefore, nobility is rooted in humility;
loftiness is based on lowliness.
This is why noble people refer to themselves
as alone, lacking, and unworthy.

The pieces of a chariot are useless
unless they work in accordance with the whole.
A man's life brings nothing
unless he lives in accordance with the whole universe.
Playing one's part
in accordance with the universe
is true humility.

Truly, too much honor means no honor.
It is not wise to shine like jade and
resound like stone chimes.

Living Wholeness

We traditionally think of wholeness as something that's complete. "The whole nine yards," for instance, implies the entire distance. "I ate the whole thing" signifies having consumed something completely. Lao-tzu, however, seems to view the concept differently: Wholeness, he writes, has roots in humility. When humility evokes our wholeness, we live the reality that we're pieces of the whole.

With this attitude, you want to exist harmoniously with the entire universe—cooperating with, and being subjugated to, other aspects of the whole. You can't even consider interfering with any piece of it because you're one with it. The moment you begin to place yourself in a transcendent position in relation to others, or to your world of the 10,000 things, you're interfering with the Tao. I encourage you to examine your concept of wholeness based upon this 39th verse of the Tao Te Ching. I can assure you that the world will appear to have changed when you see it through this lens.

Lao-tzu insists that the universe is whole; that is, it's in a state of oneness. There are no parts needing separation from this state. Sky, earth, spirit, and the 10,000 things are all parts of the whole—and what's more, that's their virtue! Now while the sky and the trees may truly be in a unified state, your ego insists that *you're* separate, distinct, and generally superior. But if you can modify your ego's viewpoint, your life will change.

When you're cooperative and looking for signs of oneness, you'll begin to see and feel the interconnectedness of everything. For example, your body is a convenient analogy for a universe all unto itself. While it is one entity, it certainly has trillions of individual, although interconnected, cells. Just one cell with an arrogant relationship to the whole makes *all* the cells suffer and ultimately become extinct, much like the individual who interferes with the Tao by polluting the sky, depleting the earth, and disrupting the equilibrium of the whole. A cancer cell that refuses to cooperate with the cells adjacent to it will ultimately gobble them up, and if left unchecked, will destroy the whole. Why? Because that cancerous cell has no relationship to the whole. It will destroy itself as it kills the host upon which it depends for its own survival. And you'll destroy yourself if you participate in destroying the Tao upon which you are dependent for *your* survival.

Each seemingly individual part of a whole is potentially dangerous (and generally useless) if it doesn't function in harmony. What's true for the chariot in this verse of the Tao Te Ching is true for you as well. Your life needs to have a relationship with the Tao, and that relationship is characterized by Lao-tzu as a bond forged by humility. In other words, wholeness and humility are one and the same, so update the way you think about your relationship to life, and play your part "in accordance with the whole."

Here's what Lao-tzu seems to be instructing as I read and interpret this verse of the ancient Tao Te Ching:

Cultivate your relationship with the planet.

Live in the spirit of wholeness, knowing that you have a role as one of the parts of the Tao. Remind yourself that you cannot interfere with the Tao and live a life of greatness. This means respecting the environment in every way by living in an Earth-friendly manner as a part of its oneness. Become an advocate for conservation. Make time to pick up and recycle trash. Drive an environmentally friendly automobile, or better yet, walk in peace to as many places as possible. Wholeness means maintaining a sense of balance with the all-providing, gentle, nonpushy Tao. In humility, you're able to feel your own tiny role in this great drama orchestrated by your Source. You'll see what Lao-tzu means by: "A man's life brings nothing unless he lives in accordance with the whole universe."

**Change the way you think of yourself from being separate
to seeing yourself in all that you encounter.**

As you live in wholeness, notice how you begin to feel a connection to all of life, rather than the separateness that your ego prefers. See yourself in everyone you encounter, in every creature on our planet, in the forest and the oceans and the sky—the more you do, the more you'll want to stay in a state of cooperation rather than competition. You'll also feel more inclined to reject the concept that there is a "them." Practice this way of being and notice that the type of happiness that may have eluded you for a lifetime is part of the oneness you begin to enjoy.

Here's how Rumi expressed this sentiment:

*If you put your heart against the earth with me, in serving
every creature, our Beloved will enter you from our sacred realm
and we will be, we will be
so happy.*

Do the Tao Now

Go for a walk today and think in wholeness terms with all that you encounter during a 30-minute period. See yourself in those you might otherwise have judged, including the very old, very young, obese, disabled, or indigent. As you look at them, remind yourself, *I share the same originating spirit with every one of these people.* This will help you feel whole by shifting from your ego to the virtue of the Tao.

40th Verse

Returning is the motion of the Tao.
Yielding is the way of the Tao.
The 10,000 things are born of being.
Being is born of nonbeing.

Living by Returning and Yielding

I see one of the greatest teachings of the Tao Te Ching here in the shortest of its 81 passages. If you can master the wisdom in these four lines, you'll be as happy, content, and centered in the Tao as any sage.

With the first word, *returning,* you're being nudged toward an understanding of the basic principle of your existence. Without needing to leave your body, you're asked to die while alive. You accomplish this by realizing that you're one of the 10,000 things that has appeared in the world of form. What Lao-tzu is expressing here in the 40th verse is what contemporary quantum physics has confirmed many centuries later: Particles do not come from particles at the tiniest subatomic level. Instead, when the infinitesimally small specks are collided in a particle accelerator, there's nothing remaining but waves of "particle-less" energy. In order for you, a much bigger speck, to form, you must have come from an originating spirit.

Now Lao-tzu may have known nothing of quantum physics in the 6th century B.C., but he was teaching an essential truth even then: It's spirit that gives life. So to truly live out your destiny as a piece of the originating Tao, you must shed your ego and return to spirit—or you can wait until your body dies and make your return trip at that time.

Six centuries after Lao-tzu dictated the 81 verses of the Tao Te Ching, the man who wrote a huge percentage of the New Testament also spoke of whence we come. Formerly called Saul of Tarsus, he became known as Saint Paul, an apostle of Jesus Christ. In his letter to the people of Ephesus, he wrote: "You were created to be like God, and so you must please him and be truly holy" (Eph. 4:24). This is an invitation for us all to return to what we came from, which is loving, kind, and not exclusive in any way.

How is this accomplished, according to Saint Paul and Lao-tzu, who emphasizes this point in many of the verses of the Tao Te Ching? You do so by yielding your ego, surrendering, and being humble. To that end, in his letter to the people of Corinth, Saint Paul quotes Jesus directly: "My grace is sufficient for you, for my power is made perfect in weakness." Paul then goes on to say himself, "Therefore I will boast all the more gladly about my weaknesses, so that Christ's power may rest on me. That is why, for Christ's sake, I delight in weaknesses, in insults, in hardships, in persecutions, in difficulties. For when I am weak, then I am strong" (2 Cor. 12:9–10). Indeed, yielding is the way of the Tao, as well as the key to an uplifted existence, according to virtually all spiritual texts that have survived over the centuries.

When you truly change the way you think about all of life, the world begins to look very different. You begin seeing everyone and everything as if they have round-trip tickets: You know they all arrived from spirit, and you know they must return. All that composes also decomposes, and whether anyone else understands that isn't important to you. You find the awareness that life on Earth is a death sentence to be a liberating and amusing viewpoint. You're choosing to live every day, each moment that you have and as much as you can, as the nonbeing aspect of yourself.

As a being of spirit, you decide to use your "return ticket" while you're still in physical form by keeping yourself in precisely the same loving status that you occupied before entering this world of boundaries. As you take your return journey, you not only get to lose your ego-identification card, you have the added bonus of regaining the power of your Source, which is the all-creating power of the universe. You merge into the oneness of a being who dissolves ego concerns, and the world that you now see is perfect and infinite in nature. There is no more worry, anxiety, or identification with your possessions— you're a free person. You're a spiritual being first, last, and always.

This is what I feel that Lao-tzu is telling you in this brief yet profound teaching of the 40th verse of the Tao Te Ching:

Monitor your direction, emphasizing returning and yielding.

Mentally make an effort to assess every step you're taking in all aspects of your life—including in your career, your relationships, and your health—in terms of directionality. That is, ask yourself, *In which way am I truly moving? Am I getting away from my originating place, or am I returning to it?* As you make this assessment, you can be more forthright about returning to, rather than moving away from, the Tao. A resolution to exercise or eat more nutritious foods is a step taking you back to the well-being from which you originated. A decision to suspend your ego and take an interest in another person is a movement of moving back to the Tao. A determination to be generous rather than hoard is a choice to be in the return motion. All of these actions come from your thinking first about the direction in which you're moving—*away from* your origination spirit or *back to* it.

Surrender!

This is what yielding is all about. Recognize that your little ego does nothing and that the Tao creates everything, including you. As I sit and write these words in my magical writing space, I know that I don't own what mysteriously appears on the paper. I've surrendered. I know that God writes all the books, composes all the music, and erects all the buildings. I bow to this all-creating power. While it appears that all of the 10,000 things are born of the world of beingness, as I think about it more, the beingness itself came from nonbeing. It is to this glorious state of nonbeing spirituality, or the Tao, that I yield. I encourage you to do the same, and then peacefully observe how it all flows together perfectly.

Do the Tao Now

Strategically place a picture of a yield sign, frequently found as a traffic device, within your field of vision. Each time you look at this sign, use it as a reminder for you to return to the Tao. At least once each day, rather than continuing a disagreement, cede on the spot. In the midst of talking about your own achievements or basking in the light of your ego, stop and become an instant listener. The more you yield each day, the more you return to the peace and harmony of the Tao.

41st Verse

A great scholar hears of the Tao
and begins diligent practice.
A middling scholar hears of the Tao
and retains some and loses some.
An inferior scholar hears of the Tao
and roars with ridicule.
Without that laugh, it would not be the Tao.

So there are constructive sayings on this:
The way of illumination seems dark,
going forward seems like retreat,
the easy way seems hard,
true power seems weak,
true purity seems tarnished,
true clarity seems obscure,
the greatest art seems unsophisticated,
the greatest love seems indifferent,
the greatest wisdom seems childish.

The Tao is hidden and nameless;
the Tao alone nourishes and brings everything to fulfillment.

*L*iving *B*eyond *A*ppearances

This verse of the Tao Te Ching influenced my choice of the title for this book. By changing your thoughts so that they harmonize with the Tao, you see that what you've called "reality" is in fact an outward form, an appearance only. In the beginning, your new way of regarding oneness is clouded by old ego-inspired habits. What you've been accustomed to still resonates within you as real, and your Tao-inspired world may not be consistently recognizable. But you will begin to look beyond what only *seems* to be your truth and move into a direct experience of the Tao, uncluttered by your previously limited views.

Reread the first section of this 41st verse of the Tao Te Ching, noticing your response. Ask yourself whether you're a great, middling, or inferior scholar when it comes to understanding and applying the wisdom of the Tao. For example, I can unabashedly proclaim myself a great scholar after so many years spent studying and writing it. And the more I've studied, the more diligently I've practiced. I've become highly attuned to the infinite variety of daily opportunities to employ the principles of the Tao. As you examine your own thoughts, you may discover an aspect of yourself that wants to learn how to utilize these ancient teachings. Thus, you can move from being a person who knew very little about the Tao, and might even have ridiculed it, to being a great scholar.

The application of the Tao each day determines the greatness of a scholar, rather than whether he or she intellectually understands these paradoxical-sounding concepts. Lao-tzu points out that without the ridiculing laughter of inferior scholars, the Tao couldn't even exist. Talk about paradoxical concepts!

In *A Warrior Blends with Life: A Modern Tao,* Michael LaTorra comments on this 41st verse:

> The Way is only attractive to those who are already wise enough to know how foolish they are. Sarcastic laughter from other fools who believe themselves wise does not deter the truly wise from following the Way. Following the Way, they do not become complicated, extraordinary, and prominent. Rather they become simple, ordinary, and subtle.

As you elect to live the Tao each day, what you experience within and around you will be different from what it appears to be. You will go way beyond surfaces into the blissful world of the Tao, and it's vital that you choose to stay in this truth regardless of how it all seems. Others will make fun of you, but remember the paradox that without that ridiculing laughter, it wouldn't be the Tao.

You'll experience times of darkness, but your new vision will eventually illuminate your inner world. And when it seems as though you're moving backward, remember that "the Tao is hidden and nameless." If it was knocking at your door, or readily accessible like a pill to swallow, it wouldn't be the Tao. So when life looks difficult, stop and realize that you're only one thought removed from being at peace. You'll know what Lao-tzu meant when he said that the easy way seems hard, and true power seems like weakness. You don't have to struggle or dominate others in order to feel strong.

A person in the Tao sees the world quite differently, knowing that inner peace is power. Less effort is actually easier—work gets done when you lighten up internally and let yourself be moved along by the ceaseless Tao, rather than by setting goals or meeting standards set by others. Allow the Tao, and see the purity and clarity that originates from this vantage point. The outward appearance of anyone or anything may appear tarnished, but a Tao view will remind you that essential goodness is always there. It's hidden and nameless, though, so don't be obsessed with finding and labeling it.

In this way you become a great scholar who diligently works to live in harmony with the Tao even though it remains obscure. Apply this same insight to the times you feel unloved: When you see what appears to be indifference, know in your heart that love is present. The Tao isn't concerned with proving its fidelity. It appears to be uninterested, but it's nevertheless always there, everywhere. As your thinking changes from a position dictated by your ego to one that transcends it, you'll see an illuminated world that is truly inviting. Ego convinced you to see a cold and indifferent planet, while the ego-transcending Tao shines pure love to all that you're connected to. Allow it to work its magic in your life.

This is what Lao-tzu seems to be instructing, as I sit here asking how I might serve those who read this book:

Be diligent.

You're not an inferior scholar of Tao if you're reading these words. So if you're a middling scholar who "retains some and loses some" of this wisdom, make a commitment to work toward your greatness. Just practice a few of these insights each day. Be diligent about it—set aside your inclination to be puzzled or argumentative, and allow yourself the freedom to be a persistent practitioner. Even a small thing such as an affirmation or a rereading of a verse each day puts you on the path of living according to the Great Way. Lao-tzu simply says to live it by zealously practicing these insights.

Here are some lines from Walt Whitman to remind you that you're not who you appear to be:

O I could sing such grandeurs and glories about you!
You have not known what you are,
you have slumber'd upon yourself all your life,
Your eyelids have been the same as closed most of the time . . .

Whoever you are! claim your own at any hazard!
These shows of the East and West are tame compared to you,
These immense meadows, these interminable rivers, you are
immense and interminable as they . . .

The Tao truth is unprovable in physical terms.

Let go of your conditioned way of needing proof in the physical world before something becomes your truth. The Tao is hidden permanently and it cannot be named, so accept this as a fact. You're not going to find it in a material form; it has no boundaries, and the moment you try to name it, you've lost it. (See the 1st verse.) Just as modern scientists must accept the fact that quantum particles originate in waves of formless energy or spirit, without their ever seeing that infinite all-creating field, so too can you let go of your need to see and touch the Tao before you can believe it. By changing the way you look at the world, you'll see a realm beyond the appearance of darkness, difficulty, weakness, indifference, and death.

As the poet Rainer Maria Rilke observed,

> . . . *behind the world our names enclose is*
> *the nameless: our true archetype and home.*

Do the Tao Now

Spend an hour with a child today, taking note of how much wisdom is embodied in what appears to be juvenile behavior and beliefs. Notice his or her fascination with seemingly insignificant items, repeating the same senseless phrase, tantrums, or laughter. Jot down your impressions of the wisdom behind such so-called childish impulses and vow to be a kid again as frequently as possible.

42nd Verse

The Tao gave birth to one.
One gave birth to two.
Two gave birth to three.
And three begat the 10,000 things.
The 10,000 things carry yin and embrace yang;
they achieve harmony by combining these forces.

People suffer at the thought of being
without parents, without food, or without worth.
Yet this is the very way that
kings and lords once described themselves.
For one gains by losing,
and loses by gaining.

What others taught, I teach.
The violent do not die a natural death.
That is my fundamental teaching.

$\mathcal{L}$iving by $\mathcal{M}$elting into $\mathcal{H}$armony

The beginning of this verse reiterates what Lao-tzu has been saying throughout the previous 41 sections of the Tao Te Ching—that is, the Tao is the hidden force that brings all of the creatures and substances that comprise the 10,000 things into being, as well as being the intangible that we think of as oneness or wholeness. All carry and embrace the opposites of yin and yang, or the feminine and masculine principles. This verse reinforces the idea that blending these seemingly opposing forces is the way to achieve harmony.

Lao-tzu reminds you of the things that you probably think cause suffering and suggests that being orphaned, going hungry, or feeling worthless are high on the list. But then he says that achieving harmony in terms of the Tao involves gaining by losing. Does he mean that if you lose your home, your mom and dad, your belongings, or your sense of self-esteem, you'll gain all that you need? *What?* How is that possible?

Your infinite self that originated in, and is animated by, the Tao needs nothing to sustain itself. Parents, possessions, and self-worth are only necessary to the existence of your mortal self. Lao-tzu wants you to recognize this difference within the oneness that you are. He teaches that you gain awareness of your Tao nature through the loss of emphasis on the physical conditions of your life. In your oneness, you're likely to lose the Tao sensibility in proportion to the emphasis you place on worldly desires. At the same time, Lao-tzu emphasizes that death of the mortal self is influenced by the way you live. *You will die as you live* is the fundamental teaching for the mortal self. This is the balancing act that's required to truly melt into harmony with the Tao.

The last several lines of this verse insistently drew my attention when I was researching, writing, and meditating on this 42nd passage. I studied many translations of it, and I spent countless hours communing with Lao-tzu, gazing at his likeness in my writing space. I discovered that this particular verse was always interpreted with the same kind of dramatic emphasis. All said something similar to the following: "I take this to be the father of teachings"; "Know this to be the foundation of my teachings"; "This will be the essence of my teaching"; "Whoever says this is my beloved teacher"; and the one I used here, "That is my fundamental teaching." My conclusion is that when you're violent in any way—including in your thoughts, behavior, pronouncements, and allegiances—then you're choosing to die in the same way. Of course, you'll draw your own conclusions about the significance of this particularly dramatic instruction of the Tao Te Ching.

The insistence with which this teaching presented itself to me leads me to believe that Lao-tzu wants me to emphasize that its opposite is also true. That is, a person who embraces the Tao and eschews violence and hatred will live and die naturally . . . which is in harmony with the perfection of the Tao. So I invite you to change the way you perceive what keeps you from harmonizing with your Source. The birthing agent of all is also your ultimate place of return when you leave your body in that moment called "death." You must be willing to give up your attachment to all forms of violence in your life if you want to melt into harmony.

Here are Lao-tzu's suggestions, written through me, for embracing this fundamental teaching of the Tao Te Ching:

Remember that violence violates the harmony of life and death.

Make a decision to live harmoniously with the Tao by removing all associations that you have with violence. Stop supporting entertainment that promotes any type of it, for instance. Monitor your vocabulary to remind yourself to remove words that direct hatred

or killing toward any living creature. Explore avenues for resolving disputes peacefully, and get involved with organizations that discourage violence. Remember that the one fundamental principle of the Tao Te Ching is that if you take up savagery in any way, then you're signing up for a savage end on this planet. And this includes your mental activity as well as behavior, so seek kind and forgiving thoughts in place of revenge and hatred. Change the way you look at life to seeing a picture that's free of violence and melts into harmony as you live and die.

**Examine your attachments with the idea that
you gain by losing and lose by gaining.**

Your attachments to objects, status, your culture, and even other people prevent you from being free in the Great Way of the Tao. The more stuff that accumulates, the more you have to watch it, insure it, worry about it, protect it, polish it, distribute it, and identify with it. In other words, you lose harmony while seeking to gain. Practice giving your possessions away and loosening your need for who and what you have. Imagine strings attached to everyone and everything that you feel you own; then symbolically cut those strings and be an observer rather than an owner. This is how you melt into harmony with the Tao.

The poet Hafiz advises:

> *Start seeing everything as God
> But keep it a secret.*

Do the Tao Now

Think of one person who may have wronged you at some time in your life: someone who abandoned or mistreated you, someone who stole from or cheated you, someone who abused you or spread ugly rumors about you. Spend one day putting all thoughts of revenge aside, and instead feel forgiveness and love for that individual. Notice the difference in your body when you don't have violent thoughts . . . this is the essential teaching of the Tao.

43rd Verse

The softest of all things
overrides the hardest of all things.
That without substance enters where there is no space.
Hence I know the value of nonaction.

Teaching without words,
performing without actions—
few in the world can grasp it—
that is the master's way.
Rare indeed are those
who obtain the bounty of this world.

$\mathcal{L}$iving $\mathcal{S}$oftly

The Tao Te Ching is full of parallels to nature, and in fact the pure essence of the teachings seems to be to help us become Tao-inspired sages through oneness with the environment. The opening lines of this 43rd verse remind me of the way of water, of its softness and ability to enter everywhere, even where there's seemingly no space to do so. Water is used symbolically in many references to Taoism, such as in the title of the outstanding contemporary work by Alan Watts, *Tao: The Watercourse Way*. To live softly is to live the watercourse way.

In this verse, Lao-tzu invites you to change the way you view hardness. To you, the concept is probably equated with strength. You may work out because the firmer your muscles, the tougher you think you are. Do you consider diamonds more valuable than a soft mineral, like volcanic ash, which crumbles in your hand? Perhaps you subscribe to the idea that doing a difficult task makes you a better person. Now imagine emulating water, this basic element that is the embodiment of nature (after all, it does comprise 75 percent of both the world's surface and our physical makeup). Think about the way water courses, flowing to the lowest place, and how in order to experience it, you can't just grab a handful. You must instead relax, lightly placing your fingers inside of it.

Reflect upon how the gentle water compares to the solid stone and marble it's capable of carving through. The soft water overrides hardness—deep valleys surrounded by mountains of granite have been carved away over the centuries by the patient, quiet, moving liquid. Imagine being able to enter where no space appears to be available, and to move slowly, speaking seldom and allowing yourself to be harmoniously intact as you seek a lower, less noisy and noticeable place . . . a place where all others desire to come to you. This is the watercourse way.

There's value in the nonaction of being able to flow like water, naturally and effortlessly. I can't help but think of this when I enter the ocean to swim for an hour or so. I want to go with the current rather than swim against it, so my first choice involves seeing which way the water is coursing. As I move through the sea, emulating its naturalness, I trust my instinct and swim without trying to direct my arms and legs in their strokes. I think of it as doing, but not interfering—that is, I'm allowing my body to propel itself through the water without my mind telling it how to move. As I've changed my thoughts about "hard" and "soft," I don't have to do anything but be in the water. I've chosen to make my daily swim a soft, silent experience that requires very little action on my part. And my swimming world has changed, becoming easy, joyful, and almost effortless. I've learned "the value of nonaction," as Lao-tzu expresses it in this verse. It's performing without action!

Apply this way of seeing everything in your world: Tasks will be simplified, your performance level will increase, and the pressure to be better than others by using superior hardened strength will cease to be a factor. You'll naturally incorporate the wisdom of peaceful harmony that's found in the martial arts by letting the efforts of others become a source of your own power. Your softness will override the hardness of others.

This principle is clearly seen when you look at great champions as they perform their chosen activities. The greatest golfers are effortless in their swing. The most successful ballplayers run, jump, throw, catch, and shoot with a softness that seems to stupefy most observers—they don't use force, nor can they find words to describe how they do it. The most talented artists dance softly, without effort; paint quietly, without force; and write easily, without struggle, by allowing the words to come to them. As Lao-tzu reminds you, these are rare beings who live the master's way. These sages "obtain the bounty of this world," which is available to you, too.

As I contemplate Lao-tzu's counsel, he urges me to offer you encouragement to apply the spirit of the watercourse way that's found in this 43rd verse of the Tao Te Ching:

Introduce a soft, nonaction style to your life.

Practice the way of nonaction, or performing without effort. By letting go of your inner drive to push ahead, you'll see that you ironically do better than when you tried so hard. In your work, become more tolerant in your drive to achieve by softening your attitude and behavior. You'll see that customers and larger opportunities are attracted to you. Why is this true? Because you're allowing the perfect flow of the Tao, like the great gray heron lets the tide recede in order to reveal the nourishment he needs to live. Notice how your life changes as you change the way you look at it.

Practice performing without effort in other areas of your life, too. For example, some marathon runners say that they've learned to relax and stop pushing, letting their legs, arms, and torso simply be as their bodies begin experiencing extreme exhaustion with only a few miles to go. They report that when they shut down the mental interference and instructions, they magically cross that finish line. Soft always has its place, for it is the watercourse way . . . the way of the Tao.

Encourage desires to freely flow in your imagination.

Consider what you've wanted to have in this life as if it's behind a locked door. Examine what you've been telling yourself about the prosperity, superb health, good luck, business success, or wonderful relationships you've craved—that no matter how hard you've tried, it's all come to naught. Then imagine yourself flowing like water through the barrier of that locked room. Do it softly, gently, and silently in your mind. In other words, just spend some time getting used to practicing the watercourse way of the Tao.

As you allow softness to be part of the picture of your life, the hard way will soften. Begin to exercise this kind of effortlessness in all areas of your desires. According to Ralph Waldo Emerson, "It is the condition of Inspiration—marry nature, don't use her for plea-sure." I urge you to consider this kind of marriage.

Do the Tao Now

Have a day of silence. Don't speak aloud to anyone; instead, just observe and see if you can be in a state of softness without telling yourself or anyone else what to do. Gently consider the powerful words of Herman Melville, who once said that God's one and only voice is silence.

44th Verse

Which means more to you,
you or your renown?
Which brings more to you,
you or what you own?
I say what you gain
is more trouble that what you lose.

Love is the fruit of sacrifice.
Wealth is the fruit of generosity.

A contented man is never disappointed.
He who knows when to stop is preserved from peril,
only thus can you endure long.

Living by Knowing When to Stop

The 44th verse tells you that changing the way you prioritize your life ensures a fruitful one. I call it the "Enough is enough" section of the Tao Te Ching. When you update your view of the most important things in your life, the world around you is going to seem very different. Lao-tzu is urging you to look into your heart and examine what is truly important.

Earlier verses of the Tao Te Ching counsel that the essential mission of your life is to go back to (or get to know) your originating Source before physical death. In other words, you don't have to die to make the return trip! It's not only possible, but essential, to feel your connection to the Tao while you're still alive.

Knowing when to stop is part of the path leading you to your essential self, where the need for fame and possessions is nonexistent. You see, it's not the things or even a desire for recognition that keeps you from a living connection to the Tao—it's your *attachment* to them that gets in the way. So shift the importance you've placed on success or belongings, which has obscured your connectedness to the Tao. Begin to note the senselessness of demanding more, exhausting yourself in pursuit of what keeps you trapped in a vicious cycle of "striving and never arriving" or trying to find fulfillment. This verse implores you to know when to stop.

I'm sure that you can easily see people in your environment who spend their entire lives seeking more of everything—more possessions, money, recognition, awards, friends, places to go, substances, food—you name it. If you live with this same philosophy, you've signed up for a life of frustration and dissatisfaction because the search itself becomes your jailer. It's easy to see then why Lao-tzu advises that what you gain is far more trouble than what you lose! When you prioritize your life, you'll find that love and a feeling of abundance are not only what you desire, but these two principles are instantly available because you've changed the way you look at the world. From this new perspective, you'll feel totally loved and wealthy in all ways.

I realize that Lao-tzu is again speaking in what seem to be paradoxical words. But he's coming to you from the perspective of having changed the way *he* looked at things, and noting that what he looked at changed. He now sees love and wealth everywhere—yet he knows intuitively that he can never possess them by chasing after them, since they'll always remain just outside of his grasp. And so he looks at the Tao and sees that the Great Way keeps nothing for itself, is willing to let go of its life-giving essence, and is desirous to share with all. When *you* give of yourself, asking nothing in return and withdrawing your need for recognition, you'll experience more contentment. The fruits of wealth and love are seen right there before you when you simply stop the chase.

The beauty of the wisdom in this 44th verse is that you give away your attachment to things or ways of being, which is what I mean by knowing when to stop. If the chase is wearing out your health, stop! If the chase is wreaking havoc on your relationships, stop! If the chase is exhausting you, stop! If the chase is keeping you from enjoying your life, stop! When you know when to cease and desist, you're protected from all of those perils, and you'll enjoy a long and contented existence connecting with the Tao.

The following is what Lao-tzu asks me to offer you as a means for implementing this teaching:

Make your relationship to the Tao your top priority.

Prioritize your life by making this the essential and foremost responsibility you have. Your primary relationship needs to be with *yourself,* not your family, business, country, culture, or ethnicity.

Affirm: *The number one priority in my life is my relationship with my Source of being.* Go there first, before any other considerations, and you'll automatically discontinue demanding more of anything else. You'll begin to emulate the Tao effortlessly, living heaven on earth.

Practice knowing when to stop.

Alert yourself to recognizing when it's a good time to stop demanding, chasing, talking, walking, working, sleeping, playing, shopping, complaining, striving, and so on. By practicing cessation, you'll move into prioritizing what's important in your life in that moment. Is your business doing well? Let it stop growing. Is your stomach full? Quit eating right now. Do you have enough money saved? Give some of it away, without taking deductions or asking for credit for your generosity. The more you're attached to needing and wanting and possessing, the more you lose in your relationship to the Tao. But when you know the time to stop, you say good-bye to the troubles that accrue for those who sacrifice arriving for a lifetime of striving.

Do the Tao Now

Pick an area of your life to practice releasing an attachment by deciding when to stop. For example, plan to leave ten minutes before you think you're done in the grocery store, or refrain from buying anything that's not on your list. At work, restrain yourself from getting another cup of coffee or writing one more personal e-mail. In a relationship, don't say anything else in a discussion that's going nowhere. Those are all examples of attachment to being or doing.

You can also practice detaching by giving something away. Just recently, for instance, my son surprised both of us by doing just that. I was admiring a new T-shirt he'd just purchased, and he said, "Here, Dad, you like this one so much that even though it's my favorite, I want you to have it." It was a simple, spontaneous letting go of an attachment, and both of us felt the wealth that is the fruit of generosity.

45th Verse

The greatest perfection seems imperfect,
and yet its use is inexhaustible.
The greatest fullness seems empty,
and yet its use is endless.

Great straightness seems twisted.
Great intelligence seems stupid.
Great eloquence seems awkward.
Great truth seems false.
Great discussion seems silent.

Activity conquers cold;
inactivity conquers heat.
Stillness and tranquility set things in order
in the universe.

Living Beyond Superficialities

This verse subtly asks you to view the world with new eyes. Most likely you've been conditioned to evaluate just about everything with a cursory and fleeting glance. Here, however, Lao-tzu is asking you to stop seeing through your ego-dominated culture, and to instead begin noticing the still and tranquil invisible space within everything. When you go beyond superficialities, you become aware that what used to look imperfect, empty, awkward, or even stupid now appears perfect, full, eloquent, and intelligent.

Your previous way of thinking about the world told you that it's full of imperfections—the people in your life should be different, politicians should be aligned with your values, the weather should be more consistent and reliable, the multitudes should be more peaceful, young people should study harder, and older people should be more tolerant. The assessments are relentlessly endless, and they're all based on teachings that you've adopted. While they may seem sensible and correct, these views are simply the result of only looking at what exists on the surface. "Hold on a minute," this verse of the Tao Te Ching seems to say, "try looking at it this way. What seems to be imperfect has perfection, and what seems empty and false has a profound spiritual truth supporting it."

The paradox here is evident: Hunger does exist in the world as an element of the perfection of the Tao, and the desire to help those who are starving is also part of that perfection. You're being asked not to label what you see as imperfect, stupid, or empty; rather, look for the stillness and tranquility within you that you can bring to these superficial appearances. When you refrain from engaging in judgments based solely on looks, you paradoxically become an instrument for change.

Study the opening lines of this verse. What seems imperfect is nevertheless inexhaustible; what seems empty is endless. Imagine a pitcher out of which you could pour delicious iced tea without ever needing to refill. "Impossible!" you say, yet that's precisely what the Tao does. It never, ever runs out. It never has, and it never will. It cannot be exhausted. You are asked to be like this inexhaustible, always-full Tao—be nonjudgmental, still, and above all, tranquil. Let the world and all of its creations unfold while you remain constant with the invisibleness that allows it all to take place. Allow whatever you feel deep within you in that quiet and peaceful space to guide you in the direction that is your true destiny.

Recently I attended a talk by my friend, colleague, and mentor Ram Dass, who had a stroke in 1997 that impacted his speech. As of this writing, he still spends almost all of his waking moments in a wheelchair, and his lecture lasted approximately 45 minutes. He received a standing ovation at the end, and I personally felt so blessed and blissful by having been in the audience. There are some who might have only seen superficialities—to them, the lecture might have seemed halting and slow because of the stroke, and judged as embarrassing or even intellectually challenging. Much of my dear friend's time onstage was silent, and it certainly appeared to be awkward in comparison to his earlier speeches, which were always masterful and eloquent. But as I sit here writing, I can only say that because I changed the way I looked at this experience, the entire thing changed for me in a very dramatic way.

While Ram Dass's words were few, his message was straightforward, laconic, and direct. What might have appeared as unintelligible to others struck me as brilliance masked by circumstance. What could have been viewed as fumbling was articulate and perfect in every way. I heard a great presentation to a loving, receptive crowd that was done largely between long periods of luscious silence. Throughout this lecture, all of the audience members and I

remained still and tranquil. As Lao-tzu concludes in this 45th verse of the Tao Te Ching, it "set things in order in [our] universe."

I can feel the presence of Lao-tzu here this morning as I gaze at the drawing of that beautiful old man sitting on an ox. He seems to be urging me on to tell you how to apply this great wisdom, which comes from living beyond shallowness:

See imperfections as perfect, even if your ego-mind cannot comprehend this.

Become aware of your conditioned responses that lead you to label people, places, and circumstances as less than perfect. See the flawlessness behind the supposed defects. As I watched my children grow up, for instance, there were many times when their challenging behavior at a certain age was really a kind of brilliance. For example, I observed them refusing to eat certain nutritious foods, knowing that they needed to go through these phases in order to reach higher places. An adamant refusal to eat vegetables isn't stupid or twisted thinking—it was perfect and necessary for them at the time. You can apply this same kind of patient stillness to your world. Inch by inch, we evolve as a people toward a fuller union with the Tao.

One of history's great mystical thinkers, Meister Eckhart, poetically put it this way several centuries ago:

Every object, every creature, every man, woman and child
has a soul and it is the destiny of all,

to see as God sees, to know as God knows,
to feel as God feels, to Be
as God
Is.

Give *yourself* permission to be perfect, even with all of your seeming imperfections.

Recognize yourself first and foremost as a creation of God, which is your perfection. It has nothing to do with how you look or any so-called mistakes or failures you may have attracted to yourself, even though these superficialities will continue throughout your entire lifetime in this body. The Source of your material self, the eternal

Tao, is flawless, straight, full, and an expression of truth. When those ways that you've been taught are imperfect appear and you notice the pain you're causing yourself by disliking or judging them, call in your Tao-perfect self to tend to the so-called faults. When you surround it with love, the superficial appearance and feeling of being unloved will become tranquil.

The 13th-century mystical poet Rumi sums this up perfectly in this short observation:

> *You <u>are</u> the truth*
> *from foot to brow. Now,*
> *what else would you like to know?*

Do the Tao Now

Make a list of ten things you've labeled as imperfect, twisted, or stupid. Then take one at a time and elicit the feeling in your body that's attached to that item. Allow the sensation to be observed and to be held in your thoughts from a perspective of loving permission. Do this for as long as you're comfortable, allowing the "Tao now!" to be present. Remember as you do this exercise that the Tao is non-judgmental and provides equally to all. You can take the sunshine and bask in it, or you can burn yourself to a crisp. The Tao just is, and it doesn't care!

46th Verse

When the world has the Way,
running horses are retired to till the fields.
When the world lacks the Way,
warhorses are bred in the countryside.

There is no greater loss than losing the Tao,
no greater curse than covetousness,
no greater tragedy than discontentment;
the worst of faults is wanting more—always.

Contentment alone is enough.
Indeed, the bliss of eternity
can be found in your contentment.

Living Peacefully

If you're presently evaluating your level of achievement based on how much you've accumulated, prepare to sense a major shift in your state of personal satisfaction and contentment. Verse 46 of the Tao Te Ching invites you to discover a more peaceful and self-satisfying way of knowing success—and as your determination to acquire more begins to weaken, your new views will change the world you've known. You'll find that the experience of inner peace becomes your true gauge of accomplishment.

This 46th verse begins with a look at what happens when a planet loses its connection to the Way. Countries begin needing to conquer more territory . . . and in their quest for more land, power, and control over others, they must constantly prepare for war. Lao-tzu speaks symbolically of horses here: When connected to the Tao, the animals fertilize the fields; when disconnected from it, the beautiful creatures are bred for war.

In a modern translation of the Tao Te Ching, my friend Stephen Mitchell interprets this message in present-day terms:

> *When a country is in harmony with the Tao,*
> *the factories make trucks and tractors.*
> *When a country goes counter to the Tao,*
> *warheads are stockpiled outside the cities.*

It's painfully obvious that our world has largely lost contact with the Way as described by Lao-tzu. These days so much of our energy is placed on breeding warhorses at the expense of using our resources to fertilize our fields so that we can live in peace. The United States is chock-full of weapons of mass destruction, and we continually legislate more funding to make our weapons so menacing that they're capable of rendering our entire planet uninhabitable. The "disease of more" has created an environment that personifies Lao-tzu's observation that there is "no greater tragedy than discontentment." But even if so many of our Divine selves seem to be engulfed by the flames of unease, *you* can begin the process of putting Lao-tzu's advice to work.

When you truly understand what it means to live peacefully, satisfaction will begin to replace your desire for more. Your world will begin to become tranquil as you change your own life and then touch the lives of your immediate family, your neighbors, your co-workers, and ultimately your nation and the entire planet. Begin by simply thinking of the opening line of the famous Prayer of Saint Francis when you notice that you're demanding more of anything.

Silently say, *Lord, make me an instrument of Thy peace; where there is hatred, let me sow love.* As that instrument of peace, you'll radiate tranquility to those in your immediate surroundings, and you'll feel the flicker of a new and different success in contentment, perhaps for the first time in your life. By refusing to lose the Tao, regardless of how lost others are and what our world's governments elect to do, you're living harmoniously. *Your* connection to the Tao will make a difference, gradually inching Earth away from the precipice of discontentment that Lao-tzu called "no greater tragedy."

The sublime Hafiz beautifully sums up the kind of success I'm referring to in his poem "Would You Think it Odd?":

> *Would you think it odd if Hafiz said,*
> *"I am in love with every church*
> *And mosque*
> *And temple*
> *And any kind of shrine*
> *Because I know it is there*
> *That people say the different names*
> *Of the One God."*

Getting back to Lao-tzu, here are his messages from the powerful 46th verse that are applicable today in your personal life:

Practice gratitude and contentment every day.

When your feet hit the floor every single morning, without exception, say, "Thank You for an opportunity to live in a state of contentment." Invite the magical energy of the Tao to freely flow through you and inform your responses throughout the day. You're in harmony with your Source when you're soliciting gratitude and gratification in these ways.

Be one with your nature.

In a world that seems to produce more and more violence, become a person who chooses to be an instrument of peace. Let your nature be the "horses" that are bred to till the fields, feed the hungry, and offer comfort to the lame or less fortunate. Live as if you and the Tao are one, which of course you are when you're in your natural state.

When enough of us are able to do this, we'll reach a critical mass, and eventually the Great Way will surpass the demands of the ego. I truly believe, to use a baseball analogy, that nature always "bats last."

Do the Tao Now

Set aside time to make a conscious effort to send peaceful energy to someone or some group whom you think of as the enemy. Include a competitor; an alienated family member; a person of a different religious persuasion; or those you oppose in a government, political party, or disagreement. Then literally send something to them if that feels okay to you, such as a flower, a book, or a letter. Begin your conscious effort today, right now, to surrender to the Tao and know authentic success, which has no separation.

47th Verse

Without going out the door,
know the world.
Without looking out the window,
you may see the ways of heaven.

The farther one goes,
the less one knows.

Therefore the sage does not venture forth
and yet knows,
does not look
and yet names,
does not strive
and yet attains completion.

*L*iving by *B*eing

I encourage you to change your belief that effort and striving are necessary tools for success. In verse 47, Lao-tzu suggests that these are ways of being that keep you from experiencing the harmony and attaining the completion that's offered by the Tao. Living by *being* instead of *trying* is a different viewpoint; as Lao-tzu states, you can see and accomplish more by not looking out the window.

How is this possible? Let's look at an example to clarify this conundrum. I'd like you to place all of your attention on one of God's greatest creations. I'm referring to your heart, that always-beating, mysterious chunk of arteries, vessels, muscle, and blood that you carry with you wherever you go. It continually maintains its *thump, thump, thump* without your trying to make it beat, even while you sleep. You don't *make* it thump away—even without your conscious attention, it works as perfectly as the ocean does. Its continuous beat is even reminiscent of waves on the sea's surface.

Your heart is indeed a thing of wonder as it delivers life itself; it is essentially you. That organ in your chest is a model for understanding and applying the lesson of living by being. Your heart attains completion (your life) by not venturing forth, looking beyond its chest cavity, or striving. As you sit here reading these words right now, it's keeping you alive just by being, and you don't even feel it.

I'd like you to think of your entire self as a heart that already knows exactly what to do by virtue of its very nature. That is, you don't have to go anywhere to know the world because you already *are* the world. The moment you attempt to control the beating of your own heart, you realize the futility of such an effort. No amount of trying or striving will make any difference, for your heart operates by its natural connection to the Tao, which does nothing but leaves nothing undone.

Michael LaTorra points this out in his commentary on this verse in *A Warrior Blends with Life:*

> As the wisest of sages have always realized, the root of essential being is in the heart, especially in the heart-beat mechanism. From here, the radiance of essential being spirals upward to illuminate the head. This mechanism lies beyond any technology. You already inhabit it. . . . And through deep feelings (rather than superficial emotions) you can connect with it immediately. . . . The ultimate act that enlightens involves no action at all.

So now you know that the paradoxical state Lao-tzu describes in this verse is not only possible, but it's actually taking place everywhere right now, in billions of human hearts. The further reality is that this is true for the hearts of *all* creatures, as well as the life system of every tree, flower, bush, and even mineral on Earth. And this is only one planet in a universe that contains so many heavenly bodies that counting them is so far beyond our ability that we can't even devise calculators to undertake such a task.

The 21st century is often called "the information age": We live in a time when there's more data available on tiny computer chips than ever before in human history. We can also easily see that our efforts do indeed bring us more facts and the like. In fact, you may be one of the computer wizards whose greater efforts have made all of this possible. What's at issue here is the relationship of information to knowledge and wisdom.

Let's take apart the very name of this era—information—to explain what I mean. When you stay "in-form" (in your body and the material world), you're rewarded with information. But move *beyond* form (transform to spirit) and you'll receive inspiration. Thus, information is not always knowledge, and knowledge is not always wisdom. Wisdom connects you to your heart in your waking moments; it is the Tao at work. Lao-tzu is asking you to recognize the difference

between striving for more facts and being in the world that is complete as it is. As you live from this perspective of wisdom or connection to the Tao, the world looks so very different.

You are a single beat in the one heart that is humanity. You don't have to look outside your window or venture forth—all you have to do is just *be* in the same way that you allow your heart to be. This concept was difficult 2,500 years ago, and I realize that it may still be challenging to grasp, but you must! In a world mad for information without the grace of being the Tao, you are one of the heartbeats that keeps the Tao wisdom flowing freely . . . just by being.

Through me, Lao-tzu urges you to work at this new awareness and try out these suggestions:

Begin the process of trusting your heart.

Listening to your heartbeat, you can clearly recognize the Tao practicing the paradox of doing nothing and at the same time leaving nothing undone. Your deepest feelings are reflections of your "heart space" talking to you. You don't have to do anything to activate this internal profundity; simply let your heart speak to you. Begin noticing and appreciating its continual silent thumping—and whatever provides the energy for the beat to go on, let its presence in your chest be a constant reminder of the Tao at work.

Trust in your "sense of knowing," which is always with you.

An internal *knowing* is there independent of your venturing forth—it's there even when your eyes are closed and you're sitting still. This doesn't necessarily mean you should become a couch potato. Rather, you must allow yourself to be guided by the same Source that twirls the planets around the sun, and trust that it will direct you perfectly without your having to interfere. Experience your innate creativity while being an observer, watching in amazement as everything falls perfectly into place. Just as moving water never stagnates, you will be moved by a natural force that seeks being complete within you and without your needing to step in. You can get in touch with this knowing through the practice of meditation.

Do the Tao Now

Find or make a picture of a heart, and spend time today contemplating it as a reminder of the Tao effortlessly at work within your chest cavity. At some point during the day, allow yourself to be guided by the Tao to do something creative that comes from within, such as painting, writing a poem, taking a walk in the park, beginning a personal project, or anything at all. Just let yourself be guided without having to venture forth in any way. Then bring this magic of the Tao more frequently into all aspects of your life.

48th Verse

Learning consists of daily accumulating.
The practice of the Tao consists of daily diminishing;
decreasing and decreasing, until doing nothing.
When nothing is done, nothing is left undone.

True mastery can be gained
by letting things go their own way.
It cannot be gained by interfering.

$\mathcal{L}$iving by $\mathcal{D}$ecreasing

We live in a society that seems to say, "The more you amass, the more value you possess as a human being." Here, in the 48th verse of the Tao Te Ching, you're asked to change the way you look at this notion. Rather than validating yourself by acquiring more, you can reverse this embedded idea of *increasing* as the criteria for mastering life. The benefit of living by *decreasing* is seeing your world in a different light—one in which, believe it or not, you'll experience a greater sense of completeness.

Throughout the years of your formal schooling, you were encouraged to accumulate more of everything being made available to you: more mathematical formulas; rules of grammar; knowledge of ancient and modern history; information about the human body, the inner and outer galaxies, religion, chemical compounds, and so forth—on and on. You amassed a series of transcripts, diplomas, and degrees that summarized your voyage of collecting, gathering, and hoarding evidence of your learning. Lao-tzu suggests reexamining this legacy, for then you can base your level of success on something that appears to be the exact opposite of what you've pursued so far.

The Tao asks you to release the external indicators and symbols of your educational status. While learning is about accumulating information and knowledge, the Tao is about wisdom, which involves letting go of information and knowledge and living in harmony with your Source. In order to enliven your experience of the Tao and live by its principles, you're being asked to practice decreasing your reliance upon things.

As I've already mentioned in these pages, everything that you add to your life brings with it an element of imprisonment: Your stuff requires you to insure it and protect it from potential thieves or natural disasters; furthermore, you need to polish, paint, clean, store, and pack it, as well as move it from place to place. There's infinite wisdom in the ideas that Lao-tzu outlines in this verse of the Tao Te Ching, especially in his view that true mastery can only be gained by freeing yourself of attachments to things and, in fact, downsizing what you already have.

When you seriously think about this idea and change the way you look at accumulation, you'll realize that you can never truly own anything. Native Americans once had no term for owning land; today, the modern individual's purchase of a piece of property involves an endless cascade of legal maneuvers including title searches, liens, attorney fees, mortgages, tax stamps, and so on. We've created gargantuan hurdles for the purchase and ownership of a piece of land that we only really occupy temporarily. Lao-tzu urges you to think of yourself as a guest here, rather than a proprietor. Cease interfering with the natural world by doing as much as you can to decrease your impact on the environment. That is, live in harmony with the *no-thing-ness* state from which you emerged and to which you are destined to ultimately return.

Lao-tzu says that you must think about your lifetime, your "parentheses in eternity," as an opportunity to be in harmony with the always-decreasing Tao by putting into practice these suggestions:

See the value in subtraction, or "daily diminishing."

Begin to consciously decrease your need to purchase more things. Keep in mind that the advertising world is designed to convince you that your happiness is tied to whatever it's promoting—so instead of buying more, see how many of your accumulated possessions you can recirculate. I guarantee that you'll notice a refreshing feeling of freedom as your desire diminishes and you let go of your obsession with the material objects you've amassed. As Lao-tzu might say, you came here with *no-thing* and you leave with *no-thing,* so take great pleasure in all that has arrived in your life.

There's even greater pleasure to be had in knowing that your ability to live peacefully and happily isn't dependent on how much stuff you add to your life. Living by decreasing is the way of the Tao.

**Practice seeing joy in the natural world, rather
than seeking fulfillment in ownership.**

See the folly of ownership in a universe that's eternally composing and decomposing . . . just like you are. In essence, Lao-tzu is saying that what's real never changes because it has no form. So the more you can let things unfold naturally, the more harmoniously you're living the Tao. Enjoy the flowers, clouds, sunsets, storms, stars, mountains, and *all* the people you encounter. Be *with* the world, in it and adoring it, but not needing to possess it. This is the way of peace. This is the way of the Tao.

For more than 500 years, Kabir has been one of India's revered poets. One of his most popular observations sums up this 48th verse of the Tao Te Ching:

> *The fish in the water that is thirsty needs
> serious professional counseling.*

Do the Tao Now

Right this minute, let go of five items that you have in your possession, putting them in circulation so that others might find them. Next, pick something that has some particular value to you and give it away. It's important that it be something you really like, for the more attachment you have to an item, the greater the joy you'll feel as you let it go. This can become a practice of living a life of daily diminishing.

49th Verse

The sage has no fixed mind;
he is aware of the needs of others.

Those who are good he treats with goodness.
Those who are bad he also treats with goodness
because the nature of his being is good.

He is kind to the kind.
He is also kind to the unkind
because the nature of his being is kindness.

He is faithful to the faithful;
he is also faithful to the unfaithful.
The sage lives in harmony with all below heaven.
He sees everything as his own self;
he loves everyone as his own child.

All people are drawn to him.
He behaves like a little child.

Living Beyond Judgment

In this gently powerful verse, we're encouraged to change the way we view virtually everyone on the planet. Lao-tzu saw the potential for existing harmoniously through living beyond judgment; thus, this 49th verse of the Tao Te Ching invites us to explore that peaceful world. It's encouraging us to replace our idea of criticizing *them* with an acknowledgment of *us* without criticism. Imagine the possibilities for all of humanity if we simply eliminated prejudice and could live "in harmony with all below heaven."

You can begin changing your view of judgment as a valuable or important activity by being aware of when you're doing it to yourself. Then simply start substituting *noticing* for *judging;* from this perspective, you'll realize pretty quickly that you prefer to observe what you're doing or feeling rather than critiquing yourself. Calling your behavior "bad" or "good" just pits you against yourself and others by using competition, punishment, or dislike as your motivational markers—hatred, anger, and threats become necessary because love, acceptance, and kindness can't be trusted.

As you move away from judging yourself, you'll no longer need or want what Lao-tzu calls the "fixed mind"; thus, allegiances that pitted you against the people you thought of as *them* will begin to dissolve. The innumerable categories that helped you organize your labels become totally superfluous and unimportant when you change the way you look at their so-called value. In spite of having been conditioned by the country you were born in, the religion you were assigned at birth, the culture you were immersed in, or even the family who raised you, living beyond judgment becomes your preference. You exist in harmony with the Tao that excludes no one and has no conception of divisions and loyalties. The oneness of the Tao entices you away from any belief that others are separate.

This is the basic solution to wars and conflicts. You see, when you stop judging and instead begin to see yourself in others, you can't help but love the uniqueness of everyone as though they were your own children. Then instead of exclusions and allegiances, the oneness of the Tao graces all, unimpeded. Rather than *God bless America* (or whatever country you happen to reside in), *Allah save our people,* or *Krishna bless those who believe in you,* there's *God bless humanity—let me do all that I can to treat everyone, without exception, with goodness and kindness, as all of those whom we revere as spiritual masters taught us by their example.*

As your worldview changes, you'll extend goodness to everyone you encounter. You'll find that you can feel nonjudgmental compassion for the mistreated, even when *their* way of seeing things causes you and yours pain. You can send out kindness not only in response to kindness, but especially when you're the recipient of cruelty. Why? Because, as Lao-tzu reminds you in this poignant verse, "the nature of [your] being is kindness." It's impossible to give to others what you are not, and you are not judgmental. You see yourself in everyone, without the need to criticize them or yourself.

Change your thoughts and live beyond judgment—and don't see *yourself* as "bad" when you falter in this view or as "holy" when you succeed. Keep in mind that you're a mix of infinite openness and finite limitation, as we all are. So sometimes you just need to notice yourself judging, without then judging yourself!

This is what I feel called by Lao-tzu to offer you from this 49th verse of the Tao Te Ching:

Change the way you look at yourself.

If you pride yourself on having a fixed mind, realize that it relies on conditioning that generally shows up as prejudice. Instead, see yourself as flexible, since being open is the higher virtue. Pride yourself on extending your goodness and kindness to all sides, even

when they oppose your preprogrammed learning. Begin to see yourself as a person who *notices* instead of *judges*. Avoid taking one position and sticking to it no matter what the circumstances are; rather, be in harmony with *all* people, especially those whose opinions conflict with yours! And remember to include yourself when dispensing kindness and nonjudgment.

Change the way you look at other people.

One version of this verse says: "I trust men of their word, and I trust liars. If I am true enough, I feel the heartbeats of others above my own." Whether you call it "judging" or "labeling," notice when you think of others as evil, lazy, dishonest, stupid, or ugly. Then affirm: *I see myself in this person, and I choose to be in a space of goodness rather than judgment.* There's a Sanskrit word, *Namaste,* that can help you with this. When used as a greeting, it roughly translates to: "I honor the place in you where we are all one." So silently or verbally begin telling others "Namaste" in order to remind yourself to love everyone as your own children.

Do the Tao Now

Vow to spend a day looking for opportunities to practice kindness in circumstances that usually provoke judgment. Notice what you think or say about a panhandler, a relative whom you feel animosity toward, or even a politician or TV commentator speaking in terms that send you off in a flurry of critical thoughts. Take that opportunity to become a "noticer," decreasing your criticism while increasing the amount of courtesy and goodness in your world.

50th Verse

Between birth and death,
three in ten are followers of life;
three in ten are followers of death.
And men just passing from birth to death
also number three in ten.

Why is this so?
Because they clutch to life
and cling to this passing world.

But there is one out of ten, they say, so sure of life
that tigers and wild bulls keep clear.
Weapons turn from him on the battlefield,
rhinoceroses have no place to horn him,
tigers find no place for claws,
and soldiers have no place to thrust their blades.

Why is this so?
Because he dwells in that place
where death cannot enter.

Realize your essence
and you will witness the end without ending.

Living as an Immortal

In this passage, Lao-tzu asks you to change the way you look at your mortality. The Tao teaches that death is an insignificant detail that doesn't need to be consciously struggled with or dreaded. As this verse of the Tao Te Ching informs you, there's a "place where death cannot enter." Talk about your life changing when you change your thoughts! This is the ultimate, since the fear of death tops virtually everyone's list of anxieties.

If you see yourself solely as a physical mortal, then you're part of the 90 percent of the population that this passage refers to as "followers of life," "followers of death," or "just passing from birth to death." Here you're being encouraged to aspire to be part of the remaining 10 percent, for whom thoughts of mortality don't invade the heart space or life in general. By altering the way you see death, you'll be in that select group. You'll experience life on the active side of infinity, knowing yourself first and foremost as a spiritual being having a temporary human experience, rather than the other way around.

In this realm, you'll be gracefully adept at moving along free of the fear of life-threatening events. You'll have a knowing about yourself and your connection to the Tao that simply allows you to ride with life like a fearless downhill skier who's at one with the snow-covered mountain. Without resorting to judgment, you'll notice others who are perpetually victimized by scams, bureaucracies, indifference, natural disaster, criminals, or meddling relatives.

With an intimate awareness of your infinite essence that's centered in the Tao, you'll most likely escape from victimization yourself, and you'll lightly deal with situations that others tend to get stuck in. In other words, when you know your own endless nature and live each day with this awareness directing you, there will simply be no space within you for mortality to call the shots. If harm ever does make an attempt to inflict damage or death on you, it won't find a place to sink its hooks into.

Change how you think about death by seeing your essential spiritual beingness, and you'll be able to *enjoy* this world without the dread caused by believing you are *of* it. When you know your immortality through the flow of the Tao, you won't even need to assign it a worldly concept or formal religion. And when the time comes for you to remove the worn-out coat you call your body, Lao-tzu says that "you will witness the end without ending."

Contemplate the teachings of the Tao Te Ching and realize that you can never really be killed or even harmed. With this view of life, you'll be able to clear your inner battlefield of the army of beliefs that continually try to march on your essential self. Fear and dread are weapons that can't hurt or threaten you. Even the natural elements symbolized by rhinos' horns and tigers' claws can't inflict damage because they butt against and tear at a space that has no solidity for them to inflict pain. You dwell in a place that's impenetrable to death—no longer are you clutching at the 10,000 things and treating your short journey from cradle to grave as your one and only ultimate life experience. Now you are the infinite Tao, living your real essence.

Although Lao-tzu lived 25 centuries ago, he is still very much alive. I feel him urging you to heed the following bits of wisdom:

Create affirmations.

Remind yourself, *No one dies, including myself.* Affirm that you can never be harmed or destroyed, for you are not your body. If you stay connected to this reality, you'll automatically deflect dangers that may have previously been able to invade your physical space. For example, as the Indian saint Muktananda lay dying, his devotees are said to have surrounded him, pleading, "Please don't leave."

Muktananda replied, "Don't be silly—where could I go?" The great swami realized his true essence and knew that he was at an end without ending.

Die while you're alive!

In your imagination, contemplate the death of your physical shell: Visualize it lying there lifeless, and observe how you, the witness, aren't identified with this corpse. Now bring that same attention to your body as it gets up and goes about its daily tasks. Nothing could harm your human form when it was dead, and nothing can harm you now because you are not that body—you're the invisible witnessing essence. Remain in this realization, knowing that you've experienced the death of your earthly container as your primary source of identification. In this new awareness, you're impenetrable and free. Here's how Leonardo da Vinci expressed the message of this verse of the Tao Te Ching: "While I thought that I was learning how to live, I have been learning how to die." Do this now, while you're still alive.

Do the Tao Now

This Tao exercise is an inner-vision quest in which you picture yourself as immune to harm. Create your own imagined picture of danger, or draw on the 50th verse of the Tao Te Ching for threats to your life. Tigers jump at you and miss, swords are thrust at you but do no damage, bombs explode but you're unscathed. . . . Keep this image of yourself as incapable of being harmed regardless of what goes on in your body. Then use this "witness to your immortality" vision to help you activate dormant protective forces that will accommodate you in fulfilling what you've imagined.

51st Verse

The Way connects all living beings to their Source.
It springs into existence,
unconscious, perfect, free;
takes on a physical body;
lets circumstances complete it.

Therefore all beings honor the Way
and value its virtue.
They have not been commanded to worship the Tao
and do homage to virtue,
but they always do so spontaneously.

The Tao gives them life.
Virtue nourishes and nurtures them,
rears and shelters and protects them.
The Tao produces but does not possess;
the Tao gives without expecting;
the Tao fosters growth without ruling.
This is called hidden virtue.

Living by Hidden Virtue

This passage encourages you to discover that quality within you that protects, nurtures, and shelters automatically, "without ruling." Consciously living by hidden virtue probably means changing many of the ways in which you see your role in the grand scheme of things. And a natural starting point would be the way you explain the mystery of how life begins.

If you had to describe your creation, you'd most likely say that you originated through an act of commingling between your biological parents. If that's the only explanation for your existence, then it excludes the spontaneity and mystery that living by hidden virtue offers you. Operating in this new way expands and redefines your conception and birth, and the world changes as a result of your modified viewpoint.

Living by hidden virtue allows you to get the most out of life because it means seeing that it's your choice and responsibility to decide how you're going to spend it. *Not* living by hidden virtue, on the other hand, ensures that your role in a family or culture is assigned at birth (or even conception), with predetermined expectations about how you should and will function. Your days become filled with stressful attempts to please those to whom you're biologically related. You experience the nagging self-criticism that you're disappointing a parent or grandparent, along with unsettling desires to be free of the pressure of your gender or placement in a designated family. Trying to operate within this belief system can consequently keep you trapped in an unpleasant and intolerable role of servitude and obsequiousness.

In the 51st verse of the Tao Te Ching, Lao-tzu asks you to expand your vision and begin to see yourself as a creation of the Tao. Imagine that the tiny seedling that was you didn't come from another particle, but rather from an invisible Source. And this Source that sprung you into existence, herein called "the Way," has no preconceived doctrine dictating what you should do, whom you should listen to, where you should live, or how you should worship. The Source, your great Mother, has no investment in the choices you make during your individual journey—it knows that the seedling that was you is perfect and free to complete itself in whatever way it chooses. This Mother, which is the Tao, has no expectations for you . . . no demands, no battles or wars for you to fight, no history to live up to.

The Chinese refer to this hidden entity that brought you into existence as *Te*. I'm referring to Te here as "virtue" or "character." And Jonathan Star's translation of the Tao Te Ching interprets it in this verse as follows:

> *Though Tao gives life to all things,*
> *Te is what cultivates them.*
> *Te is that magic power which*
> *raises and rears them,*
> *completes and prepares them,*
> *comforts and protects them.*

Te, then, is the virtue that's deep within you and all of creation. This isn't a force that guarantees the physical shell will never die; it's more a characteristic that allows you to move through the material world in your body, perfectly aligned with the creative originating force. Read this verse as a reminder that you're protected and completed by your ultimate originating Source, which isn't the same as guaranteeing your security in this phenomenal world. Helen Keller

was speaking of this very thing when she stated, "Security is mostly a superstition. It does not exist in nature . . ."

The 51st verse is about learning to trust by changing your view of life to include Te, or hidden virtue. It's about seeing yourself as a member of a family of oneness, with the same parents as all other creatures. It's about feeling your total freedom—to produce without possessing, and to keep from becoming a possession yourself. So give without expecting, and don't be victimized by the expectations of others.

Here are suggestions offered to you by Lao-tzu as I gaze at the great master's picture before me and feel as if we were one:

Practice feeling safe and protected.

Live each day trusting in the hidden virtue that's both *within* you and that *caused* you. Keep in mind that the feeling of being secure, shielded, and nurtured won't come from anything you might possess. Instead, it will arise when you know that you're in constant contact with a virtuous power that lies within every cell of your being. This hidden force is responsible for your very presence.

You sprang into existence by virtue of Tao; and while your every breath and action aren't commanded to do so, they nevertheless pay homage to the inner virtue that is your life. That power is in my hand as I write these words, and it's in your eyes as they read this page. Trust in it. Worship it. Feel safe in the force that remains hidden. This is all you need to feel complete.

Remember that the Tao produces—it doesn't possess.

Do the same and you'll achieve the wisdom of this verse. Be a caretaker, not an owner. Don't attempt to control anyone; instead, foster growth without dominating or ruling. When you're in a supervisory role, allow others to activate their hidden virtue as much as possible. Just as you wish to feel protected and trust in that invisible force that animates you, so does *everyone* you encounter. I emphasize this word because there are no exceptions.

Witter Bynner's translation of this 51st verse of the Tao Te Ching states:

All created things render, to the existence and fitness
they depend on . . .
Do you likewise:
Be parent, not possessor,
Attendant, not master.
Be concerned not with obedience but with benefit,
And you are at the core of living.

I urge you to remember the phrase "Do you likewise," and live by hidden virtue.

Do the Tao Now

Plan a day of letting go: Let go of thinking, and discover the all-embracing nature of the mind. Let go of preconceptions and ideas, and experience how things really are. Let go of needing to control others, and discover how capable they really are. Take time to find your answers to the question *What might really happen if I let go?* As you do this exercise, you may be surprised to discover that you find more of the hidden virtue in your life, which then changes the way you see yourself.

52nd Verse

All under heaven have a common beginning.
This beginning is the Mother of the world.
Having known the Mother,
we may proceed to know her children.
Having known the children,
we should go back and hold on to the Mother.

Keep your mouth shut,
guard the senses,
and life is ever full.
Open your mouth,
always be busy,
and life is beyond hope.

Seeing the small is called clarity;
keeping flexible is called strength.
Using the shining radiance,
you return again to the light
and save yourself misfortune.

This is called
the practice of eternal light.

Living by Returning to the Mother

This verse tells you that it's valuable and important to realize that your life is more than just a linear experience happening in time and space. That is, you more or less currently view your time on Earth as a straight line from conception to birth—you'll move through predictable stages of development, concluding with death, where you'll meet up with the mystery that awaits you on the Other Side. Lao-tzu is inviting you to see that your existence is a return trip to the place where all the planets' creations emerge. He wants you to realize that you have the ability to enjoy this mysterious *beginning* before your physical *ending*. This mystery, which is in each and every one of the 10,000 things, is referred to by Lao-tzu as the "Mother," or the symbol of what lies beyond all that seems to begin and end.

Start your journey back to the Mother by contemplating the first two lines of this verse of the Tao Te Ching: "All under heaven have a common beginning. This beginning is the Mother of the world." Let this thought filter into your physical being and create a state of awe about your existence, which emerged out of *no-thing-ness*. Know that this unseen Source that births every single thing also birthed you. Like electricity streaming through a conduit, the mysterious nothingness flows through and sustains all of life, including you. It's a constant invisible, soundless, odorless force, which isn't immediately available to your sensory self.

It's vital that you spend a few moments each day getting to know your (and my) eternal Mother, which you can do by simply acknowledging her presence and silently communicating with her. Once you decide to know and honor her, you'll begin to change the way you look at all of her children, including yourself. You'll view all of the 10,000 things as offspring of the Mother, and you'll look beyond the temporariness of their appearances to see the Tao unfolding. This is what Lao-tzu means when he asks you to know the children not as separate from their Mother, but as the Mother herself. So see all of creation as originating in the Mother, and then "go back and hold on to" her.

How do you embark on this return trip to your eternal Mother? Lao-tzu advises that you close your mouth and seal your ears to ensure that your spirit isn't frittered away on worldly activities. In other words, spend time with the maternal part of yourself, and seek clarity by noticing the Tao in the small and the large. Practice abandoning rigidity, and instead cultivate elasticity to improve your strength. Lao-tzu concludes by telling you that this way of seeing the world is "the practice of eternal light." See that light in the tiniest insect, and even in the invisible particle that forms that little creature's leg. It's the same light that beats your heart and holds the universe in place—so allow yourself to not just be in awe of the insect but to *be* that insect. In this way, you find clarity through "seeing the small," and you'll improve the power of your new way of seeing through your flexible viewpoint. Change your linear thoughts about your presence here on Earth, and begin to see your life change right before your eyes!

Lao-tzu offers the following to you, through me, to aid you in "the practice of eternal light" in today's world:

Open mouth—spirit escapes. Closed mouth—spirit connection excellent!

Think of your mouth as a gate that guards your spirit: When you speak to others, become conscious of the need to close the door and allow your spirit to be safely ensconced within you. Make the same mental shift with your ears: Keep them sealed when it comes to rumors and petty conversations. Use fewer words; commit yourself to long periods of listening; and eliminate giving advice, meddling, and participating in gossip.

Cultivate your strength with the flexibility of consciously deciding when to involve your speaking and auditory senses. When you're inclined to get into other people's business, remember that your eternal Mother's one and only voice is silence. Do likewise, and you'll feel yourself holding on to her in freedom and bliss, thus returning while living!

Seeing the smallest mystery reveals the grandest mystery.

By being attentive to smallness, you cultivate your desire for clarity. Noting the same spark in microscopic creatures that animates you is a way of exploring life as a return trip rather than a dead end. What seem to be the tiniest mysteries of life lead to an experience of the shining radiance that comes from an appreciation for all that you encounter. You and the Mother who birthed you and everything else are one. By seeing the small, you gain this clarity, which is the return trip you're encouraged to make while alive. Now your world begins to look very different, as you see originating spirit everywhere. Nothing is viewed as ordinary, inferior, or unwanted anymore.

Do the Tao Now

Plan a day dedicated to examining the smallest life-forms that you can find. Become a witness to a spider creating a web, a sand crab scurrying along the beach, or a fly buzzing about on the wall. Take an imaginary trip through your insides, examining the life-forms that reside in your intestines, in your bloodstream, or in the lining of your eyes—all creatures that you'd need a powerful microscope to be able to see. Meditate on the Mother birthing these little bacteria in order for you to exist. Experience the way viewing your body through the infinitesimally tiny life that's part of you affects you. Living by returning to the Mother will provide you with a clarity you've never experienced before.

53rd Verse

If I have even just a little sense,
I should walk in the Great Way,
and my only fear would be straying.

The Great Way is very smooth and straight,
and yet the people prefer devious paths.
That is why the court is corrupt,
the fields lie in waste,
the granaries are empty.

Dressing magnificently,
wearing a sharp sword,
stuffing oneself with food and drink,
amassing wealth to the extent of not knowing
what to do with it,
is being like a robber.

I say this pomp at the expense of others
is like the boasting of thieves after a looting.
This is not the Tao.

*L*iving *H*onorably

Imagine that you were able to view the world from a position of complete honor and oneness: Everywhere you looked you saw the Great Way . . . and saw all of it as you. From this perspective, every person who's ever existed, or will ever exist, is a part of you, birthed by your Source. All of life—the creatures, the land, the oceans, and the vegetation—are connected by the Tao. From this perspective, your world would change dramatically. If a critical mass of humanity had this same perspective, seeing the whole globe as part of ourselves would translate to the same respect for every form of life that we have for our individual bodies. And this unity would make the scene that Lao-tzu is describing in this passage impossible.

Despite all of our technological advances, the words that the great Chinese master wrote 2,500 years ago still apply. Unfortunately, we're far removed from walking the Great Way, for we continue to see great divisions rather than a sense of unified oneness. As Lao-tzu admonishes at the end of this verse, "This is not the Tao."

One of my favorite translations of this 53rd verse of the Tao Te Ching was written in 1944 by Witter Bynner. He expresses it perfectly:

> *See how fine the palaces*
> *And see how poor the farms,*
> *How bare the peasants' granaries*
> *While gentry wear embroideries*
> *Hiding sharpened arms.*
> *And the more they have the more they seize,*
> *How can there be such men as these*
> *Who never hunger, never thirst,*
> *Yet eat and drink until they burst!*

You can see that these conditions still exist today: Whole continents of people experience starvation, while a few in positions of power live in opulence and grandeur. Weapons of destruction receive funding, while millions live in poverty. Leaders sit down to overflowing plenitude, while the masses scrounge around for ways to feed their families and heat their homes. We have a long way to go before traversing that smooth and straight Way of the Tao, for we still take "devious paths" and see the all-too-painful results of this choice every day.

But I'm not writing these words to try to change the world in one fell swoop; rather, I'm doing so to encourage you to change the way you see *your* world. If you make that modification, others will gravitate toward living honorably as well. When enough of us do this, we'll reach a critical mass that will eliminate "the boasting of thieves after a looting."

Begin by seeing yourself as the environment, rather than as an organism within it. I've even coined a word to describe when life-forms are whole, rather than separate: *environorganisms.* Understand that you can't survive apart from what it *seems* isn't part of you—for you absolutely are the air, the water, the plants, the animals, and everyone else on the planet. Change your worldview to one that completely understands that when anyone else is starving or living in poverty, so are you. See yourself in all others and you'll find the compassion, love, and willingness that replaces your belief in your uniqueness and differentness.

Lao-tzu was obviously distressed by the conditions of hard-heartedness and indifference that he observed in ancient China, so he appealed to all to live honorably through the emulation of the Tao rather than from the ego perspective of separateness. And now he asks *you* to change the way you look at the blatant imbalances in

your world, noting how your world changes to align with the Tao when you live honorably.

Here is a suggestion, which you can apply to your life today:

Make compassion the essential foundation of your personal philosophy.

Feeling guilty about what you've amassed or wallowing in sadness over the plight of the starving won't change things, but making compassion the essential foundation of your philosophy will. This is one of the most significant ways of initiating the growth of a critical mass. As that mass grows, kind hearts and actions will realign our planet: Like-minded leaders will emerge, and gross inconsistencies will be reduced and eventually eliminated. Mother Teresa was an outstanding example of how one person's way of seeing the world can change the world itself: "[I]n each [person I see]," she said, "I see the face of Christ in one of his more distressing disguises."

"Walk in the Great Way" by doing charity work or supporting candidates for public office who embody compassionate action. And vow to make a difference on a daily basis throughout your life, which might be as simple as refusing to join in denouncing others or categorizing them as "evil" or "defective." After all, so many of the wars that currently rage on our planet are rooted in religious hatred that perpetuates the imbalances pointed out in this verse of the Tao Te Ching.

In the following excerpt from the Koran, the great prophet Mohammed tells the followers of Islam to practice compassionate action. You can use his teaching to make a daily difference during your own life:

Behave beneficently toward the neighbor
that is a kinsman and the neighbor that is
a stranger and the companion by your side.

He who behaves ill toward his neighbor is not
a believer, nor can ever be one.

One who eats his fill while his neighbor
is hungry by his side is not a believer.

Do the Tao Now

Make a daily practice of opening your heart in compassion when you see someone less fortunate than yourself. Give him or her a silent blessing rather than a thought of scorn, ridicule, blame, or indifference. Do the same when you learn how many of "them" were killed in any skirmish—rather than rejoicing about the dead enemies, say a silent prayer of love and compassion.

Live honorably; it "just [takes] a little sense."

54th Verse

*Whoever is planted in the Tao
will not be rooted up.
Whoever embraces the Tao
will not slip away.*

*Generations honor generations endlessly.
Cultivated in the self, virtue is realized;
cultivated in the family, virtue overflows;
cultivated in the community, virtue increases;
cultivated in the state, virtue abounds.*

*The Tao is everywhere;
it has become everything.
To truly see it, see it as it is.
In a person, see it as a person;
in a family, see it as a family;
in a country, see it as a country;
in the world, see it as the world.*

*How do I know this is true?
By looking inside myself.*

Living as If Your Life Makes a Difference

In this verse of the Tao Te Ching, you're invited to see your role in the transformation of the planet. Instead of perceiving yourself as one insignificant individual among billions of people, you're urged to see yourself as the Tao itself. "We Are the World" is *everybody's* theme song. You *do* make a difference!

When you live with the joyful awareness that you potentially have an infinite effect on the universe, you'll radiate Tao consciousness. You'll be like a wave of energy that illuminates a room—everyone will see the light and become affected. Those who were unaware of their Tao nature will notice the difference, and those who *were* aware—but not living as if their lives mattered—will be attracted and begin changing. So recognize and live your life as part of the Great Way, and help bring balance into the world.

In this 54th passage, Lao-tzu is advising you to see your divinity and revel in your magnificence. Know that in the silent space within you, where the Tao animates every breath and thought, your life makes a difference. The following is what he advises in the language of the 21st century:

Choose an area to concentrate on making a difference.

Don't entertain doubt about your impact on the world; instead, develop a vision for Earth and convince yourself that you are perfectly capable of contributing to this vision, whether it's grandiose or small. See a world without hatred, disrespect, or violence; where the environment is respected and cared for; and where cancer, AIDS, starvation, child abuse, weapons of all kinds, or any other detrimental or demeaning scenarios disappear.

The anthropologist Margaret Mead addressed this idea in the following observation: "Never doubt that a small group of thoughtful, committed citizens can change the world. Indeed, it's the only thing that ever has."

Realize how much your life matters.

It's said that when a butterfly flaps its wings, that energy flows thousands of miles away. Therefore, everything you think and do extends outward and multiplies. Live your life knowing that the difference you choose to make is toward wholeness, not destructiveness. Even if no one sees or acknowledges it, an act of unkindness contains energy that impacts our entire universe. And a silent blessing or thought of love toward others contains a vibration that will be felt throughout the cosmos.

William Blake's vision expresses this idea:

To see a World in a Grain of Sand
And a Heaven in a Wild Flower,
Hold Infinity in the palm of your hand
And Eternity in an hour.

Be conscious of how very much you matter to all of creation.

Do the Tao Now

Dedicate a day to extending kind thoughts and acts toward your family, your community, your country, and the world. In your family, encourage someone who's struggling with low self-esteem. In

your community, pick up litter and recycle it without judgment. In your country, spend a few moments in silent prayer, sending loving energy to those who are in positions of power—then do the same for the world, including any so-called enemies.

55th Verse

He who is in harmony with the Tao
is like a newborn child.
Deadly insects will not sting him.
Wild beasts will not attack him.
Birds of prey will not strike him.
Bones are weak, muscles are soft,
yet his grasp is firm.

He has not experienced the union of man and woman,
but is whole.
His manhood is strong.
He screams all day without becoming hoarse.
This is perfect harmony.

To know harmony is to know the changeless;
to know the changeless is to have insight.
Things in harmony with the Tao remain;
things that are forced grow for a while,
but then wither away.
This is not the Tao.
And whatever is against the Tao soon ceases to be.

Living by
Letting Go

Perhaps you've observed people who seem to get all the breaks, appearing to be impervious to the onslaughts that wreak havoc in many lives. For example, do you know someone who seldom if ever gets sick, in spite of spending the flu season in close contact with people who are coughing and sneezing? How about those who emerge unscathed in the middle of a crime spree? You might say that these lucky few seem to have guardian angels that protect them from the provocations of the symbolic "deadly insects," "wild beasts," and "birds of prey" mentioned in the opening lines of this passage. But Lao-tzu knows that these men and women are simply in harmony with the Tao, just as some individuals appear to have the right people show up in their lives at the right time, while others seem to have a knack for making money materialize just when it's needed most.

Lao-tzu says that we should look to infants, who haven't yet taken on the ego belief that they're separate from their originating Source. Consequently, they have what could be considered "magical" powers: They can scream all day and never lose their voice like a screeching adult would. Even with undeveloped muscles, they can fashion a firm grip. Furthermore, babies are pliable and virtually immune to harm from a fall that would break the bones of a grown-up. All of this is called "perfect harmony" by Lao-tzu.

Verse 55 of the Tao Te Ching invites you to realize that what you call luck isn't something that randomly happens—it's yours for life when you decide to live by letting go. You attract the cooperative power of the Tao when you release the need to control your life. So change your thoughts and see how *your* life changes to a very fortunate one indeed.

Let go and exist in harmony with the Tao in order to build up your immune system and be "lucky" about resisting disease and illness. I know that letting go for protection sounds paradoxical, and I suppose you could think of it like that. But try seeing it as a way of allowing life's natural rhythm to flow unimpeded through you. Living by letting go means releasing worry, stress, and fear. When you promote your sense of well-being in the face of what appears as danger to others, your alignment with your Source frees you from pushing yourself to act in a forceful manner. Lao-tzu reminds you here that "things that are forced grow for a while, but then wither away."

Attain the protective nature that's alluded to in this powerful verse, and realize the changeless with these insights for the world you're living in today:

Visualize yourself as indestructible.

Activate an inner picture that will carry you through perceived dangers. In this visualization, remove the image of your physical body and instead see the part of you that's as constant as a spirit or a thought. This is your essence, and it's incapable of being harmed in any way. From this perspective, you're not threatened by anything, from criminals to cancer, from a common cold to a wild beast. When you live in harmony with the enduring part of yourself, it will contribute to an overall sense of being indestructible. Declare yourself to be that lucky person who goes through life unscathed by freeing yourself from trying to control your perception of looming danger.

Change the way you look at your potential for becoming a lucky person.

Rather than telling yourself: *With my luck, things aren't going to work out for me,* affirm: *I am open to allowing what needs to happen. I trust luck to guide me.* This change in your thinking will serve you by

guiding you to live in the flow with the Tao. Peace will replace stress, harmony will replace effort, acceptance will replace interference and force, and good luck will replace fear. You'll become what you think about, so even things that you previously believed were evidence of bad luck will now be viewed as what helps you move toward greater harmony.

Living by letting go will allow you to appreciate Lin Yutang's wry observation in *The Importance of Living:* "If you can spend a perfectly useless afternoon in a perfectly useless manner, you have learned how to live."

Do the Tao Now

Dedicate a week to charting incidents of "things working out" without your having to control or "make" them happen. This will mean consciously choosing situations where you curb your automatic impulse to control the outcome. Relax when you want to tense up, and trust in as many situations as you can. At the end of the week, notice how changing the way you think has changed your life.

56th Verse

Those who know do not talk.
Those who talk do not know.

Block all the passages!
Close your mouth,
cordon off your senses,
blunt your sharpness,
untie your knots,
soften your glare,
settle your dust.
This is primal union or the secret embrace.

One who knows this secret
is not moved by attachment or aversion,
swayed by profit or loss,
nor touched by honor or disgrace.
He is far beyond the cares of men
yet comes to hold the dearest place in their hearts.

This, therefore, is the highest state of man.

*L*iving by
*S*ilent *K*nowing

This is probably the best-known verse of the Tao Te Ching. In fact, the opening two lines ("Those who know do not talk. Those who talk do not know") are so popular that they've almost become a cliché. Nevertheless, the passage's essential message is little understood and rarely practiced.

Lao-tzu is calling you to live in the highest state of silent knowing, that place deep within you that can't be communicated to any other. Consequently, you might want to change your thinking about whom you consider to be wise or learned. Persuasive speakers with a good command of the language, who are forceful in their pronouncements and confident in their point of view, are generally considered to have superior knowledge . . . but Lao-tzu suggests that precisely the opposite is true. Those who talk, he says, aren't living from the place of silent knowing, so they do not know.

As you modify the way you look at this presumption, you'll see several differences in the way your world appears. First, you'll note that those who are compelled to pontificate and persuade are almost always tied to an attachment of some kind—perhaps it's to a point of view, to being right, to winning, or to profiting in some way. And the more talking they do, the more they appear to be swayed by such attachments.

The second thing you'll notice takes place within you: You begin to see *your* inclination and desire to persuade and convince others. Then you begin to listen more attentively, finding yourself in "the secret embrace" of the "primal union" that Lao-tzu describes. Your need to be knowledgeable or dominant is replaced by the deep realization that it's all irrelevant, and you lose interest in seeking approval. Living in silent knowing becomes the process that casts your existence in a different light—you have less of an edge and feel settled, softer, and more centered.

As you change how you think about what it means to be intelligent and wise, you'll come into contact with the irony that sums up this wonderfully paradoxical section of the Tao Te Ching. Lao-tzu says that the sage who lives by the Tao is "far beyond the cares of men," yet holds "the dearest place" in his heart. I'd sum it up this way: *Those who care the least about approval seem to receive it the most.* Since such individuals aren't concerned with how they're perceived, either honorably or in disgrace, they don't seek praise or run from it. While their calm wisdom may make them appear to be aloof, they actually end up gaining the respect of everyone.

You have this place of silent knowing within you right now. And the following is what Lao-tzu suggests for adapting the paradoxical language of this verse of the Tao Te Ching to your world:

Block all the passages!

Get honest with yourself about wanting to win the favor of others. You don't have to prove anything to anyone, and you'll never succeed by droning on and on. Remember that "those who talk do not know," or as one translation of this verse simply states, "Shut your mouth." Silence is your evidence of inner knowing. Talking to convince others actually says more about your need to be right than their need to hear what you have to say! So rather than trying to persuade others, keep quiet . . . just enjoy that deeply satisfying inner awareness.

Use the acronym *BUSS* to remember the four directives of this verse.

— *Blunt your sharpness.* Do this by listening to yourself before you let your judgments attack someone else. A better course of action

is to just listen, and then silently offer loving compassion to both yourself and the other person.

— *Untie your knots.* Detach from what keeps you tied to worldly patterns. Untie the knots that bind you to a life that's dedicated to showing profit and demonstrating victory, and replace them with silently contemplating the Tao in "the secret embrace."

— *Soften your glare.* Notice when your need to be right is glaringly obvious, and let the soft underside of your being replace your rigid stance. Your impulse to glower at external events is alerting you that you're out of touch with your inner silent knowing.

— *Settle your dust.* Don't kick it up in the first place! Realize your inclination to stir up dust when you feel a diatribe about to erupt on how others ought to be behaving. Stop in the middle of pounding the table or angrily screaming and just observe yourself. Since your emotions are like waves on the ocean, learn to watch them return to the vast, calm, all-knowing Source.

Do the Tao Now

Spend an hour, a day, a week, or a month practicing not giving unsolicited advice. Stop yourself for an instant and call upon your silent knowing. Ask a question, rather than giving advice or citing an example from your life, and then just listen to yourself and the other person. As Lao-tzu would like you to know, that's "the highest state of man."

57th Verse

If you want to be a great leader,
you must learn to follow the Tao.
Stop trying to control.
Let go of fixed plans and concepts,
and the world will govern itself.

How do I know this is so?
Because in this world,
the greater the restrictions and prohibitions,
the more people are impoverished;
the more advanced the weapons of state,
the darker the nation;
the more artful and crafty the plan,
the stranger the outcome;
the more laws are posted,
the more thieves appear.

Therefore the sage says:
I take no action and people are reformed.
I enjoy peace and people become honest.
I do nothing and people become rich.
If I keep from imposing on people,
they become themselves.

Living Without Authoritarianism

In this and some of the following chapters of the Tao Te Ching, Lao-tzu counsels the rulers of 2,500 years ago on how and why to pursue a high quality of leadership. His advice is pertinent today, in the 21st century, to *all* forms of leadership, including government, business, and, in particular, parenting.

The essential message in this 57th verse is to *allow* rather than *interfere*. Now I don't interpret this to mean letting an infant crawl into traffic or leaving a child alone near a swimming pool—obviously, you must be sensible when supervising those who could harm themselves or others. What I believe Lao-tzu is conveying here is that allowing is quite often the highest form of leadership. He states that "more people are impoverished" in societies with excessive restrictions and prohibitions; the same can be true in families with commandments that must be obeyed without question. The more authoritarian any system is, the more outlaws will appear.

On the other hand, when children are encouraged to explore and exercise their inquisitiveness, they're inspired to be their best with little need for regulation. So when you change the way you view the need for rules, family members will tend to make decisions based on what's best for everyone rather than themselves. See what happens, for instance, if you drop an absolute curfew time for your teenagers, asking them to just be sensible about when they come home and to notify you if they're going to be later than normal. You may find that because you didn't impose yourself on them, they end up coming home even earlier than when they had a strict curfew governing their conduct.

Examine the restrictions that you enforce in your family. Remember that effective parents don't want to be leaned on; they want to make leaning unnecessary. After all, you want your children to be responsible, healthy, successful, and honest—not simply because you're there to monitor them, but because it is within their nature to do so. So set an example and let them see that it's possible to be self-sufficient and enormously successful. Allow them to learn to trust in their highest nature, rather than having to thumb through a rule book to decide what's right.

Change the way you look at the need for edicts, laws, and prohibitions, and see yourself as someone who doesn't need to rule with an iron fist. Then enjoy taking this revised view of your leadership abilities into every area of your life where you're considered to be "the boss."

What follows is some 21st-century advice based on this verse that was written 2,500 years ago:

Practice the art of allowing yourself.

Begin by letting yourself be more spontaneous and less regimented in your daily life: Take a trip without first planning it. Go where you're instinctively guided to go. Tell the authoritarian part of you to take a break. Introduce a different side to yourself and the world by affirming: *I am free to be myself. I do not have to live by anyone else's rules, and I release the need for laws to regulate my behavior.*

Practice the art of allowing others.

Catch yourself when you're about to cite a rule as a reason for saying no to a child or someone you supervise, and instead consider the ramifications of saying nothing and just observing. When you change the way you look at your role as a leader, you'll find that very few edicts are necessary for people to conduct the business of their lives. Everyone has a strong sense of what they want to do,

what limits they have, and how to actualize their dreams. Be like the Tao—allow others, and enjoy how your nonauthoritarian leadership inspires them to be themselves.

Do the Tao Now

Make time to do something you've never done before—it could be walking barefoot in the rain, taking a yoga class, speaking before a group at a Toastmasters Club, playing a game of touch football, jumping out of an airplane in a parachute, or anything else you've always wanted to do. Recognize that you've created restrictions for yourself that keep you from new and expanding experiences, and find the time now to close your personal rule book and plunge in where you've never before wandered. Also, make time to give those in your charge an opportunity to do the same, enjoying how much they accomplish with minimal or no action on your part.

58th Verse

When the ruler knows his own heart,
the people are simple and pure.
When he meddles with their lives,
they become restless and disturbed.

Bad fortune is what good fortune leans on;
good fortune is what bad fortune hides in.
Who knows the ultimate end of this process?
Is there no norm of right?
Yet what is normal soon becomes abnormal;
peoples's confusion is indeed long-standing.

Thus the master is content to serve as an example
and not to impose his will.
He is pointed but does not pierce;
he straightens but does not disrupt;
he illuminates but does not dazzle.

*L*iving *U*ntroubled by *G*ood or *B*ad *F*ortune

The world of the 10,000 things is also called "the world of the changing." You see it in your ever-altering life, even as you want everything to be stable and predictable. However, all things on our planet are in constant motion. As Albert Einstein once observed, "Nothing happens until something moves." This 58th verse of the Tao Te Ching stresses that there's another way to see the world, one that virtually guarantees that you'll be untroubled by good or bad fortune. Instead of only noticing the constantly shifting energy pattern of the material world, this verse invites you to let yourself focus on the unchanging Tao.

Like most humans, you probably want your surroundings to be permanent, steady, reliable, secure, and predictable. However, your reality unequivocally insists that you take into account the opposite and unpredictable that are present in every experience you have. After all, even the landscape that surrounds you is far from orderly: Mountain ranges go up and then down into valleys. Trees tower over shrubs, and cloud formations are ominously black at times and fluffy white at others. In every perfectly sunny day, there's a storm hiding, and in every rainstorm lies a drought waiting its turn. Up and down and the unexpected are the norm of nature; hills and dales are the way of the 10,000 things.

Change your view of the peaks and valleys of all of life to an attitude that allows you to discover what's hidden in both of those experiences. Begin to see *wholeness* rather than *good* or *bad fortune*. See opposites as parts of oneness, rather than disrupting surprises. In a world of pure Taoist unity, there's no good or bad luck; it's indivisible. What you're calling "bad" fortune has "good" just waiting to emerge because it's the other half.

Lao-tzu's advice for applying the 58th verse to today's world would probably include the following:

See wholeness in place of good or bad fortune.

When anyone is in the midst of an experience you believe is fortunate, such as a blissful relationship, financial success, excellent health, a great job with a new promotion, or children excelling in school, know that all is subject to change. Accumulated wealth has poverty hidden in it; popularity has nonrecognition camouflaged in it, too. And, of course, the same is true during the periods that are generally thought of as unfortunate.

Your life itself is the perfect place to personalize your ability to live untroubled by good or bad fortune, for you have the opportunity at every stage to see wholeness. So rather than calling youth an aspect of "good fortune" and old age a mark of "bad fortune," know that the youth you were is part of the wholeness of your old age. The elderly individual you may become is part of the wholeness of your development through the levels of change that are your physical existence. Life has death concealed in it. So know your own heart and let your conduct be consistent with the Tao by not imposing your will—be pointed, straight, and illuminating without piercing, disrupting, or dazzling.

When bad fortune feels so troublesome that you can't get unstuck, see good fortune leaning on it.

When you feel overpoweringly discouraged during a trip through the valley of despair, it can feel as if that's all there is. If you're unable to see a circumstance or situation as part of a larger picture, remind yourself that good fortune is leaning on this bad one, just as morning follows the darkest night. With wholeness as a backdrop, rely on your knowledge of day following night at these times. Keep

in mind that when you've reached the valley floor, the only direction you can go is upward. Things definitely will get better; your luck must change; scarcity has to turn into abundance. This is because good fortune is invisibly there in all moments of despair, and you want to learn to live untroubled by them both.

Do the Tao Now

Spend a day noticing what aspects of life fall into the categories of "fortunate" or "unfortunate." List them under their titles at the end of the day, and then explore each of them when you won't be interrupted. Allow yourself to either feel each one physically in your body or see it as an image that presents itself to you. Without trying to change it in any way, allow yourself to observe the subject with your eyes closed. Just as if it were a kaleidoscope (or life itself), watch it and permit it to flow through you—the way the clouds drift in the sky, night turns into day, rain evaporates . . . and how confusion comes and goes when you're living untroubled by good or bad fortune.

59th Verse

In governing people and serving nature,
nothing surpasses thrift and moderation.

Restraint begins with giving up one's own ideas.
This depends on virtue gathered in the past.
If there is a good store of virtue, then nothing is impossible.
If nothing is impossible, then there are no limits.
If a man knows no limits, he is fit to lead.

This is the way to be deeply rooted and firmly planted in the Tao,
the secret of long life and lasting vision.

Living by Thrift and Moderation

There are four words that crop up repeatedly in many of the translations of this passage of the Tao Te Ching: *restraint, frugality, moderation,* and *thrift*. Here, Lao-tzu is advising you to examine the way you look at these qualities in relation to your supervisory and parenting roles—he doesn't say that you should sit on the sidelines and do nothing, but he does counsel you to practice self-control. When you cultivate a style of leadership that creates "a good store of virtue, then nothing is impossible," for there are no limits.

Living in thrift and moderation means being in harmony with the world through your generous nature. Rather than continually prodding, directing, giving orders, setting down rules, and demanding obedience, it's important to be a leader who accumulates a warehouse full of virtue by living in accordance with the Tao. When that's what you have to give away, you'll naturally interfere less. Feel joyful knowing that the example you're modeling is helping others make the right choices, as this is the essence of Tao leadership. As Lao-tzu specifically states, "If a man knows no limits, he is fit to lead."

People whose lives are run by rules, dogma, and fear can only do what they've been told to do . . . nothing more. The options for self-direction are nonexistent for the blindly obedient, so practice restraint, moderation, frugality, and thrift when making pronouncements about how others must behave. Children raised in families where that blind obedience is demanded have the highest levels of prejudice when they become adults. Why? Because they've been taught to "prejudge" what's acceptable, according to someone in a position to lead them. That's why it's so vital to give your kids an example of leadership that encourages them to make choices based on higher standards.

I have a gift from my daughter Saje that I've placed on my desk, which I've titled NOTHING IS IMPOSSIBLE. It's a green plant growing out of a rock—there's no dirt or earth, only hard rock, yet it thrives, despite what all of us have been taught to believe. When Saje gave this to me, she remarked that it reminded her of me because I've always said that I refuse to believe in anything being impossible. My plant helps me remember that nature knows no limits, and that I am as much a part of nature as both the rock and the greenery growing within that hard stone.

Lao-tzu reminds you that "if nothing is impossible, then there are no limits." So practice living without limits by gathering virtue and modeling it. When you do, you'll see the "lasting vision" in those you've been selected to lead in one way or another, and they'll see it in you, too. And put the wisdom of this 59th verse to work for you by taking these suggestions:

Gather as much virtue as you possibly can.

For years I practiced gathering virtue without realizing it. I sent hundreds of thousands of books to individuals and organizations at my own expense, getting into the habit of beginning each day with this act of love. I spent a great deal of time giving away much of what I earned, almost all of it anonymously. I didn't realize it at the time, but what I was doing was accumulating virtue, or what I facetiously called "God points."

I then found that not all of my life was to be peaks and mountaintops. Yet when I succeeded in getting out from *under* what felt like a mountain, I was virtually unscathed. This is because I was so deeply rooted and firmly planted in the Tao that my original vision was to be a lasting one, impervious to external circumstances.

Practice moderating your ego.

Change the way you look at your life by moderating your ego. See yourself as a being who gives rather than collects, and live on what you need rather than practicing conspicuous consumption. You'll begin to see that your purpose has more to do with Tao consciousness than ego directives. When you moderate your demands and use only what you and your family require, you'll gather virtue points by serving rather than accumulating. Lao-tzu reminds you that this is "the secret of long life and lasting vision."

William Shakespeare described this more than 2,000 years after Lao-tzu's passing in his play *The Third Part of Henry the Sixth:*

> *My crown is in my heart, not on my head;*
> *Not deck'd with diamonds and Indian stones,*
> *Nor to be seen. My crown is call'd content;*
> *A crown it is that seldom kings enjoy.*

Do the Tao Now

Make a commitment to gather five God points today. Imagine how the Divine Source of all 10,000 things must be operating in order to maintain the creation cycles of life, and do five things that match up to it. Pick up a piece of someone else's trash, which is an example of excess; anonymously give a gift to someone in need; or perform any other actions that help you accumulate virtue and remain deeply rooted in the Tao.

60th Verse

Governing a large county
is like frying a small fish.
You spoil it with too much poking.

Approach the universe with the Tao
and evil will have no power.
Not that evil is not powerful,
but its power will not be used to harm others.
Not only will it not do harm to others,
but the sage himself will also be protected.

If only the ruler and his people would
refrain from harming each other,
all the benefits of life would accumulate
in the kingdom.

*L*iving with *I*mmunity to *E*vil

Your assignment in this verse of the Tao Te Ching is to change the way you view the presence of evil in your personal world, as well as the entire planet. You can do so by acquiring an inner awareness that evil simply can't impact you if you're centered within the protective net of the Tao. If you live in accordance with the Great Way, refusing to have injurious thoughts directed either toward yourself or others, then the powers of wickedness and wrongdoing will be rendered impotent.

The Tao isn't about destruction or visiting harm on anyone; rather, it gives sustaining energy to everyone, without exception. When people violate this principle, they're only successful when others respond in kind. This is when war erupts and dissension becomes present in the family and the community. Negativity then begets more negativity, and the leader or ruler will ultimately be destroyed as the larger grouping falls into chaos.

Update your viewpoint on the presence of malevolence in the world to one that emphatically affirms: *My loved ones and I cannot and will not be impacted by the presence of evil anywhere in the world.* Your inner landscape will immediately begin to change as well. So when you see or hear reports of violent thinking and action, your immediate reaction must be, *This is not about me. I choose not to have any thoughts of harm directed to anyone by me. I am a being of light*

287

and love, and therefore the only thoughts that can emerge from me are in harmony with the great loving Tao. In other words, whatever comes your way because of other people won't evoke a plan of revenge and hatred. That's because you've made yourself immune to negativity by being Tao centered.

Now you may think that this sounds too simplistic, but imagine if large numbers of people began thinking this way—and then imagine if rulers began to emerge from this kind of consciousness. As Lao-tzu says in this verse, "If only the ruler and his people would refrain from harming each other, all the benefits of life would accumulate in the kingdom." Ultimately, our world must live by this principle or humanity will cease to exist . . . and it begins with you.

As Tao awareness grows one person, one family, one community, and one country at a time, priorities will shift. Our energies will go into building more environmentally sensitive vehicles and homes rather than instruments that reflect a belief that we can do whatever we want to the planet without repercussions. We'll find ways to destroy the stockpiles of unimaginably horrendous weapons of mass destruction. Cooperation will replace hatred and thoughts of harm. It will come about, as Lao-tzu states, when rulers and people change the way they think about harming each other.

As you reexamine this passage of the Tao Te Ching, see how it can impact your daily life. When negativity feels like it's directed right at you, retreat to that place of kindness and love within and deflect that energy. Remember, it's impossible to pick a fight with someone who refuses to fight! So your refusal to enter into battle is your most potent weapon against evil. You can change an angry person's attempt to inflict harm by refusing to lower yourself to the level of their abusive thinking. From an enraged motorist's curse to the harsh words of a disgruntled clerk or upset family member, these outbursts are easily shifted when you stay centered inwardly. Become immune to such harmful thinking and action by knowing that none of this is about you.

As he dictated this 60th verse some 2,500 years ago, Lao-tzu was thinking about all of humanity. He knew that hurtful behavior could be rendered impotent if enough people were willing to live in ways that encourage cooperation and a spirit of love in place of competition and revenge. Now he asks you to implement the wisdom of this verse by making the following changes in the way you think about evil and its potential impact on you and the world:

Bolster your immunity to negativity by controlling yourself in the midst of noxious thinking.

Catch yourself when you have judgmental thoughts that could be considered harmful for yourself or others. For example, if you see yourself as unworthy of respect, that's a damaging thought directed at you. Change it to the following affirmation: *I deserve and anticipate receiving only Divine love. This is what I attract.* When you're confronted with any reports of hatred and evil on our planet, suspend your fantasies of revenge toward the perpetrators. Change your mental energy to something like: *I send loving, kind thoughts to all and trust that this love will help them see the folly of their hatred.* Be conscious of all of your thoughts, changing them midstream if necessary. Become one person who brings the benefits of the Tao to our world.

Declare yourself immune to injurious entreaties.

Visualize a protective shield all around you, guarding you against what's perceived as evil in the world. Your shield is permeable only to energy that harmonizes with the Tao. Love, kindness, and help can all get through—but if any harm comes near you, it will be repelled by your shield. This means you create a great sense of faith in the Tao. With this kind of inner trust, when evil rages around you, it won't be able to impact you directly. Become the sage, the leader who governs your life and the lives of those around you, and who can't be hurt. Declare it, practice it in your every thought, and walk freely in the midst of danger. This isn't having a false sense of security; instead, it's an awareness that you and the Tao are one.

Do the Tao Now

The next time you think that you're the target of a harmful thought from a stranger, a family member, or a co-worker, make every effort to remember to respond from your inner nature, which is the Tao. Send back a loving, kind response, and then retreat to a silent and peaceful knowing that you've begun the process of immunizing yourself from harm. By practicing with even a seemingly innocuous statement, you'll witness how effective this is. Approach the universe with the Tao in your heart rather than reacting defensively.

61st Verse

A great country is like the lowland,
toward which all streams flow.
It is the reservoir of all under heaven,
the feminine of the world.
The female overcomes the male with stillness,
by lowering herself through her quietness.

So if a great country lowers itself before a small one,
it wins friendship and trust.
And if a small country can lower itself before a great one,
it will win over that "great" country.
The one wins by stooping;
the other, by remaining low.

Living by Remaining Low

Most of us have been taught that it's important to tower over lesser folks in virtually all of life's endeavors. We're told to "get to the top," "stand out in the crowd," "be the best," and "honor champions" who defeat challengers. We're expected to pay homage to those who make the most money, collect the most material objects, and evoke the most fear and obedience because of their positions of power; and those who deign to live among the "commoners" are the least deserving of our respect. This passage of the Tao Te Ching invites us to reevaluate these beliefs.

Look at the ocean: It's the most powerful force on the planet because it stays lower than the streams, which are necessarily and inescapably drawn to it. As the rivers flow downward to become one with it, the sea is able to be the great reservoir of all under heaven. This is what Lao-tzu refers to throughout the Tao Te Ching as the "great Mother" or the "feminine of the world." That female energy, or yin, is the true receptor of all; by remaining quiet and still, it ultimately overcomes male (yang) efforts to subjugate and conquer.

In the 61st verse of the Tao Te Ching, Lao-tzu speaks of the advantages of leading by remaining low, using entire countries as his examples. He makes the case for nations both large and small to be like the great ocean. As he observed warring territories attempting to vanquish each other by exerting their strength, he saw that peace and harmony could only be possible if the territories behaved in accord with the Tao—that is, by subjugating their egos rather than their neighbors.

Lao-tzu was addressing countries and their political leaders in this chapter, but countries are made up of individual men and women. We need to become a critical mass of individuals who are willing to model the wisdom that the great Chinese master offers us. We all must learn the value of making a dramatic change in the way we think of ourselves and each other. Yes, it may require a complete about-face on our part, but if we begin to lessen ego-dominated thinking, sooner or later the world will get the message that Lao-tzu proposed in ancient times. Nations all over the globe will find that leaders with feminine yin energy are beneficial. After all, this is the way of nature . . . it is the Tao at work.

You can apply the wisdom of this verse in the business world or with anyone you encounter by updating the notion that towering above others in the yang approach of masculine domination is the way to get ahead. Instead, see the value of living as if you can win trust and friendship through a yin approach of feminine receptivity and stillness.

As you try on these new attitudes and behaviors, quietly watch as the energy from the following suggestions begins to influence your reality:

Reassess your personal view of what constitutes strength.

Can you see power in humility, stillness, and remaining low and out of sight? In martial arts, the strongest conqueror is the one who uses the least force and converts the lunges of his opponent into his own might. Look at the story of violence throughout human history: Those obsessed with positions of power ultimately resort to brutality, and then incur the same kind of violence on themselves. And so it is in your personal life.

By staying calm and under the radar, others will ultimately flow to you, joining with you in creating friendship and trust. As you stay in this yin, feminine, Divine-Mother mode, you'll radiate energy and strength and win over others . . . including those with an aversion to change. Think of yourself as the ocean and stay low enough to allow all others to stream down to you and create a "great country" wherever you elect to settle.

**Emulate those whose greatest impact on humanity
used the least violent methods.**

There are many examples to be found for living by remaining low, replicating the example of stillness and yin energy. Jesus Christ, Buddha, Mohammed, Zoroaster, Saint Francis of Assisi, Gandhi, Mother Teresa, and others of the highest spiritual persuasion serve as wonderful role models for us. By demonstrating the exact opposite of what has become known as power by force, they changed the course of human history. Furthermore, they are remembered with the highest esteem by all people.

You can become a similar leader of the Tao in your immediate environment, smiling inwardly as you see yourself as that low, patient ocean. All those who wish to tower above you in conquest will ultimately flow down to you.

Do the Tao Now

Each day as you grapple with how to be an effective leader in your family, in your country, and in the world, apply the following advice from Sai Baba. This is what he counsels readers to do whenever they question what action to take or how to think:

> *When head fast eyes are horrified*
> *by the cruelties of life . . .*
> *When your mouth is parched*
> *and you can hardly speak,*
> *The first sip of cool water*
> *I am soothing you.*
> *Think of me.*

In a moment of crisis, silently say *Think of me* to your mental image of the person who won you over by stooping and remaining low. You'll immediately find your way, as if that individual were directing you to overcome the struggle, addiction, or ego-dominated thoughts that seem to take you away from your feminine, Tao nature.

62nd Verse

The Tao is the treasure-house,
the true nature,
the secret Source of everything.
It is the treasure of the good man
and the refuge of the bad.

If a person seems wicked,
do not cast him away.
Awaken him with your words,
elevate him with your deeds,
repay his injury with your kindness.
Do not cast him away;
cast away his wickedness.

Thus when a new leader is chosen,
do not offer to help him
with your wealth or your expertise.
Help him to meditate on the principle;
offer instead to teach him about the Tao.

Why did the ancients make so much of the principle?
Is it not because it is the Source of all good,
and the remedy for all evil?
It is the most noble thing in the world.

Living in the Treasure-house of the Tao

Imagine having access to a very special place where we could re-treat and commune with the sacred Source of everything. Here we'd find "the treasure of the good man" and a space where the bad man goes to be forgiven. This is where great rulers and the wisest among us would meditate for guidance to carry out awesome responsibilities, where we'd be given the secret for casting out all wickedness without personally needing to cast out anyone ourselves. In this wonderful locale, we would absolutely know the Source of good as well as the remedy for evil.

As I studied and contemplated this passage, I began calling it the "Count your blessings" verse. It reminds me that I can access a sacred treasure-house deep within me, as can you and all other conscious beings. It reminds me to change the way I see the appearance of dark-ness in our world today. It reminds me that within me is the won-drous wellspring of the Tao. It reminds me to be willing to change the way I view myself and my role here as one of the 10,000 things.

You can modify your conditioned way of viewing most things by looking at all that appears to be weighted with hatred, wicked-ness, and evil. According to Lao-tzu, no one is evil or wicked; rather, those who live in contradiction to the Tao's teaching only *appear* to be so. Instead of casting them aside, you must reconnect them to the Great Way. So stay centered by thinking and behaving in ways that harmonize with the all-loving, all-knowing Tao, keeping in mind that this Source doesn't inflict harm on, exclude, or judge anyone—it just gives life.

Where you perceive negativity, alter your view to see pure love and kindness that's mistakenly being directed to seek a sacred place in the material world. That energy is powerful, and it's moving away from its Source instead of returning and replenishing in the spiritual cycle that is its originating point. When you've succeeded in changing how you perceive so-called wickedness, invite others to see the difference as well. Thanks to your new point of view, you'll be quite comfortable discussing the difference between material-world satisfactions and the riches of the Tao. And if requested, you'll even be able to offer a map or path to the sacred treasure-house of the Tao.

In a translation of the Tao Te Ching by Gia-Fu Feng and Jane English, the 62nd verse concludes with the following words:

Why does everyone like the Tao so much at first?
Isn't it because you find what you seek and are forgiven when you sin?
Therefore this is the greatest treasure of the universe.

Here's what Lao-tzu offers you in this "Count your blessings" gem of a verse:

Practice seeing the door of the treasure-house opening to you.

See yourself as a Divine creation of the eternal Tao, with the entrance to a sacred space always available to you. Know that what you've thought of as negative can never be if it's able to enter the treasure-filled Tao. Visualize a house that's opening its front door to you and welcoming you to bask in the sacred warmth of its interior, and imagine leaving all angst and fear behind as you walk in. Make this home of the Tao a private retreat that you're free to enter with this meditative visualizing technique. It is divinity itself, and it can be your sanctuary at any time.

**Practice forgiving, and avoiding judgment, when
you see reprehensible or evil-minded ways.**

Take Lao-tzu up on his advice for dealing with those who appear
to be wicked people by mentally separating the individuals from
their toxic behavior. Remember that they are Divine creations of
the Tao who simply believe that ego should control life. In your
thoughts, erase the vileness, the wrongdoing, and the addictive or
harmful actions; and allow those folks to just be there apart from
their malevolent behavior. See the unfolding of the Tao in them,
and picture them as innocent children who are overstimulated by
ego's temporary stronghold. In your mind, forgive the evil conduct,
and make every effort to wrap loving arms around the children you
see before you.

Lao-tzu urges you to treat yourself in a similar manner: Cast out
any behavior you dislike about yourself, allow your pain to be felt,
and absolve yourself. With these behaviors removed, visualize embracing yourself, and notice the radiant being of light who is yourself in your imagination. Practice elevating yourself with your Tao
deeds and doling out kindness to others as well as yourself. This is
how you apply this verse of the Tao, which is indeed the remedy for
all evil.

Do the Tao Now

Today, make the decision to help one other person, if only for a
few moments, to meditate on this verse's principle. But do so without mentioning the Tao Te Ching or this book. Possibly send out
an expression of love where you might have chosen anger. Or mail
a greeting card with a particularly meaningful verse of the Tao to
someone who's assumed a new position of leadership. Whatever you
do, your motivation is to help that man or woman unlock the door
to his or her treasure-house by offering keys in the form of your own
Tao-centered thoughts and behaviors.

63rd Verse

Practice nonaction.
Work without doing.
Taste the tasteless.
Magnify the small, increase the few.
Reward bitterness with care.
See simplicity in the complicated.
Achieve greatness in little things.

Take on difficulties while they are still easy;
do great things while they are still small.
The sage does not attempt anything very big,
and thus achieves greatness.

If you agree too easily, you will be little trusted;
because the sage always confronts difficulties,
he never experiences them.

Living Without Difficulties

This verse conveys so much with an economical use of words. Every time I read what Lao-tzu is saying here, I feel that it's impossible for me to experience difficulties in my life if I'm willing to accept his sage advice. He counsels that we learn to think in moments, rather than in days, weeks, months, years, decades, or a lifetime. All we ever get is right now—that's it. So we must avoid the inclination to magnify tiny events or worry about a future that may never arrive. It's the little things that make all the difference in our world, and keeping life simple replaces chaos. As Lao-tzu reminds us, "See simplicity in the complicated . . . do great things while they are still small."

I've followed that advice while working on this book. As you might imagine, writing individual essays on the 81 verses of one of the most revered and enduring spiritual texts has been a daunting task! A project like this involves at least a year of daily researching, reading, writing, and revising. Yet instead of focusing on the challenges of this project, I choose to "see simplicity" and "take on difficulties while they are still easy." I immerse myself in a single verse in the morning, allowing the words to flow through my heart and onto the page. I feel like I've mastered the ironic conclusion of this 63rd passage, which says that difficulties are not experienced when they're confronted.

This, then, is the wisdom of this verse: There's no such thing as difficulty when you live in the present moment, doing only what you can right now. So examine your thoughts about what you call the troubles in your life. Can you shift to thinking of every undertaking as not only manageable, but easy and small as well? After all, how do you pursue a difficult course of study that will take several years to complete? By not projecting yourself into the future or using your present moments to worry. How do you get through the long, difficult process of giving birth to a child? Moment by moment. I've watched my wife do just that during the years she was either pregnant or nursing, delivering five children in eight years. As Lao-tzu teaches, if you don't attempt anything big, you will achieve greatness.

Almost every morning I do a 90-minute hot yoga class with 26 postures and two breathing exercises. Now an hour and a half of intense activity in a room that's more than 105 degrees can seem not only big, but very difficult as well. I've learned to change the way I think about this daily routine that I enjoy so much, and now I find it to be easy. As the first breathing exercise begins, I keep my mind and body totally focused on what I'm doing in the opening moment. If my mind wants to wander to what I'll be doing in an hour, I just bring it back to the present. I look in the mirror and remind myself that this exercise or posture is small and simple. *Bingo*— difficult is out of the picture!

By practicing in the present moment and training myself to stay in a state of simplicity, I've made my 90-minute yoga class a snap. I've achieved what I consider to be greatness in the little progressions and improvements that have evolved naturally. It's work without doing, and nonaction in action because I've confronted what might have been thought of as tough. The result is that I don't experience difficulty.

Lao-tzu urges you to change the way you look at your 21st-century world by doing the following:

**Look for the simplicity in what you call complicated
by seeing that in *this* moment, it's not hard.**

Change your preoccupation with tomorrow, along with all of the tomorrows that comprise your future. My friend Byron Katie (whose husband, Stephen Mitchell, created a wonderful translation

of the Tao Te Ching that I've incorporated in this book) gave me my favorite definition of *insanity:* "To believe that you need what you don't have is insane." I'd add, "Believing that you can't be content and happy now because your future appears to you to be difficult is another form of insanity."

Look at what you have and realize that you're obviously fine in this moment! *A Course in Miracles* states this idea so well: "You have no problems, though you think you have."

Think small.

Change your notion of "thinking big" to "thinking small and getting big things done." Examine whatever it is that seems so enormous that it terrifies you to start. Then shift your thinking to see what can be done today in your precious present moments, completely ignoring the overall picture. Your accomplishments will magnify into greatness when you undertake the small; by doing so, you'll paradoxically see huge results.

Do the Tao Now

Set aside some time today to focus on the biggest challenge in your life. Break down whatever it is to one thing that can be done today, right in this moment. Erase the big picture—simply do what you can now and let everything else fade. Write the opening paragraph of your novel. Lay out your blueprint for the home you want to build. Sign up for one course at a local educational institution. Go for a two-minute run. *Be in the now.* See how doing the Tao at this moment brings big results by paradoxically staying small and simple.

64th Verse

What is at rest is easily managed.
What is not yet manifest is easy to prevent.
The brittle is easily shattered;
the small is easily scattered.

Act before things exist;
manage them before there is disorder.
Remember:
A tree that fills a man's embrace grows from a seedling.
A tower nine stories high starts with one brick.
A journey of a thousand miles begins with a single step.

Act and destroy it;
grasp it and lose it.
The sage does not act, and so is not defeated.
He does not grasp and therefore does not lose.
People usually fail when they are on the verge of success.
So give as much care at the end as at the beginning,
then there will be no failure.

The sage does not treasure what is difficult to attain.
He does not collect precious things;
he learns not to hold on to ideas.
He helps the 10,000 things find their own nature
but does not venture to lead them by the nose.

Living by Being Here Now

"A journey of a thousand miles begins with a single step" is the most famous line of the entire Tao Te Ching. It's quoted so often because it encourages us to avoid procrastination and just begin from where we are, right here, right now. A tiny seed planted and nurtured grows into a forest; a marathon begins by taking that first stride. In my opinion, the German poet and playwright Johann von Goethe nicely summed up this ancient teaching with these rhyming words:

> *Only engage, and then the mind grows heated,*
> *begin it, and then the work will be completed.*

The essence of the widely known 64th verse of the Tao Te Ching is this: Every goal is possible from here! With the emphasis on *from here!* This is particularly applicable to problems that seem overwhelming. When you change the way you think about them, your new and unique perspective will cause the enormity of the things before you to diminish.

"The sage does not treasure what is difficult" because he breaks it down into easily managed steps. Rather than taking over and directing others or attempting to do everything himself, the follower of the Tao finds a way to manage problems *before* they exist, and *prior to* disorder breaking out. Lao-tzu is encouraging us all to do the same.

Reexamine how you view the challenges you face, as well as those of your family, community, and country. Sense in your heart how easily preventable many of them are when you deal with things before they exist, and when you refuse to be attached to the ideas that are largely responsible for these problems.

There are three steps to enlightenment that most people traverse:

1. The first is *through suffering.* This is when the big problems of your life become so overwhelming that a long period of misery ensues because you "treasure what is difficult to attain." Ultimately, you come to a place where you can look back at those huge obstacles —such as illness, accidents, addiction, financial loss, children's struggles, and divorce—and see in retrospect that they were actually gifts disguised as problems. Yet this is not the way of the Tao; this is not how a sage conducts his life.

2. The second is *by being in the present moment.* Here you've moved closer to the Tao by asking yourself when a crisis erupts, *What do I have to learn from this experience right now? I know there's a gift hidden for me in this misfortune, and I'll focus on looking for it.* While this is Tao-centered thinking, it's not all that Lao-tzu wants to convey in this 64th verse.

3. The third is *by getting out in front of big problems.* This means that you act before difficulties occur, sense disorder coming your way, and manage it in advance. *This* is the way of the Tao. "The small is easily scattered," says Lao-tzu. So here you're the acute observer who's totally in tune with nature. With foresight, you anticipate an argument, play it out in your mind in a split second, and are able to neutralize the negative energy because you were in front of it. You've responded by not acting in your former problem-producing ways and are thus harmonized with the Tao. At this stage you *prevent* difficulties rather than solve them.

This verse invites you to master the third or Tao-centered method. Here are some suggestions for doing so:

**Remind yourself of the inherent value in practicing
the most enduring line from the entire Tao Te Ching:
"A journey of a thousand miles begins with a single step."**

Forget about the end result: When you arrive where you thought you wanted to be, you'll just begin a new journey. So enjoy each step along the way and keep in mind that every goal is possible from here. Just do one thing, one day at a time.

Here's an example of this from my own life: It has now been almost two decades since I've had a drink containing alcohol. Had I thought about not drinking for 20 years, it would have been overwhelming and really difficult—yet I've done it, one day at a time. I can't speak for the next 20 years, but one thing I'm absolutely certain of is that today, and today alone, I will not be taking a drink. One step . . . one moment . . . one day at a time . . . is the Tao in action.

Become a master anticipator.

Decide that you're perfectly capable of preventing trouble from cropping up in your life long before it manifests into your material world. Anticipate your own health, for instance. Become conscious of prevention rather than waiting for challenges to materialize. By taking care to be nutritiously sound as a way of life—such as by taking supplements that remove toxins from your body, cleansing your colon, eating more fruits and vegetables and fewer animal products, exercising, and meditating—you're out in front of big problems. You're foreseeing what you need to do while you're capable of scattering the small, managing your health in harmony with the Tao long before there's disorder. Find other areas of your life to practice being a master anticipator!

Do the Tao Now

Take one habit that you'd like to see removed from your life, such as something that you believe constitutes a weakness or perhaps even an addiction. Just for today, and with no promises about tomorrow or the future, take a single step to transcend this habit.

Don't smoke or drink caffeine, just today. Eat only veggies and fruit, just today. Speak warmly to hostile neighbors, just today. Notice at the end of this one day how you feel. Then, and only then, decide if tomorrow morning you wish to continue practicing the wisdom of the Tao Te Ching, which was itself written one word and one day at a time, and has lasted for more than 25 centuries.

65th Verse

The ancient ones were simple-hearted
and blended with the common people.
They did not shine forth;
they did not rule with cleverness,
so the nation was blessed.

When they think that they know the answers,
people are difficult to guide.
When they know they do not know,
people can find their own way.

Not using cunning to govern a country
is good fortune for the country.
The simplest pattern is the clearest.
Content with an ordinary life,
you can show all people the way
back to their own true nature.

Living by Staying Simple-hearted

If you are currently in the important position of ruling a country, I encourage you to take this wisdom especially to heart. If you're not, I suggest studying this passage of the Tao Te Ching from the perspective of your personal life, which most likely involves leading others.

Supervising or parenting shouldn't mean imposing bureaucratic rules or impressing others with your supposed intelligence and superiority. A truly influential person isn't cunning, doesn't "shine forth," "rule with cleverness," or instill fear in those he or she is designated to oversee. As Lao-tzu explains, "When they know they do not know, people can find their own way." In other words, the effective leader guides others to their own nature.

The realization you're invited to consider here is that your job is to help others know that they *don't* know! If they believe that they do have knowledge, then they'll never find their way back to their Tao nature. That's because they're relying on ego input, which tells them that their true essence is their identification with the physical or material world. One who lives according to the Tao knows that ego is a false master, drawing people away from knowing their true nature.

Implement the teachings of this verse by refusing to convey superiority or intellectual ingenuity. Instead, show others how to live from the Tao perspective by being willing to admit that you don't know what's best for them, nor do you even know with any degree of certainty how your own life should go. Let other people know that you're willing to ask for guidance. Show them that you're not "in charge," either of them or of what happens to you. Allow them to see a man or woman who's humble, lives peacefully in the cycles of life, and stays simple-hearted.

As you change the way you look at leadership, you'll see that individuals who are willing to surrender their egos enjoy a connection to their Tao energy and become simple-hearted leaders. Their only task is to help everyone in their sphere of influence realize that they also do not know! Lao-tzu seems to smile wryly as he informs you of this wondrous paradox.

Blend in with those whom you feel compelled to supervise by trying on these new ways of thinking and being:

**Be willing to proudly say to those in your charge,
"I don't know."**

This phrase is a symbol of strength rather than weakness, so use it freely. When you teach others to do the same, they'll begin to allow their highest selves to be guided by the Great Way. Keep in mind that nature never forces anything to grow, but is silently and invisibly ever present. Do the same to the best of your ability by not forcing yourself and your ideas on anyone (with sensible precautions for those too young or too immature to take on adult responsibilities).

The simple truth is that neither we nor anyone else really know what's ideal for ourselves or others. There's a silent destiny always at work; there are fortunes as well as *mis*fortunes in every life, independent of our particular opinions.

Practice keeping your life simple and uncomplicated.

Model this behavior for those you feel obliged to lead. Rather than analyzing a situation from every angle, trying to come up with the most viable solution, trust your first instinct and take the simplest and least problematic route. Don't "pole-vault over mouse turds"—

by the time you've discussed the many options available to you, the problem itself could have been long behind you had you simply disposed of those rodent droppings with a simple tissue and dumped them into the garbage! Here's some great advice for you, as well as the leaders of countries who are often so mired in bureaucratic red tape that they become paralyzed: *Keep it simple.*

Do the Tao Now

In as many ways as possible, demonstrate your understanding of what Lao-tzu meant by asking leaders to be "content with an ordinary life." Spend a day without the label of "parent," "supervisor," or "boss," and put yourself on an equal footing with those who usually look to you for direction. Think of yourself as one of those you lead—in fact, pretend that you are him or her for one day. This will give you an awareness of how to put the Tao to work right away.

I've found that when I practice this with my children, they respond according to their own best and true nature. For example, when I simply say to my teenage daughter, "I know that you're perfectly capable of being responsible and sensible while I'm out of town, and I love that about you," I remove the "authoritarian parent" label and treat her the way I'd want to be treated. When this becomes the norm, it's obvious that Lao-tzu is correct: "The simplest pattern is the clearest."

66th Verse

Why is the sea king of a hundred streams?
Because it lies below them.
Humility gives it its power.

Therefore, those desiring a position
above others must speak humbly.
Those desiring to lead must follow.

Thus it is that when a sage stands above the people,
they do not feel the heaviness of his weight;
and when he stands in front of the people,
they do not feel hurt.

The sage stays low
so the world never tires of exalting him.
He remains a servant
so the world never tires of making him its king.

*L*iving by *E*mulating the *S*ea

Unlike the perception of God as an old white man Who created a universe where your behavior may cause you to be sentenced to damnation for eternity, the Tao is perceived as a natural energy. The Source of life isn't seen as a deity monitoring earthlings like a king or dictator, since it doesn't dole out punishments or withhold rewards. Lao-tzu taught that the Tao only asks you to live in harmony with nature.

For Lao-tzu, nature's great symbol is water, and he refers to it in many of the 81 passages. When you emulate that element, you'll begin to see that judgment and exclusion have no place in the Tao. Be like the sea, advises Lao-tzu, and the world will never tire of exalting you. The essential message presented in this verse and in many others of the Tao Te Ching is that the ocean is king of all because it knows to stay low. All streams must ultimately flow to the sea, and in the process, it becomes a servant to all. The teachings here are clear: Be humble. Never put yourself above others or see yourself as superior to anyone. The highest power is a yielding valley. Become a servant, not a dominator.

When even the tiniest waterways are left alone, they uniquely carve out a path that leads them to the sea. And the great ocean never lords its greatness and power over the rivers and streams: It doesn't rise above them and demand devotion, nor does it threaten them with punishment or extinction if they refuse to cooperate. The sea knows instinctively that the streams and rivers will naturally gravitate toward that which stays low.

Using this metaphor throughout the Tao Te Ching, Lao-tzu reminds you that people also tend to be instinctively drawn to those with intrinsic majesty that emerges from humility and staying low. And this position isn't uniquely held by the great master. Peter, a servant and apostle of Jesus Christ, offers an almost identical message in the New Testament, centuries after the death of Lao-tzu:

> Be shepherds of God's flock that is under your care, serving as overseers—not because you must, but because you are willing, as God wants you to be; not greedy for money, but eager to serve; not lording it over those entrusted to you, but being examples to the flock (1 Pet. 5:2–3).

Change the way you think about yourself and others as model leaders by looking to the massive life-giving sea, who's patient, accepting, and lower than the streams that flow to it. Then imitate that water power yourself by suspending your ego and releasing the need to lord anything over anyone. The people you're entrusted to lead will gravitate to you and the watercourse way of the Tao's natural flow.

You're advised to learn from the way water behaves and imitate it as much as possible in your life. Here are ways to apply the wisdom of emulating the sea in your life today:

Never assume that you know what's best.

Even if you're older, wiser, and richer than others and have more influence and power than they do, never assume that you know what's best for anyone. Instead, imagine yourself as the great ocean that allows and encourages the smaller streams to come to you. Stay low, speak softly, and remain humble—and let others be in control of their lives as much as is humanly possible. By seeing yourself as the all-receiving sea, you remove your ego from the picture and thus become like one of the leaders referred to in this verse of the Tao Te Ching. No one should feel the heaviness of your directions or be hurt by your instructions.

A situation that allowed me to implement this advice occurred on the day I wrote this essay. I live on Maui, and my 90-year-old mother is in Florida, where my daughter Saje also resides. My mother was experiencing a stomachache and nausea from some strong medication she'd taken, so I phoned my daughter to see if she had any suggestions for getting some yogurt to her. Saje's immediate response was, "We have some yogurt right here—I'll take it over to Grandma's." Rather than giving her an order and instructing her to tend to her grandmother, I allowed my daughter to be of service while I stayed in the lowest possible place.

Remain a servant.

See yourself as someone who's on this planet to assist others. Look for opportunities to be of aid, particularly to those who need your leadership. Remember that the great sea serves everyone by being a life-supporting receiver of all who wish to partake of her bounty, so practice emulating her by expressing the Tao.

Do the Tao Now

Dedicate a day to leading by serving, as opposed to giving orders. Find occasions to stifle your learned habit of interfering and telling others what to do, and allow them to flow to you instead. Commit to this principle further by encouraging someone to make the decision rather than following your orders.

67th Verse

All the world talks about my Tao
with such familiarity—
what folly!
The Tao is not something found at the marketplace
or passed on from father to son.
It is not something gained by knowing
or lost by forgetting.
If the Tao were like this,
it would have been lost and forgotten long ago.

I have three treasures, which I hold fast
and watch closely.
The first is mercy.
The second is frugality.
The third is humility.

From mercy comes courage.
From frugality comes generosity.
From humility comes leadership.
Now if one were bold but had no mercy,
if one were broad but were not frugal,
if one went ahead without humility,
one would die.

Love vanquishes all attackers,
it is impregnable in defense.
When heaven wants to protect someone,
does it send an army?
No, it protects him with love.

Living by the Three Treasures

You're being invited to change your life by seeing it through the prism of this ancient verse of the Tao Te Ching, which instructs you on the three things you need for a Tao-styled life of success:

— *Mercy* is the name used here for the first treasure, but additional terms such as *compassion, good-heartedness, love, kindness,* and *charity* have been employed in other translations. You've very likely been weaned on a model of achievement that's measured by accumulation, accomplishment, and the acquisition of power and influence over others. Successful people are usually considered to be narrowly focused on their own goals, oblivious to anything but getting to the top, and ruthless in preventing anyone else from getting what they're after.

Lao-tzu, however, says that the first and most important treasure is what true courage stems from, not from a heartless and callous attitude. He even tells you that boldness without mercy is a prescription for death! So you're encouraged to think of others first by being willing to serve and exhibit kindness and love, even toward your enemies, instead of seeking external indicators to prove that you're successful.

Shakespeare speaks of the first treasure in *The Merchant of Venice:*

The quality of mercy is not strain'd,
It droppeth as the gentle rain from heaven . . .

But mercy is above this sceptered sway,
It is enthroned in the hearts of kings . . .

The great playwright then reminds us with his next lines why Lao-tzu made mercy the top priority of the three treasures:

It is an attribute to God himself;
And earthly power doth then show likest God's
When mercy seasons justice.

Mercy, compassion, and kindness are all attributes of God and the Tao. Lao-tzu saw this truth many centuries before Shakespeare did.

— The second treasure is *frugality,* or what was referred to in other translations as *economy, moderation, thrift,* or *simplicity.* Now frugality and moderation don't generally spring to mind when those at the pinnacle of achievement are described; however, according to Lao-tzu, being satisfied with less rather than more results in great generosity. So be willing to take only what you need, and don't accumulate or hoard. The less attached you are to your stuff, the easier it is to be generous; the more you cling to it, the more you feel you need, and the less concerned you are with the welfare of others.

— The third treasure necessary for a successful life is *humility,* which other translations refer to as "not presuming to be above nature," "daring not to be ahead of others," and "not always trying to be number one." From this quality, Lao-tzu reminds us, comes true leadership that radiates Tao energy.

Often our perception of strength, power, and triumph is influenced by the yang masculine qualities of arrogance, loftiness, and self-importance. So when you change the way you think about enlightened leadership, you can discover what genuinely successful

people have learned before you—that is, that we're all instruments for Tao or God or whatever you call the energy that writes the books, delivers the speeches, makes the lifesaving discoveries, and so on. Humility is akin to surrendering to a force greater than your ego, giving credit to that Source, and being grateful for any wisdom and influence that's given to you by that power. Be humble; stay low; and be a generous, grateful leader.

Here are some ways to apply these three treasures to your daily life:

Live in harmony with the myriad manifestations of the Tao.

The key to living in harmony is compassion and mercy. You're not in competition with anyone, so don't feel as if you must defeat another person or compare yourself on any level. Extend mercy and compassion toward every form of life, including yourself! When you radiate love and respect for all, you'll be aligned with the Tao, which will protect you as if you were a baby in the arms of a loving mother.

See the hidden strengths of simplicity and humility in those whom you may have previously judged to be weak or ineffective leaders.

Those who practice frugality and refuse to hoard or engage in conspicuous consumption deserve to be viewed as strong examples of how to guide others—whereas those who speak and act forcefully while stockpiling more and more goods are not in harmony with the Tao. Moreover, such individuals' actions tend to contribute to more dissension, and as Lao-tzu reminds us here, those who go ahead with boldness and without deference will die (and, I hasten to add, will lead others to their deaths as well). As you notice examples of simplicity and humility in those who are in positions to lead, make every effort to emulate the same qualities in your own daily interactions.

Do the Tao Now

Choose a conversation in which you can practice the three treasures by using an economy of words. While attempting to make a point in conversation, for instance, stop yourself after a moment or so and use your talking time to listen. You'll be employing all three of Lao-tzu's treasures at one time: You'll have *mercy* for the person with whom you're conversing by being *frugal* with your words and *humbly* refusing to be ahead of or above your conversational partner.

68th Verse

A good soldier is not violent.
A good fighter is not angry.
Good winners do not contend.
Good employers serve their workers.
The best leader follows the will of the people.

All of them embody the virtue of noncompetition.
This is called the virtue of noncontending.
This is called employing the powers of others.

This since ancient times has been known
as the ultimate unity with heaven.

*L*iving by *C*ooperating

This verse of the Tao Te Ching asks you to reconsider what you think you have to do to be a winner. In the Western world, getting ahead most often implies having to be in a state of contention and competition—basically, you must defeat the other guy by getting what you want before he does. Lao-tzu asks you to change this kind of thinking by embodying "the virtue of noncompetition," which can work for you even in a society where conquering and being number one are so highly valued.

The Tao Te Ching teaches that all of the 10,000 things emerge from the same state of nonbeing. Here there's only oneness, which implies complete collaboration, not competition. Who can there be to defeat if you see yourself in everyone? You'd be picking a fight with yourself! Lao-tzu asks that you follow his advice and choose to live by cooperating.

Believe it or not, this can actually work to your advantage in athletic competitions. Rather than thinking of an opponent as the enemy and employing anger and mental and physical violence, remind yourself of Lao-tzu's words in the opening of this verse: "A good soldier is not violent. A good fighter is not angry. Good winners do not contend." Instead, such individuals view their opponents as a part of themselves and as crucial members of this dance of life. So rather than being angry and hateful toward opponents in a tennis match or football game, see them as a part of you that's working to help you achieve excellence. Without them, you couldn't improve, get a good workout, or become victorious.

Do as Lao-tzu advises and "[employ] the powers of others" to elevate yourself to the status of winner. That is, cooperate with your opponents by wanting them to play at a high level—the best they're capable of. Shift your focus from being upset or self-reproaching to the task at hand. See the ball, move the ball, or remain upright and balanced in a martial-arts contest. When anger isn't a component, your game will go to a new level. And this is true off the athletic field as well: What you fight weakens you; what you cooperate with strengthens you. So change your thinking about competing to cooperating in all areas of your life, including your work.

I practice this concept by thinking of every person whose purpose is to help improve the quality of life on our planet as being my partner, on my "team." I cannot conceive of anyone out there whom I'm in competition with for any external prize. If they sell more books than I do, I applaud their good fortune; in fact, I'll tell as many people as I can to buy their products. If they make more money, get more publicity, or reach more people, I celebrate by thinking, *My teammate has helped me with my mission.*

When I play a close tennis match, I silently send love and encouragement to my opponent. When I'm less stressed, less angry, and less violent in my thinking, I'm living in the moment that Lao-tzu calls "the ultimate unity with heaven." My level of excellence soars, regardless of the outcome on the scoreboard.

This is what Lao-tzu recommends to you from his 2,500-year-old perspective:

Declare that you're not going to fight.

Don't fight colds, illnesses, or even serious afflictions. Don't fight with family members, or against political opinions. Don't fight addictions, and most important, don't fight yourself. Instead, make the shift to living by cooperating. If you have cancer or arthritis cells in your body, talk to them from that perspective: "If you insist on living in my body, I wish to live in harmony, peace, and total health with you; otherwise, I invite you to take up residence elsewhere." This may sound strange, but it puts you back in harmony with the Tao, which isn't violent, hateful, or angry.

Also, when it comes to your children and other family members, see yourself as their ally, daily practicing the "virtue of non-contending."

Practice seeing yourself in everyone else.

If someone you love is hurting, you experience their pain. Therefore, whenever you say or do something that's harmful to someone you love, you're doing something to harm *yourself*. Extend this awareness to all of humanity—after all, you share the same origination spirit or Tao with every living being in the universe. When you see your own spirit in a cooperative embrace with all others, you'll know what Lao-tzu means by "the ultimate unity with heaven."

Here are some marvelous words from Pablo Casals that express this thought:

> When will we [teach our children] what they are?
> We should say to each of them: Do you know what you are? You are a marvel. You are unique. In all the years that have passed, there has never been another child like you. Your legs, your arms, your cunning fingers, the way you move.
> You may become a Shakespeare, a Michelangelo, a Beethoven. You have the capacity for anything. Yes, you are a marvel. And when you grow up, can you then harm another who is, like you, a marvel?

Do the Tao Now

Affirm that you'll think of your opponent as an extension of yourself in your next competitive encounter. Vow to mentally send that person love, surround him or her in light, and pray that he or she will perform at the highest level. Then note how your own performance improves and carries you to a new level of excellence.

69th Verse

There is a saying among soldiers:
I dare not make the first move
but would rather play the guest;
I dare not advance an inch
but would rather withdraw a foot.

This is called
going forward without advancing,
pushing back without using weapons.

There is no greater misfortune
than feeling "I have an enemy";
for when "I" and "enemy" exist together,
there is no room left for my treasure.

Thus, when two opponents meet,
the one without an enemy
will surely triumph.

When armies are evenly matched,
the one with compassion wins.

Living
Without Enemies

Imagine a world with a common heritage that bonded all beings on the planet—a world that didn't know the word *enemy*, where everyone happily agreed that we're all one people, originating from the same Source of nonbeing. Picture a world that understood that harming anyone would be analogous to harming oneself. Unfortunately, while there's never been such a state of affairs among humans during the entire written history of civilization, this is the vision of Lao-tzu in the 69th verse of the Tao Te Ching. And it's *my* vision for what's possible when we work at being Tao-centered people, with Tao-centered leadership.

This grand vision begins right here, right now, with you! Remove the concept of "enemy" from your life, and model this behavior for those around you. Ultimately, the ripple effect will move everyone around the globe toward an "enemy-less" world.

Recently, a deranged man armed with guns and ammunition barricaded himself in an Amish schoolhouse in Lancaster County, Pennsylvania, where he proceeded to murder several girls. As the peaceful, Tao-centered, Christian members of this close-knit community grieved over their unspeakably horrific losses, they invited the family of the killer to mourn with them at the mass funeral and prayed for the killer as well.

As the Amish leader said, "We have no enemies; we are all God's children, and forgiveness is at the very core of our Christian faith. If we can't forgive those who are lost and would do harm to us, then our faith would be meaningless." These beautiful words are so similar in feeling to what Lao-tzu wrote in this verse: "There is no greater misfortune than feeling 'I have an enemy,'" and "when two opponents meet, the one without an enemy will surely triumph."

So how can you have an opponent without an enemy? In her illuminating book *The Tao of Inner Peace,* Diane Dreher offers a response to that question. Keep this in mind as you apply the 69th verse of the Tao Te Ching to your life: "The old perception of conflict as combat only narrows our vision, limits our choices, pulls us into endless struggles between competing polarities." She then adds, "Making enemies gives away our power, keeps us from taking responsibility for our lives. Instead of resolving conflict, we focus our attention on fearing, hating, and lashing out at perceived 'enemies.'"

The lesson from Diane's brilliant book, as well as this verse of the Tao Te Ching and the statement of the Amish community leader, is that *conflict* doesn't have to mean *combat.* In other words, someone with a contrary point of view doesn't have to be the enemy. Imagine if every general took these words of the Tao Te Ching to heart and practiced them: "I dare not make the first move . . ." There's no way war could exist.

Lao-tzu advised that if war ever does become inevitable, one should practice defense rather than offense. One should never initiate hostilities, but recognize in the heat of battle that the battle itself is something to grieve about. With no concept of "enemy," and a heart that's filled with compassion, one stays harmonized with the Tao. The presence of combat, whether verbal or physical, is an indication that contact with the Tao has been lost. There should be no celebration, and every war and battleground conflict should be treated as a funeral, with compassion ruling the day.

As I sit here contemplating the visage of Lao-tzu, he seems to say that a world free from foes isn't as impossible as you may believe. This is how you can put this wisdom to work for you now:

Refuse to think of anyone as your adversary.

Reread the most important line in this verse: "[W]hen 'I' and 'enemy' exist together, there is no room left for my treasure." Your treasure is your peace of mind and your Tao connection, so your competitors in business, your opponents in an athletic match, and the members of a competing political party are not your foes. And those people whom a government declares are your enemies are most assuredly not.

Affirm: *I have no enemies. There are people with whom I have strong disagreements. I may even be required to defend myself and my way of life, but I will not think of them as adversaries.* Recall Lao-tzu's statement that the person "without an enemy will surely triumph." Be that individual right now.

Vow to never start a fight.

Stay on the defensive side of disputes, aligning with Lao-tzu's advice to "play the guest" rather than make the first move. See *colleagues* where you once saw *combatants* by finding yourself in them. Convey compassion and caring toward your perceived adversaries, who are actually representing a part of you. Refuse to start a fight, reminding yourself that you'd be battling with yourself. Find a way to see oneness in a holy encounter, since all of us are of the Tao.

Do the Tao Now

Reproduce these words found in Anne Frank's diary, written as she was being hunted by the Nazis: ". . . in spite of everything I still believe that people are really good at heart. . . . I can feel the sufferings of millions and yet, if I look up into the heavens, I think that it will all come right."

Post this for everyone in your family to see.

70th Verse

My teachings are very easy to understand
and very easy to practice;
yet so few in this world understand,
and so few are able to practice.

My words have an ancestor;
my deeds have a lord.
The people have no knowledge of this,
therefore they have no knowledge of me.

This is why the sage dresses plainly,
even though his interior is filled
with precious gems.

Living a God-Realized Life

I pondered this 70th verse of the Tao Te Ching for a week, reading and rereading more than 50 interpretations of it. I was particularly drawn to this phrase in *The Essential Tao*, Thomas Cleary's translation:

> *Those who know me are rare;*
> *those who emulate me are noble.*

I also asked Lao-tzu for direction, trying to determine what his message is for the 21st century. I knew that the master never would have spoken from a need to have his ego massaged. He was, after all, the original Tao master, enjoying a life centered in the Great Way rather than ego and encouraging everyone to do the same.

Try to imagine what it must have been like for this Divine avatar to walk among his people in ancient China: He'd take incredulous note of their warlike behaviors, all the while having an internal awareness of what was possible for all of his fellow human beings if they would only change the way they looked at their lives. Freedom, peace of mind, contentment, and virtually every other principle that I've described in these 81 essays were only a thought away. I can imagine that some 500-plus years later, Jesus of Nazareth might have felt the same sentiment that Lao-tzu expressed here in verse

70, something to the effect of, *This is oh-so easy, so simple to understand and to practice, yet so few are willing or able to grasp the essence of heaven on earth.*

I can almost feel the frustration that Lao-tzu is expressing in these lines as he urges us to live a Tao-centered existence, rather than an ego-centered one. I've titled this brief essay "Living a God-Realized Life" because this is what I believe he's asking you to do throughout the 81 passages, and particularly here in number 70. "My words have an ancestor; my deeds have a lord," he says, and then immediately follows with the thought that the people just don't get it, so they clearly "have no knowledge of me." Lao-tzu's ancestor is the Tao, and the lord of his deeds is that very same nameless Source. He seems to be musing, *I think like God thinks; I speak as God, the creator of the universe, would speak; and therefore I act in accordance with these God-realized principles.*

I urge you to do the same, which *is* oh-so easy if you just surrender and allow this life-sustaining Tao energy to guide you. Stop fighting, eschew violent thoughts and deeds, and give up trying to control others or the world. Stay humble; don't interfere; respect your creative genius, as well as that of others; and, above all, return to your invisible Source and shed your troublesome ego while you're still alive and incarnated as one of the 10,000 things. If you do all of this, you will naturally live a long life in joyful, nonjudgmental peace.

Think of how the great spiritual masters have been portrayed by artists throughout the centuries: Lao-tzu wears a simple robe, Jesus is outfitted in plain clothes and sandals, Saint Francis sports almost tattered rags, Buddha looks like a peasant with a walking stick, and Mohammed is depicted as a simple man. Then look at the how the *followers* of the greatest spiritual teachers have been portrayed— living in the lap of luxury, opulence, and conspicuous consumption in golden palaces. The great sages dress plainly even though they conceal the most precious commodity within themselves.

And just what is this great treasure hidden within these masters? Verse 67 explained that it is God realization in the form of the three treasures: mercy, frugality, and humility. You don't need gold-embroidered costumes and temples strewn with riches—both of which were the result of the sweat of countless servants and slaves— to house these treasures. Dressing plainly keeps the sage in harmony with the simplicity of this message.

This is what I hear Lao-tzu saying between the lines of this 70th verse, expressing the bewilderment that he feels as so few people seem to grasp his beautifully simple message:

Know the Tao Te Ching.

Change your mind about being one of the vast majority who doesn't understand or practice the teachings of the Tao Te Ching. Lao-tzu tells you that there's so little to do—all you need to remember is that your holiness is a piece of the Tao. According to *A Course in Miracles,* "Your holiness reverses all the laws of the world. It is beyond every restriction of time, space, distance, and limits of any kind."

Declare yourself to be one of those who possesses this knowledge, and be willing to practice God realization every day.

See God everywhere.

Make it your daily practice to seek the invisible force of God in everything you see and hear. In the 14th century, Meister Eckhart offered some advice on how to put this 70th verse of the Tao Te Ching into daily life: "What is the test that you have indeed undergone this holy birth? Listen carefully; if this birth has truly taken place within you, then every single creature points you toward God." He further advised: "If the only prayer you said in your whole life was 'Thank You,' that would suffice."

Practice saying *Thank You, God, for everything.* This is the way to God realization.

Do the Tao Now

Plan a day to be like the sage who dresses plainly, without jewelry, makeup, or fancy clothes. In fact, head out for the day in a pair of shorts and a T-shirt. Wherever you go, stay in this "plain" mode and notice how irrelevant the attention paid to dress and looks seems. Tune in to your feelings as you go about your business unconcerned about how others view your appearance.

71st Verse

Knowing ignorance is strength.
Ignoring knowledge is sickness.

Only when we are sick of our sickness
shall we cease to be sick.
The sage is not sick but is sick of sickness;
this is the secret of health.

*L*iving *W*ithout *S*ickness

There's quite a paradox present in this passage, which has been expressed throughout my many readings of the Tao Te Ching as variations on "only when your sickness becomes sick will your sickness disappear." Lao-tzu seems to be saying that one must actually become ill in order to avoid illness.

Once again I've thought long and hard about this short verse. I've played with these words over and over in order to grasp their essential meaning for you, and for myself as well. Finally, I've meditated with Lao-tzu's image before me, asking what he meant by this puzzling 71st verse. His answer is what I based the rest of this chapter on.

First of all, what does the word *sickness* imply? For me, it means that something in the body or mind is out of balance with the well-being from which it originated—that is, it's not in agreement with the Tao. Conditions such as fevers, aches, wheezing, sniffling, breathlessness, coughing, unusual fatigue, and fainting are indications of the presence of illness; and the equivalent of such symptoms in our thinking could be fear, anxiety, anger, hatred, worry, guilt, stress, impatience, and so on. These are signals that our thoughts are out of balance with our Source, which is pure love, kindness, patience, contentment, and all of the other expressions of Tao-centeredness that appear in these 81 essays on the Tao Te Ching.

The sage in this verse has looked long and hard at illness, and has come to realize that it represents a physical manifestation of non-Tao thinking. A fever, a cold, an ache, or a pain are all identical to the non-Tao expressions of impatience, fear, anger, or any other ego-driven impulse. Since the sage has seen where thoughts like these lead, he refuses to participate in such folly. Thus, he has looked at poor health and vowed: *I will not think in ways that bring that about. I'll stay centered in the natural well-being of the Tao because to think a sick thought is to allow sickness to crop up.* Consequently, he's sick of sickness, and the result is the secret of perfect health.

Allow me to provide you with an example of this. My colleague and friend Radhika Kinger recently returned from a visit to Puttaparthi, India, where she was in the presence of Sathya Sai Baba, a God-realized master who lives and breathes all of the Divine messages presented in the Tao Te Ching. Here's an excerpt from the letter she sent me afterward:

> I just returned from Puttaparthi after spending a week there in Sai Baba's Divine presence. I was saddened to see Sai Baba in a wheelchair due to multiple fractures in his hipbone. According to the doctors, no normal human body can survive such physical agony. But Sai Baba remains ever so blissful and completely unaffected by his physical condition.
>
> A devotee asked Sai Baba how is it that a God-realized being has to undergo physical suffering. Why doesn't he cure himself? To this Sai Baba replied, "My life is my message. People today need to learn to give up body attachment and experience their divinity within. Pain is a natural phenomenon. But suffering is a 'choice.' I do not suffer, as I am not the body."

Sai Baba looked at his condition and declared himself to be sick of such a thing being in his life. Suffering with illness just isn't an option when one lives in harmony with the Tao.

With years of addictive behavior behind me, I can tell you that the wisdom of this verse of the Tao Te Ching was largely responsible for my getting back to the purity and well-being from which I originated. I became sick of my sickness, as I was no longer willing to go through the withdrawals and shame that accompanied it. I saw my affliction not so much in the material world, but in the invisible world of my thoughts, which kept leading me back to the illness.

When I finally changed the way I looked at all of this, I was able to bring about the seeming paradox of no longer being ill by getting to the point of being sick of it. And this is truly the secret of health.

Here's how Lao-tzu would instruct you to put this wisdom to work for you here and now:

Have a happy mind.

An ancient Chinese proverb says that if a man has a happy mind, he will a have a happy body. A happy mind is sick of sickness—it refuses to anticipate that things will get worse. It sees a sniffle, a stomachache, back or knee discomfort, and fatigue as messages to follow the body's signals back to a natural state of well-being. A happy mind thinks of the body as capable of healing infirmities because it knows that it isn't a human creation, but a product of the Tao. A happy mind trusts the capacity of the body to live without sickness or suffering. So use *your* happy mind to work with you to stay healthy.

Examine your habits.

What daily habits distance you from your natural state of well-being? Any addictions, no matter how serious or minor they might seem, are beckoning you to be totally fed up with them. Get sick of being weakened by destructive pursuits. You know what they are, and you know when you've habitually let yourself become ill from food, alcohol, or drugs; or from the guilt and shame that results after a binge. Remember that "ignoring knowledge is sickness" and examine your fixations, vowing not to ignore your awareness of what they are.

Do the Tao Now

Dedicate a day to really listening to and trusting the messages from your body, and then listen to what your *mind* tells you about those signals. Introduce your mind to the possibility that the body is signaling a request that you can grant, such as a nap or a walk along the beach, for instance. Cultivate the Tao-centered happy mind, which will not entertain sickness thoughts.

72nd Verse

When people lack a sense of awe,
there will be disaster.
When people do not fear worldly power,
a greater power will arrive.

Do not limit the view of yourself.
Do not despise the conditions of your birth.
Do not resist the natural course of your life.
In this way you will never weary of this world.

Therefore, the sage knows himself
but makes no show of himself;
loves himself
but does not exalt himself.
He prefers what is within to what is without.

*L*iving with *A*we and *A*cceptance

This verse of the Tao Te Ching alerts you to two components that work together for a harmonious life: a sense of awe and total acceptance. Without these combined forces, you're unlikely to see the presence of the Tao.

As I wrote about this verse, I found myself reading from Saint John of the Cross, a 16th-century mystical poet who lived a life of awe. I've reproduced a few of his lines to give you an idea of how this feeling manifested in a Divinely spiritual man:

> *My Beloved is the mountains,*
> *And lonely wooded valleys,*
> *Strange islands,*
> *And resounding rivers,*
> *The whistling of love-stirring breezes,*
>
> *The tranquil night*
> *At the time of rising dawn,*
> *Silent music,*
> *Sounding solitude,*
> *The supper that refreshes and deepens love.*

This morning I sit here in my sacred space on Maui feeling an urgency that actually feels like the rapture in Saint John of the Cross's words. I sense the presence of Lao-tzu urging me to hurry up so that he may convey to you what he means by having a sense of awe. It is so profound as to usher into your life a timeless awareness of the arrival of a greater power.

I feel that power right now in my beautiful surroundings. The sound of mynah birds fill the air as the ocean rolls in undulating waves, much like the heartbeat of our planet. The colors are absolutely breathtaking: the bright blue sky; the shimmering green palm trees, sea grass, and ficus plants; the dreamy oranges and purples mixing in the distant clouds; and topping it all off, a rainbow that appears to be connecting the nearby island of Lanai with my front window.

When words appear on my blank sheets of paper, I'm awash with bewildering waves of pleasure at how I'm being used by an invisible Source. I know that I'll soon be in the ocean, propelling myself along the shoreline, looking down at the creatures playfully moving about in the salty water and wondering where they sleep. How do they get here? How can they breathe without air? Do they ever stop moving? Will they be here after I'm gone? And then I'll emerge from the ocean and walk along the sand, feeling the sun on my body and questioning how it stays up there, how we keep moving around it while spinning once every 24 hours, why the ocean doesn't tip upside down while the whole planet is turning over and over, and if the stars and the universe itself will ever end.

The reason it's crucial to have a sense of awe is because it helps loosen the ego's hold on your thinking. You can then *know* that there's something great and enduring that animates all of existence. Being in awe of that something staves off disasters because you have no fear of worldly conditions. You're kept grounded in the otherworldly power that manifests a trillion miracles a second, all of which are oblivious to your ego.

The 72nd verse of the Tao Te Ching also asks you to accept yourself and your individual concerns. With three very emphatic suggestions, Lao-tzu tells you to avoid self-limits, accept your body as a perfect creation, and allow your life to unfold in accordance with its own nature.

I love the metaphor of nature as a guide to sagelike acceptance. In fact, throughout the 81 verses, Lao-tzu emphasizes being in harmony with the natural world, telling you that's where you connect with the Tao. As Meister Eckhart, a 13th-century Catholic monk and scholar, put it: "God created all things in such a way that they are not outside himself, as ignorant people falsely imagine. Rather, all creatures flow outward, but nonetheless remain within God."

And in John 15:4–5, the Bible advises you to "stay joined to me, and I will stay joined to you. Just as a branch cannot produce fruit unless it stays joined to the vine, you cannot produce fruit unless you stay joined to me. I am the vine, and you are the branches."

Learn about the Tao by being in perfect harmony with the environment. Think of trees, which endure rain, snow, cold, and wind—and when the harsh times arrive, they wait with the forbearance of being true to their inner selves. As Deng Ming-Dao writes in *365 Tao: Daily Meditations:* "They stand, and they wait, the power of their growth apparently dormant. But inside, a burgeoning is building imperceptibly . . . neither bad fortune nor good fortune will alter what they are. We should be the same way."

In order to do so, we must accept ourselves as being a part of the 10,000 things. And we must love that same burgeoning, imperceptible inner nature that will bear fruit. Or, as Lao-tzu concludes this verse, "He prefers what is within to what is without."

Love yourself, make no show of yourself, and quietly remain in awe and acceptance. Here are some suggestions on how to make this your reality:

See the miraculous in *everything.*

Change your view of the world to one of awe and bewilderment. Rather than looking for miracles, shift to seeing everything as miraculous. By being in a state of awe, you won't be able to mentally experience boredom or disappointment. Try seeing the invisible Tao flowing through and supporting everyone and everything: A rainstorm becomes a miraculous event, the lightning a fascinating display of electrical fireworks, the thunder a booming reminder of the invisible power of nature. Live the mystery by beginning to perceive what average eyes fail to notice.

**Focus on loving the life you have now
in the body you've got!**

Tell yourself that you love everything about the physical shell you've incarnated into. Affirm: *My body is perfect, born at precisely the right time, and this is the perfect age now. I accept myself as I am. I accept my role in the perfection of this universe at this time. I surrender to the natural course of my body's destiny.*

See your body through the eyes of totally accepting thoughts and, as Lao-tzu says, "In this way you will never weary of this world."

Do the Tao Now

List five natural occurrences in your daily life that you've been taking for granted. Then spend some contemplative time allowing each into your consciousness. The sky, some flowers, a tree in your yard, the moon, the sun, the fog, the grass, a spiderweb, a crab hole, a lake, a shrub, a cricket, your dog, anything that occurs naturally . . . let yourself radically appreciate the miracle you hadn't been noticing. Write, draw, or photograph some observations that you've gleaned from this new perspective of awe and bewilderment.

73rd Verse

Bold action against others leads to death.
Bold action in harmony with the Tao leads to life.
Both of these things
sometimes benefit
and sometimes injure.

It is heaven's way to conquer without striving.
It does not speak, yet it is answered.
It does not ask, yet it is supplied with all that it needs.
It does not hurry, yet it completes everything on time.

The net of heaven catches all;
its mesh is coarse,
but nothing slips through.

Living in Heaven's Net

Once again you're asked to see the Tao through a paradoxical lens. After all, what *is* "the net of heaven"? It is the invisible world wherein all of the 10,000 things originate. And while it appears to have many openings—ways to escape the inevitability of the intentions of the Tao—no one and no *thing* can exist beyond what the Tao orchestrates.

Here in this 73rd verse, you're encouraged to be a respectful, cautious being under the net of heaven. All the translations I've studied say the same thing in different words. Here's one, for instance, that's brief and to the point:

> *Reckless bravery: death.*
> *Cautious bravery: life.*
> *Therefore the sage behaves in a cautious manner.*

So Lao-tzu is asking you to change the way you look at bravado and courage. Rather than seeing these qualities as admirable, he asks you to be less of a dauntless hero and more vigilant and alert in order to live the Great Way. Note that the way of heaven is to eschew bold actions and remain cautious.

Lao-tzu offers you four examples of how the net of heaven holds everything within its grasp without having to be forceful or reckless, and you're encouraged to emulate that in all of your undertakings:

1. "It is heaven's way to conquer without striving." See how the Tao is peaceful, silent, and always the conqueror. No human can command the sun to cool down, ocean currents to stop, winds to subside, rain to cease, or crops to quit growing—this is all handled naturally and perfectly without any effort by the Tao. Nature always wins because the Tao simply does it all without needing to attack or strive. Be like this and relax in heaven's net.

2. "It does not speak, yet it is answered." Heaven's net is invisible and silent—the force that provides you with every breath and holds the universe together at the same time does so without commanding, yelling, or even mildly cajoling. So be in harmony with heaven's way by being more cautious and reserved. Listen more and speak less, trusting that your answers will come to you without any notice and most assuredly without any screaming.

3. "It does not ask, yet it is supplied with all that it needs." You have an infinite supply of all that you will ever need available to you, so you needn't demand anything or even ask for it. All is in Divinely perfect order with heaven's way, and you are a component of that perfect order. Your supply will arrive if you require less and welcome all that shows up. You simply cannot slip through heaven's net, no matter how many holes you may perceive there to be. Everything is arriving on schedule—by trusting in this, you'll be guided to a rendezvous with your destiny, and you'll marvel at how it all comes together without your asking or demanding.

4. "It does not hurry, yet it completes everything on time." How can the Tao hurry up? Imagine giving such a request to heaven: "I'm tired of winter and insist that you bring me spring flowers in the middle of these long freezing nights. I want my potatoes today, even though I only planted the seeds yesterday. Hurry up, I insist!" The Tao works with Divine timing, so everything is completed precisely as it should be. You're invited to slow your pace so that it

harmonizes with heaven's way. Even if you think that what you want is late, in reality it is all on time.

The more you hurry, the less you get done. Try rushing through a shower after running a 10k and notice how your body continues to sweat profusely. Then try slowing your mind down, relaxing, and allowing the water to course over you—and notice how your body feels clean without sweating in precisely the same amount of time that you used in your hurry-up mode. Even if your ego doesn't grasp it, this is the truth: *Everything is on time under heaven's net.*

What follows is Lao-tzu's advice for you today, as you peruse this 73rd verse of the Tao Te Ching some 2,500 years after it was written:

Don't see caution as a weakness or an expression of fear.

Instead, view it as a way to step back and allow events to unfold naturally. Bravery is a fine quality, but *reckless* bravery—that is, where you rush in without thinking—is a sure way to invite disaster. In this provocative verse, Lao-tzu is telling you to think before you act. Allow heaven's way to do the conquering without your having to fight or defeat anyone. Very often your first impulse is dominated by your ego's need to win and conquer.

I saw this as a competitive tennis player. By not striving, I'd often emerge victorious over younger, stronger, and sometimes more talented players. The reckless overhitting of the ball by my opponent would cause him to make unnecessary errors, while I stayed in the backcourt and simply returned the ball in what appeared to be effortless harmony. And this created more of a desire to win in my recklessly brave opponent, causing him to make even more mistakes. I call this "young man's disease."

Be an active listener.

Rather than attempting to control others by speaking frequently and loudly, allow yourself to become an active listener. Many of the answers you seek (and the results you expect) from others will surface if you can remember not to speak or even ask. Try living in accord with nature, which listening—rather than pushing, striving, or demanding—will help you do.

Do the Tao Now

I decided to go for a one-hour nonaction walk today after rereading this 73rd verse, to simply observe how everything under the net of heaven is working perfectly. I noticed the silent sun nourishing the land and providing light for us all. I stepped back and watched bees flitting back and forth between flowers, and stood there amazed by the invisible life force growing green bananas in a clump at the top of a tree. In all, I was just an observer of the Divine, invisible, silent, effortless Tao at work—realizing that while it's in no hurry, it's still getting everything done on time. Those green bananas will ripen in due course; but today I just loved the energy that creates, nourishes, and prepares them to appear for my breakfast someday!

Today I urge *you* to take a similar nonaction walk for an hour, and note how nothing slips through the net of heaven.

74th Verse

If you realize that all things change,
there is nothing you will try to hold on to.
If you are not afraid of dying,
there is nothing you cannot achieve.

There is always a lord of death.
He who takes the place of the lord of death
is like one who cuts with the blade
of a master carpenter.
Whoever cuts with the blade of a master carpenter
is sure to cut his own hands.

*L*iving with *N*o *F*ear of *D*eath

What happens when we die? Is death the vehicle that returns us to our Source of being, or does it signify the end of consciousness and all of life? One thing is absolutely certain: This subject is an absolute mystery to us. Some Tao scholars have referred to death as a place of oneness wherein time, space, and all of the 10,000 things cease to have meaning. Thus, what dies is our *human identity*. There's still someone underneath the external layers, though, so when you know and understand who that formless someone is, your fear of dying will evaporate. You can live on the active side of infinity by knowing your infinite Tao nature, which probably means that you'll alter the way you think about birth, life, and death.

Move from wanting to see permanence in your life to realizing that *all* things change due to the nature of this being an ever-modifying world. There's nothing external to hold on to; after all, the moment you think you have it, *it* becomes something else. This is as true for your earthly packaging as it is for your worldly treasures. Whether you realize it or not, the body you were in when you began reading this essay is different now, and it will become different again the moment you attempt to make it remain the same. This is the nature of our reality. If you can get comfortable with it, you'll reduce—and ultimately eliminate—your anxiety regarding mortality. As Lao-tzu promises: "If you are not afraid of dying, there is nothing you cannot achieve."

Your Tao essence has to be infinite because it came from a world of infinite possibilities. You're not a thing that's solid and permanent; in fact, there's nothing like that in the world you incarnated into! You are real, and what's real never changes. Yet your real self isn't in this world, but is the part of you that is the Tao. When you live in harmony with the infinite Tao, death is irrelevant—so know your highest self and understand that there's nothing you can't achieve.

The second part of this verse deals with killing, or taking another being's life. Lao-tzu is quite specific here, saying, "There is always a lord of death." At the moment of your coming into the world, everything you needed for this journey was handled by the lord of life *and* death. Just as your birth was Tao energy, your body type, skin color, eyes, ears, and every other physical aspect of you are expressions of the Tao. This includes your death, which has been choreographed, determined, and allowed to unfold in Divine timing. In other words, killing isn't your job, not ever—not of another person or any other being. Since death is as much a part of the Tao as life, it must be allowed to be in accord with nature, not performed as an ego decision.

I learned this lesson years ago while changing court sides in the middle of a tennis match in which I'd been playing at an exceptionally high level. While taking a drink of water, I noticed a bee lying upside down, apparently in the final throes of its short life. I assumed that it was suffering, so I stepped on it to avoid prolonging its agony. As I began to play again, I couldn't get that bee out of my mind: *Did I do the right thing? Who am I to decide this little creature's fate? Who am I to become an executioner, even to such a seemingly insignificant creature as a tiny insect?* And everything on the tennis court began to take on a different energy from that moment on.

Previously my shots had been landing on the lines, and presently they were out by inches. The wind seemed to shift and work against me. I was now moving more slowly and making uncharacteristic errors. Ultimately, what looked like a sure victory turned into a complete letdown and an embarrassing defeat because my role as the well-intentioned murderer of a small bee had been occupying my mind. I've since changed the way I see death, and I no longer

deliberately kill anything. I've decided that it's not my job to decide another's death ever since my day of awakening with that bee! Even if that bee only had a few minutes of life remaining, it is the job of the "lord of death," or the great Tao, to make that determination.

I just spoke with my dear friend Lauren, who's in the throes of watching her cat, who's been with her for 19 years, get ready to pass on. She asked for my advice about having Sweet Pea euthanized to avoid prolonging her suffering. After I read her this verse and told her my own experience with that tiny bee, Lauren elected to hold Sweet Pea in her lap until death claimed her. A reverence for life as a form of the Tao helps us all realize that we're not in charge of death decisions.

Lao-tzu's legacy is summed up magnificently in the words of T. S. Eliot, from his poem "Little Gidding":

> *We shall not cease from exploration*
> *And the end of all our exploring*
> *Will be to arrive where we started,*
> *And know the place for the first time.*

This is death—nothing to fear, nothing to do.

This is what I believe Lao-tzu is saying to you in this profound verse of the Tao Te Ching:

Discontinue fearing your death.

It makes as much sense to think about your death in fearful terms as it does to perceive the color of your eyes in such a way. The Tao is in it all—birth, life, and death. Reread the T. S. Eliot quote, as well as the 40th verse of the Tao Te Ching (which I titled "Living by Returning and Yielding"). By returning in death, you'll truly know the Tao . . . for perhaps the first time.

Examine the ways you kill.

Make a decision that you're no longer going to serve in the capacity of executioner, including even the smallest and seemingly most insignificant creatures, and then act on it. Live this principle by allowing the lord of life and death to decide when the return trip is to be made. Don't make this a crusade; just make your own commitment to exist in harmony with the Tao. And by all means, don't impose your beliefs on others, for noninterference is one of the major positions of the Tao Te Ching.

Do the Tao Now

During meditation, practice dying while still alive. That is, leave your body, discard it, and float above the world. This will help you disconnect yourself from feeling that your physical shell is who you are. The more you are the observer rather than the object of what you see, the easier it will be to remove your fear of dying. Do this for just a few minutes daily. Remember that you are *not* this body—you are a piece of the infinite Tao, never changing and never dying.

This excerpt from Neale Donald Walsch's *Communion with God* elaborates on this thought:

> Which snowflake is the most magnificent? Is it possible that they are all magnificent—and that, celebrating their magnificence together they create an awesome display? Then they melt into each other, and into the Oneness. Yet they never go away. They never disappear. They never cease to be. Simply, they *change form.* And not just once, but several times: from solid to liquid, from liquid to vapor, *from the seen to the unseen,* to rise again, and then again to return in new displays of breathtaking beauty and wonder. This is *Life, nourishing Life.*
>
> This is you.
>
> The metaphor is complete.
>
> The metaphor is real.
>
> You will make this real in your experience when you simply decide it is true, and act that way. See the beauty and the wonder of all whose lives you touch. For you are each wondrous indeed, yet no one more wondrous than another. And you all will one day melt into the Oneness, and know then that you form together a single stream.

75th Verse

When taxes are too high,
people go hungry.
When the government is too intrusive,
people lose their spirit.

Act for the people's benefit;
trust them, leave them alone.

*L*iving by
*D*emanding *L*ittle

This verse was intended to help the ruling classes and the no-bility manage the realm. Understand that during the warring-states period in ancient China, rulers used onerous methods to impose order on the masses: They tended to keep all of the tax money that was collected from the people for themselves, flaunting their good fortune in the faces of the impoverished. Those who were overtaxed and overburdened would lose their spirit and sense of loyalty and ultimately rebel against the laws imposed upon them.

This book you're holding in your hands isn't intended as a so-cial commentary to enlighten political leaders who take advantage of their positions (although I'd certainly invite any of them to take heed of Lao-tzu's advice!). Rather, I wrote it to help *you* apply the inherent wisdom in each of the 81 verses of the Tao Te Ching. So you're invited to change the way you look at assisting others to stay inspired and have contented and peaceful lives.

You may believe that demanding more from those in your charge, such as your children or co-workers, creates more productivity, but Lao-tzu suggests the opposite is true. Demand little, he advises, and even leave people alone as much as possible. And the imposition of excessive taxation on the masses can have an analogous component for you to consider when it comes to how you treat those you're responsible for leading.

Government officials often vote to raise more and more money for pet projects and even their own personal benefit simply because they have the authority to do so. Since they're in charge of lawmaking, they write rules that allow them to be abusive toward the very people who pay their salaries and provide them with all of their benefits. In virtually all cases, those who are being taxed to provide luxurious lifestyle perks receive far less in the way of benefits than those who are the recipients of that tax. In other words, the rule makers and others in power are using their positions to take advantage of ordinary people. When this becomes too prevalent, those ordinary people become restless and disruptive, with scant respect for authority. As Lao-tzu puts it "People lose their spirit."

Rather than demanding more because you're older, bigger, richer, or more powerful, leave those you're in charge of alone whenever feasible, trusting in their inherent wisdom to do the right thing. Overbearing, taxing authorities create rebellion and chaos—and you'll create the same unless you check your inclinations and reverse yourself by being *less* demanding instead of *more.*

I've practiced this approach to leadership my entire adult life by keeping the number of people who work for me and require my supervision to an absolute minimum. My demands on my manager/secretary/all-purpose assistant are few and far between, and she's been my sole employee for three decades. I allow her to negotiate contracts, to make all arrangements for speaking events, and to manage my very large business with an absence of demands from me. I don't tell her what time to come to work, what to wear, or how to talk to people; and my reward for being a boss with minimal demands is someone who's fiercely loyal, who can be depended on to do the right thing, who loves her job, and who is indispensable to me.

I behave the same way toward my editor, who has also been with me for 30-plus years. I write from my heart, allowing the words to flow onto the page, and then I send it to her. I trust this woman implicitly and allow her to do what she incarnated to do with no demands from me. My reward for being nonintrusive is to have my books beautifully and professionally polished. My editor and I also enjoy a loving, peaceful relationship, with both of us content and proud of the work we were destined to produce. While what I'm describing may seem impossible to you, it can absolutely be attained when you trust in the Tao to manage all of the details of both your professional and personal life.

The following is what Lao-tzu urges you to take from this 75th verse of the Tao Te Ching, which was originally intended for leaders of countries, but is applicable to everyone in a supervisory or parental role:

Don't overtax yourself.

Lao-tzu's reminder that excessive taxation will lead to a loss of spirit applies to you as well. If you weigh yourself down with excessive demands, you'll wear yourself out or develop symptoms of depression, anxiety, worry, heart disease, or any number of physical ailments. Give yourself a break from self-imposed pressures that burden you, allowing yourself plenty of free time to commune with nature, play with your children, read, see a movie, or just do nothing.

Trust those you're entrusted to lead.

Don't continually monitor those you're responsible for raising or supervising; instead, develop a trust in your less experienced charges. They must be allowed to use their own minds, for they also have a destiny to fulfill that's orchestrated by the Tao. So demand less and encourage more as much as you can, allowing them to pursue their own excellence and happiness. Your trust will lead to their trusting themselves *and* the wisdom that created them.

Do the Tao Now

Take a break from all that occupies your mind, including your responsibilities. Even if it's only for 15 minutes, clear your mind, empty your "demands file," and allow yourself the freedom that comes with being less exacting.

When you complete this, do the same with your children or someone who reports to you at work. Put your arm around them and ask them to go for a brief walk, just doing nothing but being together in nature. Then let them return to their responsibilities at their own pace.

If you're thinking that your child or employee needs an imperious overseer, perhaps they've become that way because you haven't trusted them to be self-reliant.

76th Verse

A man is born gentle and weak;
at his death he is hard and stiff.
All things, including the grass and trees,
are soft and pliable in life;
dry and brittle in death.

Stiffness is thus a companion of death;
flexibility a companion of life.
An army that cannot yield
will be defeated.
A tree that cannot bend
will crack in the wind.

The hard and stiff will be broken;
the soft and supple will prevail.

*L*iving by *B*ending

The thing I love most about studying the Tao Te Ching is its impeccable adherence to finding the Great Way by closely studying nature. In this passage, Lao-tzu asks us to change the we look at the concept of strength by noticing how the most solid and durable things in the natural world tend to be soft, gentle, and even weak. If we see strength as being hard, inflexible, and unyielding, he invites us to change that perception. Life, according to Lao-tzu, is defined as soft and pliable.

Some of my fondest memories of my eight children came from watching their flexible newly born bodies in awe. I could lay them on my lap and easily place their feet in their mouths or even behind their necks! They were perfect yoga masters at the tender age of only a few months or even days. When they were toddlers, I watched in amazement, often holding my breath as they bumped their heads, ran into walls without looking, and took what appeared to be nasty falls. Yet lo and behold, they'd shake it right off. What would have surely resulted in a broken hip or arm for an older person was hardly noticed by these limber youngsters.

By the same token, an older tree that's getting close to death will become hard, brittle, and susceptible to fire and harsh winds. Since the tree can't bend, a strong gust can blow it right over. As it ages, the wood becomes weaker simply because it's inflexible. Its rigidity, which some think of as strength, has actually turned it into a weak organism. Similarly, at the moment of death all creatures go into rigor mortis, which is complete stiffness and, of course, a total absence of strength.

Being pliable and able to bend goes beyond the aging process that all bodies are destined to experience. Thus, Lao-tzu encourages you to apply this principle to your thought processes and behaviors. You're reminded that rigidity and hardness accompany death, while pliability and even weakness are the companions of life. You may have been taught that strength is measured by how "hard" you are in your thinking or how inflexible you are in your opinions, and that weakness is associated with those who bend. But when confronted with any stressful situation, keep in mind that being stiff won't get you very far, whereas being flexible will carry you through.

Change the way you think about strength, not just as it relates to those in positions of power, but for yourself as well. There's a lot to be said for what we're conditioned to think of as weak: Begin to see that strength is weakness, and weakness is strength . . . just another of the Tao Te Ching's fascinating paradoxes.

Here's what Lao-tzu urges you to consider as you apply the lessons of this oft-quoted 76th verse:

Be strong by bending.

Be willing to be like palm trees in the midst of hurricane-force winds—their so-called weakness somehow gives them the strength to survive devastating storms. The same is true for the way you relate to others, so listen more, allow your viewpoints to be challenged, and bend when necessary, knowing that you're actually choosing strength. The more you think in rigid ways, refraining from considering other points of view, the more you're liable to break. As Lao-tzu reminds you, "The hard and stiff will be broken," while "the soft and supple will prevail."

Examine your unbendable attitudes.

Scrutinize your attitudes on matters such as the death penalty, legalization of certain drugs, abortion, gun or birth control, taxation, energy conservation, and any other issues on which you hold an unshakable position. Then make an effort to walk in the shoes of

those who have opposite opinions. When you consider the rebuttals they'd offer, you'll see that this old proverb has some truth in it:

This is my way!
What is your way?
The way doesn't exist.

Today, for example, I had a conversation with my daughter Serena concerning a presentation she was to make before one of her college classes. She was convinced that her conclusion was unbendable regarding a large retail chain's employment policies. There was no room for discussion—they were wrong and she was right. Yet for the sake of an intelligent discussion, I took the position of the retail giant and tried to offer that perspective to her. As our discussion continued, my daughter found herself bending just a bit. As she realized that every story has two sides, she found herself willing to listen to the opposition. Serena was able to bend in a way that made her strong.

If leaders on both sides of any matter were willing to at least listen to each other, conflicts wouldn't need to escalate to life-and-death proportions. By listening, yielding, and being gentle, we all become disciples of *life*.

Do the Tao Now

Every day in yoga class there's an exercise that reminds me of this verse of the Tao Te Ching, and I encourage you to practice it right now. Stand with your feet together, raise your hands above your head, and stretch as high as you possibly can. Now bend to the right as far as you can go, stretching for 60 seconds. Then return to an upright position and do the same on your left side. All the while, see yourself as flexible, supple, and able to bend in harmony with the Tao.

77th Verse

The way of heaven
is like drawing a bow:
The high is lowered,
the low is raised.

When it is surplus, it reduces;
when it is deficient, it increases.
The Tao of mankind is the opposite:
It reduces the deficiency in order to add to the surplus.
It strips the needy to serve those who have too much.

Only the one who has the Tao offers his surplus to others.
What man has more than enough
and gives it to the world?
Only the man of the Tao.

The master can keep giving
because there is no end to his wealth.
He acts without expectation,
succeeds without taking credit,
and does not think that he is better
than anyone else.

*L*iving by
*O*ffering the *S*urplus

If you view the ways of heaven from a distance, you'll find that nature is perfect. The Tao is at work, invisibly keeping a Divine balance. When I was in Sedona, Arizona, for instance, I took a tour of the forested areas in the steppes of the majestic red-rock mountains. After I lamented the recent fires that had decimated so many trees, the guide explained how this had actually been nature at work. "For millions of years," he explained, "when the forest gets too thick, nature's lightning strikes and thins out the forest." Without such an occurrence, the timber would choke on its own surplus. This is how our planet works.

While at times natural events such as droughts, floods, hurricanes, windstorms, and excessive rainfall can seem disastrous, they're actually maintaining balance. This is also clear in the lives of butterflies, flocks of geese, or herds of caribou and buffalo—the sport of killing upsets nature's system of dealing with surpluses. And the Tao agrees: "When it is surplus, it reduces; when it is deficient, it increases." Observe nature, says Lao-tzu: If deficiencies exist, don't continue to reduce what's already in short supply.

The lessons in these final verses relate to governing the masses by staying harmonized with the Tao. Lao-tzu seems to rail against people in positions of political power who took from the needy to give themselves more of what they didn't need. In today's world, we can see evidence of this practice in myriad ways, but especially in lawmakers voting themselves benefits to be paid for by everyone else: They give themselves 95 percent retirement packages, medical insurance for life, limousines, private parking places on public land, and free first-class travel, even as they strip the needy and serve those who have too much. And in countries where starvation is rampant, it's not unusual to see large amounts of food and supplies stacked on docks while people die from malnourishment because government representatives think they're "above" all that.

The 77th verse of the Tao Te Ching suggests thinking about the surpluses we can put back into circulation to decrease deficiencies that exist elsewhere in our world. Lao-tzu asks you and me to put the wisdom of this verse to work in our personal lives by seeing what we have but don't need as an opportunity to be "Tao people." Lao-tzu isn't asking our government, political leaders, or captains of industry, but us personally: "What man has more than enough and gives it to the world?" The answer is, only the man or woman of the Tao. When there are enough of us, there will be a pool from which we Tao-centered people emerge to govern. Then we'll put into place the way of living offered in this verse.

It's fairly simple to understand a *surplus* of money or possessions, but the word actually symbolizes much more. For example, there's the surplus of joy you feel that you can offer to yourself and your family. Then there's the excess of intellectual prowess, talent, compassion, health, strength, and kindness you can share with the world. Whenever you see deficiencies in joy, abundance, educational opportunities, perfect health, or sobriety, make your own surpluses available. Lao-tzu urges you to look at what's deficient and be an instrument of *increasing,* rather than a collector of more, which marginalizes and divides the oneness that is all of life.

Practice these new ways of being that are more aligned with the way of the Tao:

Reduce surplus.

Reduce what's in excess in your life and then offer it where it can be utilized. Begin with your stuff: clothing, furniture, tools, equipment, radios, cameras, or anything that you have too much of. Don't sell it; rather, give it away (if you can afford to). Don't ask for recognition for charitable acts—simply behave in harmony with

the Tao by reducing your surplus. Then think about your intangible abundance of health, joy, kindness, love, or inner peace, and seek ways to offer those glorious feelings to those who could benefit from your bounty.

Be an instrument of increasing.

Just as nature fills voids by maintaining the cyclical balance necessary to our world, be an instrument of increasing where you observe deficiencies. Practice giving by dedicating a portion of your earnings to be used to ease deficits, for as Lao-tzu points out, "The master can keep giving because there is no end to his wealth." If you can't offer money to those who are less fortunate, say a silent blessing for them. Offer a prayer when you hear an ambulance's or police car's siren. Look for opportunities to fill the empty spaces in other people's lives with money; things; or loving energy in the form of kindness, compassion, joy, and forgiveness.

Do the Tao Now

Plan a day when you make a point of getting rid of some of your surplus, making sure that you part with something that's useful elsewhere. Look around for things you don't need or use—for instance, I just glanced up from my writing and spotted some legal pads, three DVDs, and a toaster that I haven't used in six months. If you scan the room right now as you're reading these words, I'm positive you'll see things that you could easily categorize as surplus. So schedule a time to put some of your excess into circulation. You can also pick up those things in your line of vision at this moment and drop them off where they'll be welcomed today. Be a man or woman of the Tao!

78th Verse

Nothing in the world is softer
and weaker than water.
But for attacking the hard, the unyielding,
nothing can surpass it.
There is nothing like it.

The weak overcomes the strong;
the soft surpasses the hard.
In all the world, there is no one who does not know this,
but no one can master the practice.

Therefore the master remains
serene in the midst of sorrow;
evil cannot enter his heart.
Because he has given up helping,
he is people's greatest help.

True words appear paradoxical.

*L*iving like *W*ater

In researching, studying, and putting into practice the 81 verses of the Tao Te Ching, I've been struck by the many references Lao-tzu makes to water in its various forms: the sea, rain, fog, mist, snow, and rivers and streams. The esteemed master seemed to find his spiritual strength in all of nature, but he must have had a special reverence for water and how it functions in all of our lives. *Be like water* seems to be repeated throughout the Tao Te Ching. This element is closer to being Tao-like than anything else in this world, so it is a perfectly suitable symbol for teaching about the Great Way.

Water is as mysterious to us as the Tao is. When you reach into the river and try to squeeze it tight, you end up losing it all. Water is elusive until you cease grasping and let your hand relax and be one with it—paradoxically, you get it by letting go. Lao-tzu advises emulating this element in all of its undecipherable and mysterious ways, even if it seems contrary to what your intellect and conditioning are telling you.

Lao-tzu reiterates three themes that appear throughout this book. They are the true characteristics of water:

1. Overcome the unyielding parts of your life by yielding! Hard and rigid are overcome by the relentless application of gentle things, such as water's soft flow or steady drip. So be persistently gentle and willing to surrender, and watch the resistance of the harsh and implacable wear away.

For years, one of my family members who insisted on damaging herself and her relationships by ingesting intoxicating substances has been met by my loving but firm response. Slowly, over time, her hardness began to wear away in the face of the steady *drip, drip, drip* of gentle but resolute kindness, acceptance, and love. It can be discouraging at times, but as Lao-tzu points out in this verse, we must act just like water and use a soft approach, "for attacking the hard, the unyielding, nothing can surpass it."

2. Water appears to be something you could easily overpower. However, it's so flexible that once you push it out of the way, it will find its own level below all strong things and patiently enter where nothing solid can block its resting place. Put up barricades, erect levees, and make everything waterproof; yet with enough passage of time, the flexible quality of water will triumph. "The weak overcomes the strong" is a powerful message for you. Remember to stay flexible, willing to lower yourself in humility and appear weak, but knowing that you're in harmony with the Tao. Lao-tzu urges you to be like the master who remains "serene in the midst of sorrow," and evil will not be able to enter your heart.

3. Water is so soft that it can't be harmed, damaged, or destroyed—it simply returns to its Source to be used over and over again. Boil it until it disappears, and its vapors enter the atmosphere, ultimately to return. Drink it, and it returns after nourishing your body. Pollute it, and it will return after enough passage of time to become purified nourishment again. This is all accomplished because of the element's mutable softness.

When you stay soft and surpass the hard, you too will be indestructible. (Reread verse 43, "Living Softly.") There's nothing softer than water under heaven, and yet there's nothing that can surpass it for overcoming the hard. There's so much wisdom to be found in this analogy: Stay in your soft mode. Hang back when you're about to show how hard you can be. Try patience rather than attempting to rigidly control. Trust your innately gentle self.

I love Mary Oliver's beautiful poem "Wild Geese," in which she speaks of this:

You do not have to be good.
You do not have to walk on your knees
for a hundred miles through the desert, repenting.
You only have to let the soft animal of your body
     love what it loves.
Tell me about despair, yours, and I will tell you mine.
Meanwhile the world goes on.
Meanwhile the sun and the clear pebbles of the rain
are moving across the landscapes,
over the prairies and the deep trees,
the mountains and the rivers.
Meanwhile the wild geese, high in the clean blue air,
are heading home again.
Whoever you are, no matter how lonely,
the world offers itself to your imagination,
calls to you like the wild geese, harsh and exciting—
over and over announcing your place
in the family of things.

From his 2,500-year-old perspective, Lao-tzu reminds you of how much you have to learn from nature, particularly water, and urges you to put these ideas into practice:

Change the way you look at strength versus weakness.

See that the stereotypes of rigid, hard, forceful, cocksure, and dominant aren't attributes of strength at all. In fact, these qualities will lead you to be suppressed and overpowered by softness, or what you've called weakness. Change the way you look at all of this, and watch your world change. When you begin to admire and emulate those who stay weak and pliable, you'll see the true strength in yourself as a person of the Tao. Give up interfering and helping, and opt instead to stream like water—gently, softly, and unobtrusively—wherever you're needed.

Be soft like water.

Like water, flow everywhere there's an opening, rather than attempting to dominate with your forcefulness. Soften your hard edges by being more tolerant of contrary opinions. Interfere less, and substitute listening for directing and telling. When someone offers you their viewpoint, try responding with: "I've never considered that before—thank you. I'll give it some thought."

Do the Tao Now

Do a meditation today in which you picture yourself as having the same qualities as water. Allow your soft, weak, yielding, fluid self to enter places where you previously were excluded because of your inclination to be solid and hard. Flow softly into the lives of those with whom you feel conflicted: Picture yourself entering their private inner selves, seeing perhaps for the first time what they're experiencing. Keep this image of yourself as gently coursing water, and watch how your relationships change.

79th Verse

After a bitter quarrel, some resentment remains.
What can one do about it?
Being content with what you have
is always best in the end.

Someone must risk returning injury with kindness,
or hostility will never turn to goodwill.
So the wise always give without expecting gratitude.

One with true virtue
always seeks a way to give.
One who lacks true virtue
always seeks a way to get.
To the giver comes the fullness of life;
to the taker, just an empty hand.

Living Without Resentments

In this verse, which has been so helpful to me personally, you're asked to change the way you hold resentments following a difference of opinion or an outright quarrel. Now what causes annoyance and anger after a dispute? The generic response would be a laundry list that detailed why the other person was wrong and how illogically and unreasonably they behaved, concluding with something like, "I have a right to be upset when my [daughter, mother-in-law, ex-husband, boss, or whomever you're thinking of] speaks to me that way!" But if you're interested in living a Tao-filled life, it's imperative that you reverse this kind of thinking.

Resentments don't come from the conduct of the other party in an altercation—no, they survive and thrive because *you're* unwilling to end that altercation with an offering of kindness, love, and authentic forgiveness. Lao-tzu says, "Someone must risk returning injury with kindness, or hostility will never turn to goodwill." So when all of the yelling, screaming, and threatening words have been expressed, the time for calm has arrived. Remember that no storm lasts forever, and that hidden within are always seeds of tranquility. There is a time for hostility and a time for peace.

As the storm of a quarrel subsides, you must find a way to disregard your ego's need to be right. It's time to extend kindness by letting go of your anger. It's over, so offer forgiveness to yourself and the other person and encourage resentment to dissipate. Be the one seeking a way to *give,* in the sense that Lao-tzu describes in this verse, rather than the one looking for something to *get.*

I run a large enterprise based on the wisdom in this profound verse. My company is all about giving, so if there are any disputes about product sales, my assistant knows to let the other party have whatever they desire. If someone can't afford something, I give it away. I allow recordings of my talks and ask nothing in return. I give of my time for photographs, autographs, or anything at all. Unless I have a plane to catch, I'm the last person out of the auditorium, and I'm willing to talk with anybody who makes such a request. It's all about giving, and those who work for me know this and live by these principles.

When I asked an outsider to be a part of my speaking tour not long ago, I encountered a man who was a tremendously gifted musician and entertainer yet was living in scarcity. Despite his enormous talent, abundance just wasn't flowing into his life. After a few of our speaking dates, I noticed his inclination to be a taker rather than a giver—he consistently looked for ways to make more money on the side, excluding everyone else who was working to provide a service to those who attended the lectures.

I had a long discussion with this man about how his profiteering rather than offering was blocking the flow of abundance into his life, and I encouraged him to trust in the wisdom that Lao-tzu provides. The point here is that this was an opportunity for us to both proceed on the tour without resentment.

Regardless of anyone else's attitude, if you live with "true virtue," you'll seek a way to give. This truth completely aligns with the Tao; after all, the creator of life is always giving, never taking. So change the way you think about scarcity and resentment, and begin to truly feel the question *How may I serve?* The universe will seem to respond, *Finally, you got it—you're acting like me! I'll keep that flow coming into your life in ways that will astound and delight you.* As Lao-tzu says, "To the giver comes the fullness of life; to the taker, just an empty hand."

Here's what Lao-tzu encourages you to do to make the wisdom of the 79th verse your reality:

End on love, no matter what!

Picture yourself at the termination of a quarrel or major dispute. Rather than reacting with old patterns of residual anger, revenge, and hurt, visualize offering kindness, love, and forgiveness. Do this right now by sending out these "true virtue" thoughts to any resentments you're currently carrying. Make this your standard response to any future altercations: *I end on love, no matter what!*

Practice giving.

In the midst of arguments or disagreements, practice giving rather than taking before you exit the fracas. Offer the Tao treasures or real virtues by presenting kindness rather than a put-down, or a sign of respect instead of proving someone wrong. Giving involves leaving the ego behind. While it wants to win and show its superiority by being contrary and disrespectful, your Tao nature wants to be at peace and live in harmony. You can reduce your quarreling time to almost zero if you practice this procedure.

Do the Tao Now

Silently recite the following words from the Prayer of Saint Francis: "Where there is injury, [let me bring] pardon." Be a giver of forgiveness as he teaches: Bring love to hate, light to darkness, and pardon to injury. Read these words daily, for they'll help you overcome your ego's demands and know "the fullness of life."

80th Verse

Imagine a small country with few people.
They have weapons and do not employ them;
they enjoy the labor of their hands
and do not waste time inventing laborsaving machines.

They take death seriously and do not travel far.
Since they dearly love their homes,
they are not interested in travel.
Although they have boats and carriages,
no one uses them.

They are content with healthy food,
pleased with useful clothing,
satisfied in snug homes,
and protective of their way of life.

Although they live within sight of their neighbors,
and crowing cocks and barking dogs can be
heard across the way,
they leave each other in peace
while they grow old and die.

Living Your Own Utopia

This second-to-last verse of the Tao Te Ching might have been titled "KISS"—that is, "Keep It Simple, Stupid." Here, Lao-tzu makes a case for an ideal society where conflict isn't a problem, harmonizing with nature is practiced, and weapons may be present but are never used. The ancient Chinese master seems to say that staying close to nature and taking pleasure in the basics of life are more satisfying than pursuing technological equipment and fancy carriages. He advises readers to keep close to the land, work with their hands, and not compete with neighboring villages.

While it's clear that the world has changed dramatically over the past 2,500 years, the advice in this 80th verse offers wisdom for the 21st century and beyond. Imagine a world where weapons are vestiges of the past, displayed in museums to illustrate and warn the populace about an absurdly violent history. You'd see the conflicts on this planet exhibited from the perspective of human beings as tiny microbes living on the same body, equally dependent on it and on one another for survival, yet killing each other and destroying their host anyway. War would simply seem senselessly destructive.

When we look at the conflicts that have taken place throughout history, we cannot help but see that the hatred and rivalries in ancient and modern times make no sense. Why won't (or can't) people share the land and live together peacefully? What seems so important that it's necessary to kill each other over it? Even in fairly recent times, those individuals who were so hated that we tried to decimate them have become our allies. So what was all the killing about? Why haven't we learned to live in harmony with the life-giving Tao? The answers to these questions are obviously complex, but, unfortunately, they continue to need to be asked.

This verse doesn't negate an effort by you to create ways to live your utopia. Instead, it's offering you an escape from the vicious cycle of hatred, murder, war, and subsequent cooperation before the next cycle of violence erupts. You can return to the basics of a peaceful existence by choosing to live simply and placing less effort on needing to conquer *anyone.* When you see the inclination toward creating more war machines, vote instead for candidates who support peaceful ways for dealing with conflict.

Your personal choices also align you with the tranquil nature of the Tao. You can opt to do without some of the new technology some, or even all, of the time. You can choose to write by hand and feel your connection to your Source as the words flow through your heart onto the paper. You can choose to walk rather than drive as often as possible. You can choose to compute numbers without a calculator, and remember phone numbers as a way of personalizing your connections. You can choose to swim or bicycle for exercise in lieu of using machines.

There are many laborsaving devices that Lao-tzu may never have dreamed about, and you can eliminate them as part of your simplification routine. Maybe not having e-mail or downloading music is your way of symbolically staying close to the land that Lao-tzu speaks of in this verse. In other words, you can know what the modern world offers in the way of information and technology, while at the same time being aware of the areas of your life where you want to keep things basic. Recognize when you're feeling the effects of information overload, too many gadgets, or overcomplication, and switch to a natural environment that pleases you for whatever amount of time you choose.

Lao-tzu seems to be encouraging you to simplify as a way to heighten awareness of your Tao connection. Try out these new attitudes and behaviors to help you change the way you think about your modern life; you may in fact change the life you're living!

Practice radical appreciation.

Begin a practice of joyfully engaging with the things you take for granted. There are comforts such as your home, garden, meals, clothes, family members, and friends that you experience every day without ever appreciating them. Choose to pay attention—make the shift by giving thanks and loving appreciation. Spend more time close to home in awe over the many simple treasures that make up your life.

See paradise all around you.

Change your belief that you must travel, be worldly, and experience distant lands and people in order to have a fulfilling life. In fact, you could reside on the same street for a lifetime without ever leaving and know the bliss of the Tao. Keep in mind the thought offered by Voltaire: "Paradise is where I am." If where you are is at home, with the same people, the same photographs, and the same furniture, make it your paradise. Find joy and solace in the simple. Change your view to see the pleasure in what you have, where you're located, and who you are. Cultivate your utopia by feeling the Tao in every cubic inch of space.

Do the Tao Now

Devote a day to food! Appreciate the mysterious intelligence that created food for your health and pleasure, and say a prayer with every connection to it. Going grocery shopping, cooking, planning a dinner party, being a dinner-party guest, eating at a restaurant, grabbing a snack, or having some popcorn at the movies are just some of the opportunities to consciously explore that connection. See these food connections as a part of the endless Tao cycle, and being in your own utopia.

81st Verse

True words are not beautiful;
beautiful words are not true.
Good men do not argue;
those who argue are not good.
Those who have virtue do not look for faults;
those who look for faults have no virtue.

Sages do not accumulate anything
but give everything to others;
having more, the more they give.

Heaven does good to all,
doing no evil to anyone.
The sage imitates it, acting
for the good of all,
and opposing himself to no one.

Living Without Accumulating

This final verse of the Tao Te Ching provides the closing message of this entire collection of ideas: You came from *no-thing-ness*. The place of your origination had no things; the place of your return is one of no things. Therefore, Lao-tzu is inviting you to replace the accumulation of more stuff with the celebration of your true essence. Just as nothing is pure Tao in its formlessness, the real you is that same formlessness . . . for you are the Tao.

The Tao Te Ching attempts to attract you to a way of being that recognizes nothingness as the Tao—you could call it a God-realized way of being. In this final essay, I've chosen to propose that you access your nonbeing, Tao self by living without accumulating. This means giving more, arguing less, and releasing your attachment to everything in the world of the 10,000 things. Ultimately, living this way even means letting go of your attachment to your life and your body. But you can practice this right now, while you're still living in the world.

Saint John of the Cross speaks to this way of seeing your life:

> *To reach satisfaction in all*
> *desire its possession in nothing.*
> *To come to possess all*

desire the possession of nothing.
To arrive at being all
desire to be nothing.
To come to the knowledge of all
desire the knowledge of nothing.

All of this wisdom of nothingness comes out of the offerings of Lao-tzu, the ancient spiritual sage who wants us to experience the bliss of being all by knowing a nonaccumulating place of *no-thing-ness.*

It is difficult to imagine a world without things, yet in this final verse of the Tao Te Ching, Lao-tzu takes you through what such a world would look like. You don't need beautiful words, since there is *no-thing* for you to describe. There is *no-thing* to argue about, as there are no possessions to fight over. There's no faultfinding or blaming, for all that exists is the hidden virtue of the Tao. And finally, there is *no-thing* to collect, amass, or accumulate, which leaves you in a state of creative giving and supporting. "Heaven does good," says Lao-tzu, and *good* is a synonym for *God,* which is truly the same as the Tao.

Meister Eckhart illustrates the interchangeability of the words *God* and *Tao* in this piece:

God is a being beyond being
and a nothingness beyond being.
God is nothing. No thing.
God is nothingness.
And yet God is something.

You're encouraged in this final verse of the enduring and amazing Tao Te Ching to do all that you can to imitate heaven while you're here in form.

Try out these suggestions from Lao-tzu as you change your thoughts, and ultimately your life, forever:

Quit accumulating points for being right!

Let go of your propensity for argument and replace it with the willingness to allow anyone with whom you have a disagreement to be right. End your quarreling ways by simply telling the other

person something like this: "You're right about that, and I appreciate hearing your point of view." This ends the argument and eliminates blame and faultfinding at the same time. Change ego's need to be right by using the Tao-based statement, "You're right about that." It will make your life so much more peaceful.

Reduce yourself down to zero or *no-thing-ness*.

Observe your body and all of your belongings, and then put them into the changing-world context. Keep this statement from Mahatma Gandhi in mind: "If you would swim on the bosom of the ocean of Truth, you must reduce yourself to zero." So from a place of *no-thing-ness* or zero, become the observer, seeing what you accumulate in the world of things. From this perspective, you'll find that nothing can ever truly be real in such a world. Practice this exercise whenever you're feeling attached to your possessions or your point of view.

D. H. Lawrence dramatically captures this idea:

> *Are you willing to be sponged out,*
> *erased, cancelled,*
> *made nothing?*
> *Are you willing to be made nothing?*
> *dipped into oblivion?*
> *If not, you will never really change.*

Now glance again at the title of this book, *Change Your Thoughts—Change Your Life: Living the Wisdom of the Tao*. Be willing to change.

Do the Tao Now

I leave you with these words of Lao-tzu from *Tao Te Ching: A New Translation*, which were translated by Sam Hamill. Here's the final verse:

> *The sage does not hoard,*
> *and thereby bestows.*
> *The more he lives for others,*
> *the greater his life.*

The more he gives to others,
the greater his abundance.

Copy these words by hand, study them, and put them into practice at least once each day. You will energize the flow of the Tao in your life, in this world of 10,000 things.

Namaste,
Dr. Wayne W. Dyer

Epilogue

I close this yearlong project on a personal note to share with you how these 81 verses unexpectedly increased my personal sense of awe and incredulity concerning the power and vast wisdom in this ancient classic.

Reread the display quote at the beginning of this book, which is attributed to Confucius. Legend has it that this master was so impressed by Lao-tzu's influence that he sought him out for consultation on etiquette and rules, which was the major focus of Confucian philosophy but considered to be hypocrisy and nonsense by Lao-tzu. After meeting Lao-tzu, Confucius told his disciples that the man was a sage—a dragon with mysterious powers beyond the understanding of most people, including Confucius himself.

Throughout the writing of these 81 short essays, I felt an almost mystical attraction to Lao-tzu. In the early verses, I thought of him as a great educator offering all of us advice on how to apply his wisdom from an ancient Chinese perspective to our modern world. As time passed and I became more engrossed in his teachings, I began to feel that Lao-tzu was speaking directly to me . . . and then *through* me to you, and even to coming generations. It felt at times as if Lao-tzu was intently saying that we had to get these important messages or perish as a civilized society. As this book unfolded, there were times that I could even feel his presence.

When I concluded writing this manuscript, I had an unavoidable and painful opportunity to experience the dragonlike qualities that impressed Confucius. Through the Tao Te Ching, Lao-tzu gave me insight into the Way to confront the winds and clouds of time and space, along with what initially seemed to me to be an insurmountable crisis.

As I reread the final edit of *Change Your Thoughts—Change Your Life,* I was presented with perhaps the greatest personal challenge of my life. I felt the deep internal hurt that often drives human beings into conflicts. I felt the anger that allows people to think of themselves as victims and ultimately leads to the extremes of war that are addressed so frequently throughout the Tao Te Ching. My thoughts struggled with how Lao-tzu could speak of never having enemies—surely it would be impossible for *anyone* to stay serene and feel connected to their Source of love and well-being in the face of what I was going through. What good fortune could be hidden in this misfortune that seemed to emerge out of nowhere for no justifiable reason? Was I now to be the designated teacher for "bad men"? On and on went the questions within me as I read each verse.

Then it began to feel as if Lao-tzu's dragonlike character appeared, burning my face as I read. It was almost as if he spoke these words directly to me:

> So you think you've mastered the Great Way because you've spent a year reading and interpreting these 81 verses. Here's an opportunity to explore your mastery of the Tao. Here's something unexpected that's capable of turning you upside down and inside out spiritually, physically, intellectually, and emotionally. Apply all that I've taught you: Stay peaceful; trust your nature; know that it is all perfect; and most of all, do nothing. Live the hidden virtue of the Tao. If you feel dragged into a war, refuse to have any enemies. Don't have any violence in your mind—no revenge and absolutely no judgment. Do this while staying centered in the all-loving, all-knowing perfection of the Tao in the face of what you think of as insurmountable. Then you will be able to call yourself a man of the Tao.

I began to feel that Lao-tzu was warming me with his dragon fire, as each verse was exactly what I needed each time I reread it. What at first seemed so hopeless and devastating became my ultimate calling: to live joyously and with deep gratitude for all that the

Tao brings me. As you close this book, it is my wish that you, too, will be able to apply this great wisdom of the Tao so that you can, even in the most difficult of times, change your thoughts and enjoy changing your life as well. I may not be a Tao master, but I am a man of the Tao. However these words of the Tao Te Ching came to be written and to endure for over 25 centuries, I'm honored to have been called to help clarify them for you. I am at peace.

Thank you, Lao-tzu.

Acknowledgments

I thank the translators and authors of the following ten books:

The Essential Tao: An Initiation into the Heart of Taoism through the Authentic <u>Tao Te Ching</u> and the Inner Teachings of <u>Chuang Tzu,</u> translated and presented by Thomas Cleary

The Illustrated Tao Te Ching: A New Translation with Commentary, by Stephen Hodge

Tao Te Ching, by Lao Tsu; translated by Gia-Fu Feng and Jane English

Tao Te Ching: The Definitive Edition, by Lao Tzu; translation and commentary by Jonathan Star

Tao Te Ching: A New English Version, by Stephen Mitchell

Tao-Te-Ching: A New Translation, by Lao-Tzu; translated by Derek Bryce and Léon Wieger

Tao Te Ching: A New Translation,
by Lao Tzu; translated by Sam Hamill

Tao Te Ching, by Lao Tzu; translated by John C. H. Wu

A Warrior Blends with Life: A Modern Tao, by Michael LaTorra

The Way of Life According to Lao Tzu, translated by Witter Bynner

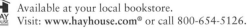

About the Author

Wayne W. Dyer, Ph.D., is an internationally renowned author and speaker in the field of self-development. He's the author of 30 books, has created many audio programs and videos, and has appeared on thousands of television and radio shows. His books *Manifest Your Destiny, Wisdom of the Ages, There's a Spiritual Solution to Every Problem,* and *The New York Times* bestsellers *10 Secrets for Success and Inner Peace, The Power of Intention,* and *Inspiration* have all been featured as National Public Television specials.

Wayne holds a doctorate in educational counseling from Wayne State University and was an associate professor at St. John's University in New York.

Website: **www.DrWayneDyer.com**

Hay House Titles of Related Interest

FOUR ACTS OF PERSONAL POWER:
How to Heal Your Past and Create a Positive Future,
by Denise Linn

HEAL YOUR BODY: The Mental Causes for Physical Illness
and the Metaphysical Way to Overcome Them,
by Louise L. Hay

KICK UP YOUR HEELS . . . BEFORE
YOU'RE TOO SHORT TO WEAR THEM:
How to Live a Long, Healthy, Juicy Life, by Loretta LaRoche

THE POWER OF PLEASURE: Maximizing Your Enjoyment
for a Lifetime, by Douglas Weiss, Ph.D.

POWER OF THE SOUL: Inside Wisdom for an Outside World,
by John Holland

REPOTTING: 10 Steps for Redesigning Your Life,
by Diana Holman and Ginger Pape

THE TIMES OF OUR LIVES: Extraordinary True Stories
of Synchronicity, Destiny, Meaning, and Purpose,
by Louise L. Hay & Friends

YOUR DESTINY SWITCH: Master Your Key Emotions,
and Attract the Life of Your Dreams! by Peggy McColl

All of the above are available at your local bookstore,
or may be ordered by contacting Hay House (see last page).

We hope you enjoyed this Hay House book.
If you'd like to receive a free catalog featuring additional
Hay House books and products, or if you'd like information about
the Hay Foundation, please contact:

Hay House, Inc.
P.O. Box 5100
Carlsbad, CA 92018-5100

(760) 431-7695 or (800) 654-5126
(760) 431-6948 (fax) or (800) 650-5115 (fax)
www.hayhouse.com® • www.hayfoundation.org

Published and distributed in Australia by: Hay House Australia Pty. Ltd.,
18/36 Ralph St., Alexandria NSW 2015 • *Phone:* 612-9669-4299
Fax: 612-9669-4144 • www.hayhouse.com.au

Published and distributed in the United Kingdom by: Hay House UK,
Ltd., 292B Kensal Rd., London W10 5BE • *Phone:* 44-20-8962-1230
Fax: 44-20-8962-1239 • www.hayhouse.co.uk

Published and distributed in the Republic of South Africa by:
Hay House SA (Pty), Ltd., P.O. Box 990, Witkoppen 2068
Phone/Fax: 27-11-467-8904 • www.hayhouse.co.za

Published in India by: Hay House Publishers India, Muskaan Complex,
Plot No. 3, B-2, Vasant Kunj, New Delhi 110 070 • *Phone:* 91-11-4176-1620
Fax: 91-11-4176-1630 • www.hayhouse.co.in

Distributed in Canada by: Raincoast, 9050 Shaughnessy St., Vancouver,
B.C. V6P 6E5 • *Phone:* (604) 323-7100 • *Fax:* (604) 323-2600
www.raincoast.com

Tune in to **HayHouseRadio.com**® for the best in inspirational talk radio
featuring top Hay House authors! And, sign up via the Hay House USA
Website to receive the Hay House online newsletter and stay informed
about what's going on with your favorite authors. You'll receive
bimonthly announcements about Discounts and Offers, Special Events,
Product Highlights, Free Excerpts, Giveaways, and more!
www.hayhouse.com®